The Starving and Exploited Masses Shall Be Victorious!

UNEQUAL EXCHANGE AND THE PROSPECTS OF SOCIALISM

Published by *Iskra Books* © 2025

10 9 8 7 6 5 4 3 2 1

Originally Published by Manifest Press, 1986

All rights reserved.
The moral rights of the author have been asserted.

Iskra Books
iskrabooks.org
Olympia, US | London, England | Dublin, Ireland

Iskra Books is a nonprofit, independent, scholarly publisher—publishing original works of revolutionary theory, history, education, and art, as well as edited collections, new translations, and critical republications of older works.

979-8-3492-7733-7 (*Softcover*)
979-8-3492-5968-5 (*Jacketed Hardcover*)

British Library Cataloguing in Publication Data
A catalogue record for this book is available from the British Library

Library of Congress Cataloging-in-Publication Data
A catalog record for this book is available from the Library of Congress

Editing and Proofreading by David Peat
Cover Design by Ruehl Muller, Ben Stahnke
Book Design by Ben Stahnke, Alessandro Zancan
Typesetting by Alessandro Zancan

UNEQUAL EXCHANGE AND THE PROSPECTS OF SOCIALISM

COMMUNIST WORKING GROUP

WITH A NEW PROLOGUE AND EPILOGUE BY
TORKIL LAUESEN

With the Original Introduction by ARGHIRI EMMANUEL
and a New Preface by HENRY HAKAMÄKI and NEMANJA LUKIC

iskra books
olympia | london | dublin

Contents

Editor's Note for the Iskra Edition   xvii

Preface to the Iskra Edition   xix
Henry Hakamäki Nemanja Lukic

Introduction to the First Edition   xxiii
Arghiri Emmanuel

**Prologue:
The Struggle Goes On: On Anti-Imperialist Praxis in the Global North**   xxvii
Torkil Lauesen

     THE ONES WE WERE   xxviii

     THE PRAXIS   xxxiv

     UNDERCOVER   xxxv

     THE SPLIT   xl

     MANIFEST—COMMUNIST WORKING GROUP (M-CWG)   xlii

     SOLIDARITY WORK   xliv

     THE DEVELOPMENT OF POLITICS   xlv

     THE HISTORY OF THE BOOK   xlviii

1 Introduction   1

     THE PURPOSE OF THEORY IS PRACTICE   1

     MARXISM—DIALECTICAL MATERIALISM   2

	Analysis of the Economic Conditions is Fundamental	3
	The Main Social Contradiction	4
	The Relationship Between Consciousness and Being	4
	The Population of the World is Divided into Rich and Poor	5
	The Consequences of the Present World Order	7
2	**The Historical Background of Unequal Exchange**	**11**
	The Development of Capitalism in the Nineteenth Century	11
	Britain's Industrial Monopoly	11
	The Contradiction Production—Consumption	12
	Marx & Engels On the Potentialities of Capitalism	13
	The New Manifestation of the Contradiction	18
	The Development of the United States of America from Colony to Advanced Capitalist Power	23
	Summary	29
3	**The Theory of Unequal Exchange**	**31**
	Introduction	31
	The Capitalist Mode of Accumulation	32
	Commodity Production—Generally Defined	34
	Simple Commodity Production	34
	Commodity Production Under Developed Capitalism	35
	Primitive Accumulation	35
	Labor-Power—Its Value and Price	36
	Productivity and Wages	40
	The Use-Value of Labor-Power	45
	The Circulation of Capital	45
	Surplus Value	47

THE RATE OF SURPLUS VALUE	47
COST-PRICE	48
THE RATE OF PROFIT	49
THE CREATION OF AN AVERAGE RATE OF PROFIT BETWEEN THE BRANCHES OF PRODUCTION	50
THE CONDITIONS FOR AN EQUALIZATION OF THE RATE OF PROFIT NATIONALLY	54
SUMMARY	55
THE WORLD MARKET	55
UNEQUAL EXCHANGE BETWEEN COUNTRIES	56
ON EXPLOITATION BETWEEN COUNTRIES	58
ON EXPLOITATION	60
SOUTH AFRICA—A CONCRETE EXAMPLE	61
GLOBAL INEQUALITY	68

4 The Validity of the Prerequisites of Unequal Exchange — 71

INTRODUCTION	71
VARIATION IN WAGES IN A DIVIDED WORLD	72
THE CONCRETE VARIATIONS IN WAGES	74
WORKING CONDITIONS	78
PRODUCTIVITY AND WAGES	80
PRODUCTIVITY AND WAGES—FINAL REMARKS	82
CONCLUSION	84
EQUALIZATION OF THE RATE OF PROFIT	84
CAPITAL MOVEMENTS	88
CONCLUSION	92
THE SIZE OF THE UNEQUAL EXCHANGE	92

5 The Possibilities of Socialism in a Divided World — 103

ON PRODUCTIVE FORCES AND RELATIONS OF PRODUCTION — 103

THE POSSIBILITIES OF SOCIALISM IN THE IMPERIALIST COUNTRIES — 104

REFORMISM — 106

THE RISE OF REFORMISM — 107

THE POLITICAL DEVELOPMENT IN THE INTERWAR PERIOD — 111

THE EFFECTS OF UNEQUAL EXCHANGE ON INTERNATIONAL SOLIDARITY — 113

THE WORKING CLASS HAS BECOME A "SACRED COW" TO THE LEFT WING — 122

CONCLUSION FOR THE IMPERIALIST COUNTRIES — 125

THE POSSIBILITIES OF SOCIALISM IN THE EXPLOITED COUNTRIES — 126

WHAT ARE DEVELOPMENT AND UNDERDEVELOPMENT? — 127

THE CONNECTION BETWEEN UNEQUAL EXCHANGE AND UNEQUAL DEVELOPMENT — 129

FOR A NEW WORLD ORDER—WHAT IS PROGRESSIVE? — 134

FOR A SOCIALIST WORLD ORDER — 136

CONCLUSION CONCERNING THE PERSPECTIVES OF SOCIALISM IN THE EXPLOITED COUNTRIES — 139

6 What Can Communists in the Imperialist Countries do? — 141

SUPPORT THE ANTI-IMPERIALIST MOVEMENTS IN THE EXPLOITED COUNTRIES! — 141

SUPPORT THE LIBERATION MOVEMENTS MATERIALLY! — 143

WHAT DO WE WORK FOR? — 144

Epilogue:
The Task of the New Stage — 145
Torkil Lauesen

THE END OF OUR PRAXIS — 145

Reflection and Evaluation	146
Evaluation of the Strategy	148
The New Global Division of Labor	152
Neoliberal Lessons for Dependency Theory	155
The Decline of Neoliberalism	157
From Neoliberal Globalization to Geopolitical Confrontation	158
The Contradiction of the End Game	160
The Current Principal Contradiction	162
"Socialism or Barbarism"	163
Anti-Imperialism Today	165
From Utopian Socialism to Realizing Socialism	166
The Prospects of Socialism	168
Advanced Socialism	170
What Can Communists in the Imperialist Countries Do?	171
There Will Come a Day...	172

Bibliography 179
Abbreviations	179
Literature	179

Works by Arghiri Emmanuel 183

List of Tables

TABLE 1.1	7
TABLE 2.1: SUGAR CONSUMPTION PER CAPITA	14
TABLE 2.2: DECENNIAL INDEX FOR LONDON'S POPULATION: BEEF AND SHEEP AT SMITHFIELD, 1801-51	14
TABLE 3.1	50
TABLE 3.2	53
TABLE 3.3	57
TABLE 3.4	57
TABLE 3.5: DISTRIBUTION OF DEVELOPING COUNTRIES' EXPORTS	60
TABLE 3.6: ROUGH INDICATION OF WHITE MINERS' SHARE IN SURPLUS PRODUCED IN THE MINING SECTOR (CURRENT PRICES AT TIME OF ORIGINAL PUBLICATION)	62
TABLE 3.7: ROUGH INDICATION OF WHITE MANUFACTURING AND CONSTRUCTIONS WORKERS' SHARE IN SURPLUS IN THOSE SECTORS (SELECTED YEARS, CURRENT PRICES AT TIME OF ORIGINAL PUBLICATION)	63
TABLE 3.8: DANISH WAGES 1973-1977 (USD)	68
TABLE 3.9	69
TABLE 4.1: HOURLY WAGES (USD)	76
TABLE 4.2: RETURN ON DIRECT CAPITAL INVESTMENTS IN DEVELOPING COUNTRIES AND DEVELOPED COUNTRIES MADE BY THE UNITED STATES, GREAT BRITAIN AND WEST GERMANY	86
TABLE 4.3: AMERICAN DIRECT INVESTMENT IN MANUFACTURING INDUSTRY. MOVEMENT OF THE RATE OF PROFIT	87
TABLE 4.4: STOCK OF DIRECT INVESTMENT ABROAD OF DEVELOPED MARKET ECONOMIES, 1967-75	89

TABLE 4.5: YEARLY ANNUAL AVERAGE RATE OF PROFIT ON INVESTED
BRITISH CAPITAL 91

TABLE 4.6: WORLD TRADE BY REGION, 1948-1982 93

TABLE 4.7: EXPORTS TO DEVELOPED MARKET ECONOMIES 95

TABLE 4.8: EXPORTS TO DEVELOPING MARKET ECONOMIES 95

TABLE 4.9: EEC DEPENDENCE ON RAW MATERIALS FROM
DEVELOPING COUNTRIES (IN 1972) 97

List of Figures

FIGURE I: REAL WAGES IN BRITAIN FROM 1850 TO 1905	20
FIGURE II	46
FIGURE III	48
FIGURE IV	49
FIGURE V	51
FIGURE VI: MINING WAGES	66
FIGURE VII: MANUFACTURING AND CONSTRUCTION WAGES	67
FIGURE VIII: VALUE OF OPEC HOLDINGS IN THE WEST (USD BILLION)	90

Abbreviations Used in Tables and Formulas

Abbreviation	Meaning	Formula
c	Constant Capital	
v	Variable Capital	
s	Surplus Value	
C	Aggregate Capital	$c + v$
V	Value	$c + v + s$
P	Price	
p	Profit	$P(c + v)$
p'	Rate of Profit	$\frac{s}{c+v}$
P'	Average Rate of Profit	$\frac{s}{c+v}$
s'	Rate of Surplus Value	$\frac{s}{v}$
PP	Price of Production	$c + v + P'(c + v)$

Editor's Note for the Iskra Edition

For clarity and semantic accuracy, some modifications to the text were made:
1. Certain terms were updated to reflect modern spellings;
2. The names of certain countries were updated to reflect modern spellings and names;
3. Tables that were inside footnotes were moved to the main text;
4. Language was added to clarify the context of specific tables;
5. Both tables and figures were renumbered to make them clearer and easier to reference. Tables follow a "chapter.number" format, with Arabic numerals, whereas figures use Roman numerals.

Preface to the Iskra Edition

HENRY HAKAMÄKI NEMANJA LUKIC

WHEN MINING THE ANNALS of radical thought in libraries and dusty boxes, two questions arise—why choose this specific text to republish, and how is it relevant today? These questions will not be answered directly and succinctly, but rather are a throughline within this preface.

Unequal Exchange and the Prospects of Socialism was penned by the incisive minds of the Communist Working Group in Denmark in 1985, as a culmination of two processes: the development of their own 'Parasite State Theory,' and the practice based on international solidarity with the national liberation movements in the Third World. This text served as a clarion call for the dissection of global capitalism's most pernicious mechanisms. Its original publication (first appearing in English in 1986) coincided with the era of Reaganomics and Thatcherism, a time when the siren songs of the free market were at their most seductive, and the specter of socialism was dismissed as a relic of a bygone age. Despite the environment present during the Cold War, the Communist Working Group, unfettered by the shackles of dogma, dared to peer beyond the horizon and envision a future where the principles of socialism could transcend the confines of national borders and permeate the very fabric of global trade. They posited that unequal exchange between the core and periphery was not merely a symptom of capitalism's excesses, but a foundational stone upon which the edifice of inequality was constructed. This perspective, once deemed radical, now resonates with an eerie prescience as we grapple with the stark disparities laid bare by the digital age and the ever-expanding reach of transnational corporations. In a time when the very concept of socialism is being re-evaluated and redefined, *Unequal Exchange [...]* serves as a beacon, guiding us through the murky waters of economic theory with a firm hand and a clear vision, forcing us to keep in mind the uncomfortable truths about the contradictions of the struggle itself. The ideas within these pages have remained potent, biding their time, awaiting the moment when the cracks in the capitalist edifice would once again allow them to seep into the collective consciousness. That moment is now, as we proudly present to you a new edition of this seminal work, replete with an extensive new prologue and epilogue by Torkil Lauesen, one of its original architects.

This re-publication is not merely an act of nostalgia or historical preservation. It is a declaration of relevance. The world has changed significantly since the first edition saw the light of day, but the core principles of exploitation and inequality that the text so masterfully elucidates remain as entrenched as ever. The 'digital age,' the entrenchment of neoliberalism, and the relentless march of capitalist globalization have not only failed to eradicate the disparities identified by the CWG, but have in many cases, amplified them. The chasm between the haves and have-nots has grown wider, and the desperation of the latter more profound. The concepts of unequal exchange, which the group dissected within this text, are as vital today as they were when the book was first released, perhaps even more so. In a time when the very fabric of society is being stretched to the breaking point by the insatiable hunger of the capitalist market, we are reminded that the struggle for a more equitable world is not anachronistic but rather a pressing imperative.

The new prologue that Lauesen has provided is an examination of the birth of the CWG, the internal dynamics of the group, and the era in which they were operating in, as well as specific actions that the group was taking. It also serves to explicate the origins of their interest in unequal exchange and the creation of the original text. Through understanding the processes of the creation of this text and the social realities under which the CWG were operating, readers will be equipped with the necessary tools to best utilize the material within.

Lauesen's new epilogue serves as a bridge between the past and the present, casting a discerning eye over the intervening decades. He dissects the evolution of the system critiqued in the original text, revealing how it has morphed and adapted to maintain its stranglehold on power. In addition, it is a call to arms, not for a return to the rigid structures of yesteryear, but for a socialism that is flexible, adaptable, and responsive to the complexities of the modern world.

The original publication comes with the intellectual endorsement and introduction by Arghiri Emmanuel, the scholar whose name is tightly associated with the term "unequal exchange," and whose work served as a theoretical basis for Wallerstein's conception of core-periphery hierarchy. Emmanuel was not merely an intellectual contributor to the ideological work of CWG, he was also a friend and sympathizer of their struggle.

The most striking difference between this and other works on the subject is the focus on the activist audience. Prior to the discussion and elaboration of unequal exchange theory, the topic was constrained within the high walls of academia, protected by technical language, and a high learning curve that prevented activist and intellectual access to it. *Unequal Exchange and Prospects of Socialism* is a bridge between the two worlds, making a very complex topic accessible and easy to understand to those who carry the struggle on their shoulders. While it reduces the complexity of the topic, it does not oversimplify it nor banalize it. As such, it received positive critique from the authorities in the field such as Samir Amin, and Immanuel Wallerstein.

With this new edition, we aim to reintroduce the ideas of *Unequal Exchange and the Prospects of Socialism* to a new generation of thinkers and activists. The book is not just a historical artifact; it is a living document, a toolkit for those who wish to understand and challenge the structures that perpetuate inequality. It is a declaration that the quest for a more equitable world is an ongoing one, that the lessons of the past are as vital to our future as the oxygen we breathe. Iskra Books is dedicated to the dissemination of knowledge that empowers the oppressed, and in this spirit, we have taken great care to ensure that this revised version remains true to its original vision while also containing notes from Lauesen that speak to the realities of the 21st century.

The book's exploration of unequal exchange is as pertinent today as it was three decades ago. The global economy, with its labyrinthine networks of trade and finance, continues to siphon wealth from the Global South to the North, perpetuating a cycle of dependency and underdevelopment. The original text's analysis of the commodity form and the nature of value in capitalist societies remains a foundational text for those seeking to understand the roots of poverty and exploitation. The re-publishing of this work is an act of solidarity with those who have and continue to fight for a better world. It is a nod to the countless individuals and communities who have borne the brunt of capitalism's depravity, and who have refused to accept their fate with quiet resignation. In the face of a system that seeks to commodify every aspect of human existence, the book stands as a reminder that another world is not only possible but necessary. It is a foundation to stand on for those who wish to dismantle the edifice of inequality brick by brick and build in its place a society founded on the principles of justice, solidarity, and human dignity.

As we stand on the precipice of a new era, with the old order teetering and the future uncertain, it is more crucial than ever to look to the wisdom of our forebears. The new prologue and epilogue by Torkil Lauesen serve not only to contextualize the original work but to breathe new life into its pages. We believe that *Unequal Exchange and the Prospects of Socialism* will resonate with a readership hungry for answers in a time of turmoil. We hope that it will inspire readers to look beyond the surface of our globalized society and to recognize the deep structural inequalities that underpin it, and, most importantly, to join in the struggle to create a more just and equitable future for all.

In the spirit of the original text, this new edition is not a definitive answer to the riddles of our time, but rather a provocation—a spark that we hope will ignite the fires of critical thinking and radical imagination. We publish it not as a final word, but as a conversation starter, inviting readers from diverse backgrounds and ideological persuasions to engage with its arguments, to challenge its premises, and ultimately, to enrich the discourse on the left. For as Antonio Gramsci once said, "The old world is dying, and the new world struggles to be born; now is the time of monsters." We believe that within the pages of this book, one can find the tools to slay the monsters of inequality and give shape to the nascent world that yearns to emerge.

Introduction to the First Edition

Arghiri Emmanuel

OFTEN IN MEETINGS, academic or other, where I was to put the case for my theses on unequal exchange and on the international exploitation which was its outcome, sincere left-wing militants, somewhat at sea, asked the same question in different forms. If this is the case, if the proletariat no longer exists in our industrialized countries, if all, or almost all wage-earners, white collars and blue collars together, have become a labor aristocracy by definition producing less value than their wages allow them to appropriate and thus becoming the objective allies of imperialism, which brings them the supplement, what, then, becomes of the political action of revolutionary marxists? To whom, to which class, to which strata of society can they therefore address themselves?

This question visibly worried them as much as it troubled me. For it is not exactly easy to say to those who have committed their lives to a cause and who have already sacrificed part of it thereto, that they have quite simply mistaken their side.

This is the question to which the members of the *Kommunistisk Arbejdsgruppe* Communist Working Group (CWG) have replied in this book. One must, they say, quite simply, put oneself at the service of the classes which have an interest in overthrowing imperialism, "[...] no matter where they are geographically." This is clearer and more distinct than anything that I have been able to mumble in answers here and there to my various questioners.

This reply is three-fold.

In the first instance, it asserts that the modern structuralist idea of history without actors is unacceptable. The social revolution is borne along by living men. It is not the forces of production which rise up against social relationships. The objective internal contradictions can only replace one structure by another by mobilizing the classes which have an interest in this change. Without that, there is but one alternative to socialism: barbarity and generalized chaos.

It is precisely because of the impossibility today of identifying these classes that the theory of a revolution without revolutionaries has been able to germinate in the minds of a part of the intelligentsia in our industrialized countries. It would have sufficed to place one-self at a point where one viewed the world as a whole to see that these vectors exist.

Thereafter, it reminds us that today the revolution is of necessity anti-imperialist. In the borderline case a social revolution in any of the countries of the center, supposing even that this could take place, would not lead to socialism but to social-imperialism. On the other hand, an anti-imperialist victory in the Third World, even without a direct socialist content, would indirectly open the way to socialism if only by the impoverishing and re-proletarizing of the center.

Nevertheless, the surest way would be a break by the underdeveloped countries both with the capitalist system internally by means of planning and with imperialism externally by the elimination of unequal exchange. The first is an internal matter, the second implies that these countries act in concert internationally.

Finally, this thesis shows that, while the conflict is international, that does not necessarily mean that it is a conflict of nations. It remains a class conflict.

But classes can only fight where they exist, not where they do not exist. Now, as a result of some historical changes which Marx could not have forecast, classes are no longer distributed "geographically" today, according to the classical intranational model. The proletariat, the true party to the cause of the socialist revolution, has practically disappeared in the affluent countries of the center. It continues to exist in the periphery.

Thus, when the people of e.g. El Salvador revolt, it is primarily against their local exploiters that they turn, and the fact that by fighting them they are led to fight their external allies at the same time in no way changes the classical schema of the class struggle. What does change is that these allies of the capitalists in El Salvador are no longer only, and not even to any great extent, the capitalists, but also, and above all, the working class in the United States. Of course this does not mean that all the conflicts in the world are dependent on the class struggle. There are major conflicts: the struggle of the Palestinians against Zionist colonization, that of the Irish Catholics against another type of "white settlers," that of the Blacks in South Africa against apartheid etc., which have nothing to do with the class struggle.[1] But this does mean that any class struggle in which the ultimate issue at stake is the socialist transformation today inevitably transcends the national level and directly implies an anti-imperialist commitment.

On the other hand, nor does this mean that the workers and the capitalists

---

1 **Author's Note:** We do not agree with this formulation. Both national and class struggle must be considered in order to understand the conflicts mentioned by Emmanuel.

of the imperialist center have straightened out everything which separates them. But what separates them is no longer an antagonistic opposition, that is to say, an opposition which can only be resolved by going beyond the existing system; it is an opposition between partners for the sharing of the spoils in the framework of the system. This is the very meaning of reformism. They are therefore natural allies in any outcome in which it is a question of confronting the suppliers of these spoils.

It is not a question of political immaturity of the masses and betrayal by the leaders. It is a question of the contrary: an awareness on the part of the masses of their true interests. No class in the imperialist countries has a stake in the overthrow of imperialism.

The fundamental process remains the same: "Accumulation of wealth at one pole is at the same time accumulation of misery at the opposite pole" (*infra* p. 29). But instead of taking place "internally" today this process takes place "internationally." The "zero-sum game," the condition for the irreducible antagonism, has moved from a national to an international level, whereas within the imperialist center a "positive-sum game" unites the classes over and above their oppositions.

Must we conclude that imperialism, far from being a "stage of capitalism," is a prerequisite therefore, according to some theses (e.g. Serge Latouche) in circulation at the moment? Should we go as far as to say that the destruction of imperialism would mean ipso facto and automatically the collapse of capitalism by the simple disappearance of the necessary condition of its existence?

Certainly not. I would even say that I do not see the meaning which these theses could have when it is a question of capitalist countries which are subject to imperialism instead of practicing it. Should we then admit that imperialism precedes and gives rise to capitalism in the two directions, both as regards its beneficiaries and its victims? Much more conventionally, Bill Warren only speaks of the "pioneering" of imperialism in the countries dominated and exploited by it, where it is a question of an acceleration of the spread of the capitalist relationships already existing in the centers of imperialism.[2] But, in both cases, how can we explain the fact that capitalism has developed in Latin America and in India much less than in Spain or in Greece? None of these countries have practiced imperialism and the last two have certainly been less subject to it than the first. These theses only take on a definite meaning if one restricts the definition of capitalism to reduce it to its special case, that of over-developed capitalism.[3] Then,

---

2 **Author's Note:** Bill Warren presents this opinion in his book *Imperialism: Pioneer of Capitalism*, Verso Edition, 1980.

3 Not to be confused with Lenin's concept of "over-ripe" capitalism. The latter concerns devel-

yes, naturally, it is easy to understand that without imperialism abroad capitalism would never have been capable of ensuring the masses at home the affluence of the countries of the center. Depriving these countries of the fruits of imperialism would not automatically overthrow capitalist relations in general in these countries, but would put an end to this aberrant, atypical, non-antagonistic capitalism which is the consumer society and, as a result, would put the normal process of the class struggle, which will destroy these relations, back on the rails.

This, rather crudely summarized and imperfectly interpreted, seems to be the position of the authors. But the latter have not been satisfied with producing a formula; they have inferred a line of political action from it and are themselves personally committed to it. They practice the "geographical delocalization" about which they speak. They have crossed the front lines and have put themselves at the service of the organized revolutionary movements in the South. The structure of this book reflects the progress of their praxis, as I have been able to witness it through personal contacts which I have had with them. Firstly to know the world, then to transform it. But [...] to know the world as it is today and not as it was in Marx's time and nevertheless to do this by using the Marxist method.

It is not very easy for me to judge the first part, which is devoted to reflection. Its convergence with my own ideas is such that I am inhibited for fear of being partial. But I admire the second part devoted to their action. Not only, and not so much for the courage that that implies and the tasks inherent to this type of adventure. But especially for the amount of moral courage that one has to have if one is not to be content with giving up one's own illusions but tries to dissipate those of others by striking head on at the wishful thinking which is so widespread, so conventional and so "respectable" as that of the present generation of young left-wing idealists in our industrialized countries.

---

opment of contradictions beyond the point where they can be managed within the framework of the system. The former concerns development of the productive forces locally and beyond what capitalism, as a world system, can and did effectively achieve on a world scale.

Prologue

The Struggle Goes On: On Anti-Imperialist Praxis in the Global North

Torkil Lauesen

One might ask oneself, why read this book, a text written nearly fifty years ago about the political economy of imperialism and the struggle for socialism? The short answer is that the struggle goes on, and that history is not only the condition of the current struggle, but also reaches into the future. Our reading of the anti-imperialist struggle in the "long sixties," has an impact on our current strategies, and thus on our actions now, and will continue to have an impact in the future. The past, the present, and the future are dialectically connected and interdependent. The ideas of socialism, from Marx and Engels, to the struggle of the Third World revolutionary movements, still have an impact, because the hope they raised drive us to act, and to realize those ideas in the future.

A longer answer to the question above can be divided into two parts. Firstly, the book was written by an anti-imperialist organization, not only as a theoretical analysis of imperialism, but also as a development of strategy and praxis, to be followed by revolutionaries in the Global North. The book reflects the experience of building an organization and developing a praxis. The continuity of the struggle is important; experience must be passed on as, at once time, we received it. Secondly, the book's analysis of the political economy of imperialism can be used as a basis for updating the perspective on how imperialism works today, again with the purpose of developing strategy and praxis for the continuing struggle. This introduction elaborates on those two answers: the organizational experiences of the group, of which I was a member, and the development of imperialism and the prospects for socialism today. In this way the first part of this introduction expands and clarifies the concluding chapter 'VI: What Can Communists in the Imperialist Countries Do?' Matters which could not be described at the time of publication are elaborated upon here. At the time we were very careful, ensuring our words were not overly specific, so as not to give hints as to our illegal activities. The second part of this introduction is an evaluation of the strategy presented in the book. On this basis an update on contemporary anti-imperialist strategy is outlined.[1]

THE ONES WE WERE

The Communist Working Circle (CWC)[2] was founded by Gotfred Appel in December 1963, as a split from the Danish Communist Party (DCP), which was loyal to the Soviet Union, at the time of the Sino-Soviet split.[3] The DCP was at the time a large party, due to its active role in the struggle against Nazi Germany's occupation of Denmark during the Second World War. The older members carried experiences and knowledge from the struggle in the 1930s and 40s. However, situated in the Scandinavian welfare state, the DCP soon slipped into reformism and focused on parliamentarism.

It was the lack of a thorough-going revolutionary spirit in the DCP, and the compromising attitude of the mother party in the Soviet Union after the 20th Party Congress in 1956 on one side, and the inspiration from the anti-revisionist faction in China and from the national liberation struggle in Vietnam on the other side, which made up the idea for the formation of CWC. Developments in China had for some time been Appel's chief interests. When ideological disputes between Moscow and Beijing emerged in the early 1960s, Appel sided with Beijing. In autumn 1963, Appel left the party newspaper to work for the Chinese embassy's journal *Bulletin*. When he was expelled from the DCP shortly thereafter, he and twenty other DCP dissidents founded the Communist Working Circle. Appel was trained at the Higher Party School in Moscow in the 50s and upon his return to Denmark he led study circles to teach new DCP members the foundations of Marxism. He had been in charge of DCP's publishing house, was a journalist at the Daily Newspaper, and was responsible for contact to the Chinese Communist Party. CWC became Europe's first Maoist organization and maintained contact with the Communist Party of China from 1963-69.

CWC hoped that once they explained the mistakes of DCP's revisionism,

---

1   See also: Lauesen, Torkil (2024), *The Long transition to Socialism and the End of Capitalism*. Iskra Books, Washington.

2   **Ed. Note:** Differentiated from Communist Working Group (CWG), whose formation is explained later in this introduction.

3   For the history of CWC and CWG, see: Kuhn, Gabriel (ed.) (2014), *Turning Money into Rebellion: The Unlikely Story of Denmark Revolutionary Bank Robbers*. Montreal: PM/Kersplebedeb.

more members from DCP would join them, but it was not so. The same negative response came from left-wing trade-unions, and workers in the large Copenhagen factories. Danish workers struggled for little more than higher wages. Socialism held no appeal and solidarity with the working classes in the Third World was not on the agenda. CWC policy had more appeal to young people in the late sixties. CWC had a strong internationalist orientation. It was the first organization in Denmark to call for a demonstration against the Vietnam War on February 8, 1965. The same year, CWC initiated a program to collect funds for North Vietnam. In 1966, CWC founded "The Vietnam Committee." This anti-imperialist solidarity work became the main source of new members and sympathizers for the organization.

This made Appel reconsider his approach. CWC would develop a unique profile within the European left. The Danish working class had no immediate revolutionary potential. The concerns of the Danish working class were very different from those of Third World workers. Danish workers demanded longer vacations, a higher pension, and a raise of 1 USD per hour—Third World workers were starving, did not have a single day off, and were lucky to earn 1 USD per day. A series of articles under the heading "Perspectives for our Struggle" were published in *Kommunistisk Orientering*. One of them explained:

> The working class has no chance of toppling the capitalist class and introducing socialism before the foundation of the capitalist class has been undermined by the struggle and at least partial victory of the peoples of Asia, Africa, and Latin America.[4]

Western Europe was not a "dry prairie" to be ignited by the revolutionary spark, as in the Third World, but rather a damp meadow. CWC's theoretical grounding for this conclusion was that the profits brought home over decades by the imperialist countries from colonies and dependent countries had in part been used to turn the former "dangerous classes" of the nation into loyal citizens. For sure, the working class wanted a higher living standard, but socialism? For this, they showed no interest. They were a labor aristocracy, in the words of Lenin. Super-exploitation[5] and other forms of value-transfer had created the foundation of an imperial mode of living in Western Europe and North America. In 1966, the essence of what is called the "parasite state theory" was outlined in a *Kommunistisk Orientering* article[6] emphasizing the consequences of

---

4   Kommunistisk Arbejdskreds (1966), 'Perspektiverne for vor kamp (part 1)' [Perspectives for our Struggle], *Kommunistisk Orientering*, Vol. 3, no. 3, p. 8. København 1966.

5   For a definition of super-exploitation, see: Marini, Ruy Mauro (1974), *The Dialectics of Dependency*, ed. Amanda Latimer and Jaime Osorio, p. 131-132. Monthly Review Press, New York: 2022.

6   Lauesen, Torkil (2018), 'The parasite state in theory and practice,' *Journal of Labor and Society*.

the theory for socialists in the rich countries:

If we want socialism to become a reality in the Western capitalist world, including Denmark, then it is our highest duty to support oppressed nations and peoples in their fight against Western capitalism, the common enemy.[7]

CWC considered the victory of the peoples of the Third World over imperialism the decisive factor which would then lead to a revolutionary situation in Europe and North America. Any weakening of the neo-colonial grip on the peoples of Asia, Africa, and Latin America would entail a weakening of imperialism and tend to revive class antagonisms and so too class struggle in the imperialist countries. In that sense, it was not just a projection of the missing revolution in Denmark made by "romantic revolutionaries" onto the Third World. The main task was still to be able to pinpoint the turn of events that would create a revolutionary situation in Denmark.

This analysis had also some organizational implications. The leadership of CWC were wondering if it was possible at all to build a revolutionary organization in Denmark, where the social circumstances were not ripe for radical change, and the wish for socialism in the working-class diminutive. If it was possible—what could such an organization look like? Would it be possible to mobilize members with the dedication and discipline needed for such an organization? What should their praxis be?

In the late 1960s, much of the anti-imperialist activities in Denmark focused on demonstrations. The young sympathizers with CWC were at the forefront of these activities. In 1969, *The Green Berets*, a film starring John Wayne about US special forces in Vietnam, premiered in Denmark at a large Copenhagen cinema. In the screening hall, chairs were smashed, and butyric acid poured on the carpet. We also participated in the militant demonstrations against the World Bank meeting of 1970. The aim was not just to protest, but to actually stop the event. Molotov cocktails were thrown through the windows of the congress center, but sprinklers prevented greater damage.

The development of the organization became a human resources management project. Out of the crowd who were attracted by the radical profile and protest actions by CWC's frontline organization "Anti-Imperialist Action Group" members were recruited. One criterion was dedication. New members were expected to prioritize political work over personal lives and careers. But dedication was not enough; discipline was another criterion. The dedicated but "wild ones" were sorted away, even though some were eager to become full

---

7   Kommunistisk Arbejdskreds (1966) 'Perspektiverne for socialisme i Danmark' [Perspectives for Socialism in Denmark], insert in *Kommunistisk Orientering*, no. 3-5, København 1966.

members. What was needed was an organization of more or less professionals, dedicated, and able to act in unity and discipline after a strategy, laid down by the leadership of the organization. There was no formal democracy in CWC, not even statutes; instead, a recognition of the experience and knowledge of the leadership. The leadership was exercised by direct contact between three to four leading members and individual members and subgroups handing out tasks. This structure was only possible due to the small size of the organization. The lack of democracy and formal rules did not seem to be a problem in the beginning, but it became one later.

What had such an organization to offer? What was the attraction, which led me—among others—to join the group, when I was offered membership?

First: the analysis. The "parasite state theory," corresponded to my everyday experiences. It explained that there was a direct connection between the wealth in our part of the world and the poverty elsewhere—imperialism. The parasite state theory also explained why the working classes in our part of the world were not interested in revolution, but only in changes to the ruling system that would grant them a bigger share of imperialist plunder. The analysis was followed up by clear strategy—support the liberation struggle in the Third World, to cut the pipelines of imperialist value transfers. My individual, uncoordinated, and emotional political approach gave way to an organized and strategic one. Furthermore, the strategy advised a concrete praxis—support the liberation struggles. Not only by words of protests, information, and demonstration, but also in deeds and material support. "Solidarity is something you could hold in your hands," as we used to say. There was a clear line between analysis, strategy and action. I knew what I had to do, and CWC offered the organizational framework.

Second: dedication and discipline. It was not only the logic in CWCs theory that appealed to me; it was also the commitment and integrity of the members. From the first encounter with a member—Holger Jensen—I felt that there was a strong correlation between what was being said and what was being done, in contrast to much of the left at the time. It was not just proclamations on "what should be done," there was a willingness to do the job. No one said "sorry, I do not have the time at the moment." Comrades came on time, well prepared, and were working tirelessly. The strong unity in the political outlook, in the small group of 30-40 more or less professional and disciplined activists, created unity in action and energy to manage a huge number of tasks. As the organization had a publishing house, membership also offered the opportunity to learn how to produce informational material from layout and reproduction, to offset printing and binding books.

Third: Schooling and theoretical development was an important component in the group. With the background of decades in the Danish Communist Party, the old comrades knew their classics. There were weekly study-groups and sometimes longer seminars. But schooling was seldom done in the form of general and abstract appropriations of Marxism. We needed methods that tied analysis and practice together. Marxism can only be properly studied when we are committed to action. Hence, the Marxist classics were brought in, to help to solve specific problems in the development of our strategy. The political economy of Marx's *Capital* was used to explain the forms of imperialist value-transfer.[8] The dialectic materialism of Mao was used to find the "principal contradiction."[9] State and class theory from Lenin were used in order to define the characteristics of the social democratic welfare state, and class struggle in the parasite state. Finally, historical materialism was used to explore how Scandinavia was integrated in the imperialist core.[10] But also, more specific limited issues were analyzed: What was the position of migrant workers in Europe? What was the "hippie culture" an expression of? For a period of a year, four comrades lived and worked in Frankfurt, and there were study trips for all members to the Ruhr industrial district of Germany in order not to limit our perception of European capitalism to the Scandinavian welfare states. On top of this—and most importantly—came the specific economic analysis of different Third World countries and their political movements, to decide who, and how, they could be supported. This was not only done by studying books.

In the late sixties, we were certain that North Vietnam and FNL (*Front de libération nationale*, in Algeria) would defy US imperialism. In the spirit of Che Guevara, we wanted to contribute to the establishment of "two, three, many Vietnams."[11] We wanted to transfer the energy from our solidarity with the Vietnamese struggle to other struggles in the Third World. This seemed very possible at the time. There were revolutionary movements in the Congo and the Portuguese colonies of Angola, Mozambique, and Guinea Bissau. There was armed resistance against Ian Smith's settler regime in Rhodesia, and militant struggle against apartheid in South Africa as well as South African rule in Namibia. There were revolutionary movements in the northeast of India, and in Nepal, Cambodia, Laos, Thailand, and the Philippines. In the Middle East, the

---

8 Lauesen, Torkil (2018), *The Global Perspective*. Montreal: Kersplebedeb.

9 Lauesen, Torkil (2020), *The Principal Contradiction*. Montreal: Kersplebedeb.

10 Lauesen, Torkil (2021), *Riding the Wave. Sweden's Integration into the Imperialist World System*. Montreal: Kersplebedeb.

11 Guevara, Ernesto Che (1967), "*Vietnam and the World Struggle for Freedom*," quoted from George Lavan (ed.), *Che Guevara Speaks*, page 159. Pathfinder, New York 1967.

liberation struggle in Palestine received much attention due to its international actions. A left-wing government came to power in South Yemen. The liberation struggle in Oman was on the rise. In Iran, there was widespread resistance against the Shah. In Latin America, revolutionary movements were active from Mexico, Guatemala, El Salvador, Nicaragua, Brazil, Uruguay, and Chile. If, in the early 1970s, one looked at a map of the world and took note of all the countries that had active liberation movements, the future of socialism looked very promising indeed. There were over forty attempted revolutions in the Third World between 1945 and 1975. The zenith was in 1968, in which the rebellions occurred in all "three worlds" at the same time: young people and students rose up in Western Europe, and the Black Panther Party was on the offensive in the USA.

To develop our strategy and to make the decision about where to concentrate our limited efforts and resources, we studied the economic and political development of a number of countries across the Global South. In addition, we traveled to Asia, Africa, and the Middle East to experience the situations there first-hand and make personal contact with the liberation movements. Our travel experiences and talks with liberation movements convinced us of their revolutionary potential. There was an objective interest in a "different world" and a subjective will for revolutionary change. By supporting the struggle there, we could contribute to a radical change of the world order.[12] As a result of Third World liberation movements' victories, we expected socialist states to emerge that would put an end to the super-profits of transnational companies and the unequal exchange between the world's rich and poor countries, and thereby foster a new urgency around the contradiction between the capitalists and working classes in our own part of the world.

In order to maximize the result of our efforts, we had to identify the regions that seemed economically and politically the most important for imperialism. We identified the Middle East as one such area. The region's oil reserves were of vital interest. The Middle East also had geopolitical importance: it lay along the transport routes to and from Asia, and it was close enough to the Soviet Union for the US to launch a military attack.

We also tried to evaluate the class struggles in the regions where liberation movements operated. Was there a revolutionary situation? Which objective and subjective forces were involved? By *objective forces*, we meant the classes that were in motion, regardless of their level of organization or involvement in revolutionary parties. They were in motion out of necessity, due to their miserable living

---

12 Lauesen, Torkil (2020), *The Principal Contradiction*, p. 126. Kersplebedeb, Montreal.

conditions. They could move in different directions, these depending on the ability of the subjective forces to analyze, organize, and mobilize. The *subjective forces* were the revolutionary organizations. In the 1970s, there were often several organizations claiming to be so in the same region. This meant that we had to study and evaluate the potential of each one. Relevant questions were: Is their ideology nationalist or class-based and socialist? What does their organizational structure look like? How do they relate to the objective forces—the masses? What are their strategies, tactics and specific practices? We needed to support the right movements in the right regions, the regions that were most important for the maintenance of imperialism.

Witnessing the living conditions in the Third World, and collaborating with Third World revolutionaries, strengthened our commitment—the wish for justice and our outrage at imperialist oppression. It sparked a feeling of personal responsibility: Third World liberation movements were no longer abstract political entities but now consisted of real life people and comrades to whom we felt obliged. We found it was our duty to support the struggle waged against neo-colonialism in the Third World, while simultaneously preparing ourselves for the outcome of this struggle in our own country.

After years as an active sympathizer, I became a member of CWC. Longtime personal knowledge was a precondition before you were let in, making it very difficult to infiltrate the group. Being a member, I felt like a little cog in a big machine fighting for a different world order. Emotions were the driving force, theory provided guidance, organization brought structure, and practice gave concrete results.

The Praxis

Huge demonstrations against the World Bank Conference in Copenhagen in 1970 made us reflect on the utility of fighting with the police in the streets. At the same time, we had our trips to Jordan, Lebanon and Mozambique, which made the needs of the liberation movements specific, and we made personal contacts which made practical cooperation possible. So, the decision was made to scale down political activities to influence the political situation in Denmark, and instead focus on material support to the Third World liberation movements. In the following years it developed into two distinct and separate forms of providing material support—legal and illegal.

Material support can consist of many things: money, equipment, medicine, weapons, and logistical assistance. But it can also consist of other forms of service: for example, studies that the liberation movements ask for but do not have the time, resources, or the data to conduct. What all forms of material support have in common is that they can be put to concrete use.

In 1971, CWC founded an organization with a rather inconspicuous name, *Tøj til Afrika* (TTA) [Clothes for Africa] to provide material support. Its members were CWC, sympathizers, and other anti-imperialists, but the goal was not to push ideology. The organization collected clothes to be sent to refugee camps run by the liberation movements in Africa and the Middle East. We also organized flea markets and ran second-hand stores to generate cash. On weekdays and during holidays, we sorted and packed them by the ton. They were then transported to Hamburg and shipped to destinations where they could be received by the liberation movements. TTA had chapters in Copenhagen and four other Danish towns, and during its heyday it had about one hundred members overall. In the 1970s, TTA supported FRELIMO in Mozambique, the MPLA in Angola, ZANU in Rhodesia, SWAPO in Namibia, and the PFLO in Oman. In the 1980s, it also supported a Black consciousness project in South Africa by the name of Isandlwana Revolutionary Effort (IRE), as well as the New People's Army in the Philippines. In addition to clothes, shoes, blankets, tents and medicine, we sent the money we made from the flea markets held every month, amounting to around hundred thousand dollars per year. This work also allowed us to spread information about the liberation struggles and recruit new sympathizers and members.

In the 80s we also established Café Liberation, run by activists, to generate a profit for the liberation movements. CWC had a printshop which produced the leaflets and posters for the collection of material, but also magazines, pamphlets, and posters for the liberation movements.

Undercover

Our relationship with the Palestinian movements began in 1969, when a group from CWC went to Lebanon and Jordan in 1969, traveling by car through Europe.[13] We were especially impressed by the analysis of the Popular Front for the Liberations of Palestine (PFLP). The slogan *"Our enemies are imperialism, Zionism, and Arab reactionaries"* spoke to us. The State of Israel is a distinct settler colonial project, but at the same time it serves a certain purpose for US imperialism. The founder of Zionism, Theodor Herzl writes in 1896 in "The

---

13 See also: Lauesen, Torkil (2022), "Solidarity is Something you can Hold in your Hand." *Journal of Labor and Society*, Vol. 25 Issue 1, pp. 123-147.

Jewish State":

> There [in Palestine] we shall be a sector of the wall of Europe *against* Asia, we shall serve as the outpost of civilization against barbarism.[14]

This factor makes the struggle of the Palestinian people important globally, above and beyond the battle for National Liberation. We did not primarily support the PFLP because it wished to establish a Palestinian nation-state, but because the PFLP envisioned a socialist Arab world. This struggle was of crucial importance. Not only because of the oil resources, but also for geopolitical reasons: The Persian Gulf and the Suez Canal are the primary transport roads from Asia to Europe.

In the 70s, the PFLP had party-cells in different Middle Eastern and North African countries. In general, the PFLP had a strong internationalist outlook. It allowed liberation movements from around the world to use its facilities. The first FSLN guerrilla fighters, the Nicaraguan Sandinistas, were trained in a PFLP camp in Lebanon. During our visits, we saw Kurds, Turks, Iranians, South Africans, and Nicaraguans in PFLP camps. In other words, supporting the PFLP meant supporting many liberation movements at once. Finally, the PFLP was a well-established organization with a lot of potential. It had a proper armed wing with training camps; it ran clinics and children's homes, and even had a pension system for families of fallen or injured *fedayeen*. It was essential for us to support organizations that did not stop at national liberation but were eager to lead the struggle further, toward economic and social liberation.

The relation between CWC and PFLP grew stronger in the early 1970s. In August 1970, *Al-Hadaf*, the PFLP newspaper, published an article by CWC with the title "Why Do We Support the PFLP?":

> If under the leadership of a petty-bourgeois class the national liberation movement results in the creation of an independent state with a flag and a national anthem of its own, political institutions and armed forces of its own—but does not result in a weakening of imperialism, can we support it? [...] We can support it, yes, we must support it, yes, but not unreservedly. We must also criticize it. And if at one and the same time there exists another movement, in the same country, in the same part of the world, which strives to give proletarian leadership to the national liberation movement, which will not stop revolution half ways, but which has set out to mobilize the working class, the working people, to fight imperialism the whole way, then there can be no doubt as to whom we must support—in the interest of socialist revolution also in our own country! In the struggle of the Arab peoples against imperialism, Zionism and Arabian reaction we are therefore unreservedly supporting PFLP. Whom else should we support?[15]

---

14 Herzl, Theodor (1896), *The Jewish State*. Jewish Virtual Library, https://www.jewishvirtuallibrary.org/quot-the-jewish-state-quot-theodor-herzl.

15 CWC (1970), 'Why Do We Support PFLP?' Translated from the Danish *Ungkommunisten*, Vol. 3, no. 6. Snylterstaten, https://snylterstaten.dk/why-do-we-support-pflp.

In September 1970, members of CWC were visiting the PFLP in Jordan at the time of the hijacking and forced landing of two aircraft in the Jordanian desert. This action was part of an effort to stop the Jordanian regime's attacks on Palestinian refugee camps. The subsequent political discussions convinced the CWC that it was important to develop its material solidarity work with the PFLP.

We were constantly contemplating how to increase the organization's support for liberation movements. One of the possibilities was to acquire funds in illegal ways. The illegal practice started as an experiment after long and thorough discussions by a central core of the membership. As the first illegal actions were considered successful it was decided to develop this practice. This, however, demanded some structural changes within the organization. In particular, security was tightened internally and in relation to outside partners. We had contacts with Palestinians living in Denmark, especially the Palestinian Workers Union (PWU); however, we stopped that because of the intelligence service's close surveillance of Palestinians living in Denmark.

We did not go directly from legal demonstrations and arranging flea markets to expropriating cash-in-transit trucks. CWC had been involved in illegal activities more or less since its founding. It assisted a group of Indonesian communists stranded in East Europe with false passports to secure them a secret return to Indonesia in order to reestablish the Communist Party after the Suharto-led massacre in 1965-66. Members had been painting slogans in support of the Vietnamese and Palestinian liberation struggles on public buildings, and participating in violent demonstrations and street fighting. There is a significant step from these kinds of activities to acquiring money for liberation movements by illegal means. However, these activities functioned as a kind of bridge, providing a selection process for determining who is interested in participating in illegal activities. These actions were also the first learning steps in careful planning and secret communication. With the CWC's decision to develop the illegal solidarity work, a more careful training scheme was implemented, starting with small and simple tasks. It could be making a false driver's license and renting a car, or stealing license plates.

This illegal practice had a double purpose. One purpose was to provide Third World liberation movements with material resources. The other was to familiarize CWC members with illegal work, which was deemed necessary in a future revolutionary situation. This was the practical extension of our twofold political strategy: first, liberation movements had to be supported in order to throw imperialism into a crisis, which would lead to a revolutionary situation in Europe. Second, a disciplined and organized group had to be ready to seize the opportunity when it occurred in our own country.

As we were in it for the long haul, for tactical reasons, we needed to work *undercover*, not *underground*. The illegal activities had to look like ordinary "apolitical" crime. We wrote no communiqués about expropriations and the like to explain or justify our actions. We knew that we didn't have any support among the Danish population. The *undercover* tactic made it possible for us to operate for almost twenty years.

Had our illegal practice been openly political, it would have forced us to go underground and we would have been chased down in no time. The Red Army Faction in Germany started out by attacking US army bases to support the anti-imperialist struggle in the Third World. Their actions were politically explicit and intended to shake up imperialism's hinterland. RAF wanted to "tear off" the "democratic mask" of the German political system, and intended their actions to serve as an inspiration to the German masses. However, the Red Army Faction were not *"fish swimming in the sea of the masses,"* to paraphrase Mao. RAF was quickly forced into a defensive underground struggle which they were destined to lose.

To successfully execute *undercover* illegal support work demanded certain skills. We were first of all required to develop secure communications, and handle surveillance by intelligence services using counter-surveillance skills, necessary because of the frequent transitions from legal and open political work to undercover illegal activities. These techniques had to be performed in an inconspicuous way, in order not to attract further attention from the police. One mistake and our cover would be blown, not only for the individual, but for the whole organization.

There were many other skills to be learnt, some of which relied on our class position, with many coming from a well-behaved middle class background: how to set up safe apartments to store material, for planning meetings and bases for actions, and making false documents and identification papers. The skills from working at the publishing house were handy in making false documents. We used disguise techniques, uniforms, wigs, false beards, and makeup. Picking locks, stealing cars, sailing a boat, and flying a plane—the list of skills we acquired is long. In the preface to a book about our group Klaus Viehmann, former member of the German "Second of June Movement," called us "Craftsmen of the world revolution."[16]

Up through the 1970s and 80s we managed to execute a series of robberies and fraudulent activities generating millions of dollars. The success was based on careful planning and execution of actions. At that time money transactions

---

16 Kuhn (ed.) (2014), *Turning Money into Rebellion*. Montreal: PM/Kersplebedeb.

were still mainly made in cash. Our first step was to analyze the flow of cash in our society, in terms of time of the month and places in the city. People draw out their salary from the banks by the first of the month. They paid their rent and other fixed expenses at the post office, and used most of their cash at department stores, within the first week of the month. The banks recollected the cash from post offices and stores. From the province cities cash was transported by train to Copenhagen central station, and from there by truck to the post office downtown, to be distributed to the bank headquarters. This information was gathered and confirmed by observation, sometimes using the "latest technology" of hidden video surveillance. The trick was to figure out when and where cash was concentrated, transported, and stored—and most importantly—easy to get access to. What was the best place and time to hit? How to get near the target without looking suspicious, and then hit quickly and precisely with a minimum use of force. Finally, we needed to have a well-planned escape route. As we continued the illegal praxis over the years, it was also important to change *modus operandi*, the way things were done, so it did not look like activities done by the same organized gang, but rather a series of different "lucky punches" by petty criminals.

The decision to embark on and execute such praxis should never be taken lightly. In political practice, there is a real dilemma between the means and the ends. What means are just and suitable to obtain the desired ends? With regard to the liberation struggle, the ends are not petty issues: the end of the exploitation and oppression of millions. Does this end justify any means? Alternatively, do the ends never justify the means? Are the means part of the end? Do the wrong means compromise the ends? You inevitably encounter these dilemmas as a political militant. The answers to these questions are not general and abstract, they have to be related to the specific situation, the time and place. The means must be adjusted to the scope of the struggle.

We justified our limited use of violence—in comparison the brutal imperialist war machine—with the significant support that these means allowed us to provide to liberation movements. We experienced the difficult situation of the liberation struggles firsthand in visits. The struggle of the Palestinians was our struggle. They were our comrades and friends. The massacre of the Palestinian Tel al-Zaatar refugee camp in 1976, and the Sabra and Shatila massacre in connection with the Israeli invasion in 1982, made a huge impression on us because we had visited these camps and talked to the people living there.

In the period from September 1970 until April 1989, I would estimate that we used one third of our time on development theory and strategy, one third on legal solidarity and information, and one third on illegal undercover work.

This balance between developing theory and strategy on one side and the different kinds of praxis on the other, is not a suggested baking recipe. The content and measurement of the ingredients of praxis and form of organization cannot be copied and pasted in time and space. Each specific situation needs a specific praxis and form of organization. Sometimes, when the world-system is under transformation, and the balance between the aspect in the principal contradiction is shifting, theoretical work has priority, in order to figure out what is going on, and adjust the strategy. In other periods praxis—action—is the priority, in order to use opportunity to make a change.

The Split

This line of work continued rather up until the 4 of May 1978, when a major crisis in the organization broke out. In 1977, personal animosities and power struggles within CWC escalated. Originally, Gotfred Appel and Ulla Hauton were CWC's undisputed leaders, surrounded by enthusiastic but unschooled militants in their twenties. By the end of the 1970s, however, many members had a decade of political experience behind them, they had traveled, organized solidarity projects, and so on. They had matured and developed their own perspectives. Some of them were bothered by CWC's internal discipline and lack of democracy that didn't allow discussions, leading to theoretical improvements and development of praxis. Neither the transformation of imperialism since the time of Lenin, nor events like the oil crisis led to adjustments of CWC's political foundations. Ideas for projects were never put into practice, because members were not used to doing things without receiving orders. Furthermore, there were personal conflicts. Ulla felt disrespected by male members. Gender discrimination was without a doubt a problem within CWC, and this was the time when the Redstockings movement was strong, also in Denmark.[17] Eventually, it all came to a head when female members, with the approval of the leadership, demanded that male comrades undergo "criticism and self-criticism" sessions. Men who refused to participate or did not respond "in the right way," were threatened with expulsion. This was serious, as the membership in CWC was central to CWC members' lives. CWC members were proud of their organization—maybe too proud, and sometimes a bit complacent. Politically, there was nowhere else to go either; all their social lives revolved around their comrades.

The criticism and self-criticism sessions lasted through the winter of 1977-

---

17 **Ed. Note:** *Rødstrømpebevægelsen* is the Danish term for the international feminist-socialist Redstockings movement, founded in New York City in 1969.

1978 and effectively put a halt to all other activities. Female members demanded the expulsion of several men. Friendships and relationships were put to a test. Eventually, it became obvious to several members, both men and women, that things had gotten out of hand.

On May 4, 1978, members under threat of exclusion were called into a general meeting for all members, except Houton—and Appel. It was actually the first time I experienced that the whole organization was gathered, in some kind of democratic process. The meeting's agenda was to end the anti-gender discrimination campaign and to analyze how things could have gone so wrong. What were the problems within our organization that had allowed this to happen? A few days later, Ulla and Gotfred were called to a meeting in order to present their views. Ulla was furious and insisted on the campaign continuing. Finally, Gotfred came to the meeting alone and suggested to suspend all CWC activities for half a year; then, the leadership would present a proper analysis of the events. The majority of the members rejected this proposal; they wanted to analyze the reasons for the anti-gender discrimination campaign and the course it had taken themselves. In the end, the members expelled Ulla from CWC after a vote. Gotfred chose to remain loyal to his partner and left the organization.

In July and August of 1978, CWC's political orientation, practice, and structure were discussed at numerous membership meetings. The balance between the anti-imperialist solidarity work, versus mingling with the local left wing and participating in political struggles in Denmark was debated. Was the illegal work the wrong track, too time consuming and risky? The development of theory continued: did "the parasite state theory" hold water at all? On the sideline, all the sympathizers did not know what was going on, and the legal support work came to a standstill.

In the process of evaluations over the months, different conclusions were drawn. It became obvious that there was disagreement about how to deal with the mistakes that had been made and how to move on. Papers with evaluations, future plans, theoretical reflections, and practical suggestions were written and discussed. It looked as if the debates would go on forever. Some of the members—including me—grew increasingly frustrated with the practical part of our work lying idle. We felt that we had a responsibility both towards the "Clothes for Africa" activists and to the liberation movements we collaborated with. They were all wondering what was happening. We wanted to continue the political evaluation of CWC's history and the development of future perspectives, but we also wanted to go back to practical work. In August 1978, we presented our thoughts and announced the founding of a new organization. The former CWC was de facto split into three groups.

Gotfred Appel and Ulla Hauton continued to work under the name CWC, which they had registered. They published the magazine *Kommunistisk Orientering* (Communist Orientation) for a year or so, but never managed to build a new group. Appel was a great Marxist, but limited himself by only sticking to the narrow cannon of Marx, Engels, Lenin, and Mao. I learned much more being part of CWC's schooling and praxis than my later university studies. However, Appel's human resource management was not good. CWC could have unleashed more energy and creativity, by a more democratic and dialogue based leadership.

Other former members of CWC founded the *Marxistisk Arbejdsgruppe*, (Marxist Working Group). They intended to continue with the analysis of CWC's past mistakes, while trying to develop a new form of organization and solidarity work. However, it was also short-lived, and folded in 1980.

The rest of us prepared for a new organization. We seized the assets of the old CWC. Things that were related to the illegal practice were relocated to a new safe location. We reestablished contact with the liberation movements we had collaborated with and explained the new situation. The majority of the "Clothes for Africa" activists in Copenhagen and the chapter in Odense decided to work with us. Later, another chapter was established in Århus. We hired office space and established a print shop.

Manifest—Communist Working Group (M-CWG)

On September 3, 1978, Manifest—Communist Working Group (M-CWG) was officially founded. In October, the first issue of our journal *Manifest* appeared. The first article, "Communist Working Group Founded," outlined our perspectives and intentions.[18] In certain ways we felt like CWC's heirs, but we also wanted to develop our own analysis, improve our practice, and democratize the organization. M-CWG's organizational goal became a bit different from the former CWC's. Even if Appel saw revolutionary development in Denmark as highly improbable, his intention and priority was to to build an organization that had the resources, the knowledge, and the discipline to act once a revolutionary situation in the country would occur. In the end, his support for Third World liberation movements had a clear Danish perspective:[19] CWC was to be

---

18 M-KA (1978), "Kommunistisk Arbejdsgruppe dannet" [Communist Working Group founded], *Manifest*, no. 1.

19 See for example: Appel, Gotfred (1968), *There Will Come a Day—Imperialism and the Working Class*. Copenhagen: Futura. Online: https://snylterstaten.dk/there-will-come-a-day-imperialism-and-the-working-class/s —Snylterstaten.

ready for the day the revolution was returning to Western Europe.

For M-CWG, supporting liberation movements was a revolutionary end in itself. Any possible revolution in Denmark was too far away and too abstract to even consider. Rather, we saw three things as crucial: to develop political analysis and theory; to spread our analysis and theory in order to mobilize more people; to expand the illegal and legal practice. We wanted to provide material support for liberation movements as an organization with a solid analysis. The Danish perspective moved further and further into the background and gave way to a thoroughly global perspective on the transition to socialism. One could say that M-CWG was a reflection of "globalization" before we became aware of it. Our new logo combined a globe with a five-pointed red star.

The establishment of M-CWG set a new energy free. We had been in the doldrums for almost a year. Now there were new possibilities. It was a small but hard-working group of more or less "full-time" activists. During the decade of M-CWG existence, a few people left; others joined. The membership was around fifteen to twenty people. Because of the illegal work, new members were only fully included after a year or so once we had gotten to know them well. There was a circle of fifty sympathizers and volunteers who helped with the legal solidarity work. Our journal *Manifest* had about 200 paying subscribers.

The way M-CWG was organized marked a rupture with the one-way centralism of CWC. We had an elected leadership and there were bi-monthly meetings for all members. We wanted to form an organization able to develop its politics by way of internal as well as external discussion. Holger Jensen was a driving force in M-CWG, as he had been in CWC, because of his dedication and energy. He died in a traffic accident in 1980, which was a hard blow to us. However, the following years proved that M-CWG had become grounded enough to continue its work. Administrative, theoretical, legal, and illegal tasks were divided on the basis of mutual agreement. This gave the organization stability and made it effective.

It is obvious that the illegal practice set limits as to how open M-CWG could be internally. Only those involved in the illegal practice knew about the details—the "need to know principle." But the decisions about which liberation movements to support were taken by the entire organization. We continued the illegal praxis up through the 80s.[20] It was time-consuming, but there were other activities.

---

20 For our cooperation with PFLP in the '80s, see: Lauesen, Torkil (2022), "Solidarity is Something You Can Hold in your Hand." *Journal of Labor and Society*, Vol. 25, Issue 1, pp. 123-147.

The offset print shop made journals for African movements; *Isandlwana Revolutionary Effort* for a South African Black Consciousness Movement, and *Liberation* for an East African organization based in Dar Es Salaam. We also printed material for "Clothes for Africa," our own magazine *Manifest*, and pamphlets and books.[21] The expenses for running the organization were exclusively paid for by member contributions, which depended on the individuals' means. In some cases, those were quite high.

SOLIDARITY WORK

Clothes for Africa continued to send tons of clothes, shoes, and tents to camps hosting refugees from Zimbabwe, Mozambique, Namibia, and Angola. We visited these camps to make sure that all the deliveries arrived. We arranged monthly flea markets. The earnings went to political refugees from South Africa or to the PFLO in Oman in the Arab Gulf. In 1983, we published a book about the conflict in the Western Sahara.[22] In 1985, we were involved in starting the Western Sahara Committee. We were also involved in the Philippines Committee, and the El Salvador solidarity campaign.

In 1987, we opened Café Liberation in central Copenhagen. The café was exclusively run on voluntary labor. All earnings went to liberation movements.

We had four criteria for deciding which movements to support:

- a socialist perspective;
- broad popular support;
- strategic significance for the struggle against imperialism;
- tactical considerations.

We wanted our limited means to be used in ways that made a difference. This is why we often supported movements during the earliest phase of their struggle, when they did not yet receive much other support. Let us name one example: in the early 1980s we supported the Black Consciousness Movement, BCM, in South Africa. The BCM's activities were carried out by students and youths in poor townships around Johannesburg. As mentioned, we printed a journal related to the movement, *Isandlwana Revolutionary Effort*, as well as fly-

---

21 See the website *snylterstaten.dk* for a list of Manifest publications.

22 M-KA (1983), *Konflikten om Vestsahara: Polisarios kamp for et uafhængigt land* [The Western Saharan Conflict: Polisario's Struggle for an Independent Country]. Copenhagen: Manifest.

ers and posters. We sent the material to Botswana, from where it was smuggled into South Africa. We also supported a pig farm and a bottle store in Botswana, which were managed by political refugees from South Africa and functioned as a base for actions on South African territory.

The Development of Politics

To advance political theory was important. We arranged study groups together with sympathizers. We installed a small library at our office in connection to the print shop. This was before the Internet age, so we subscribed to the BBC World Service, which had daily local news cables coming from the Middle East, Southern Africa, and other regions. Different members were responsible for being updated on the different regions., with monthly sharing between all members. This allowed us to keep ourselves updated on the developments in regions in which we supported liberation movements.

To develop an effective practice, we needed to study economic and political relations and to have a concrete analysis of where and how to get involved in people's struggles. Our practice was informed by strategic and tactical reflections to which we dedicated a great deal of time. The importance of politics was also present in our collaboration with liberation movements. We would always discuss international politics first; only after would we go on to practical matters. We developed our political perspectives together. We also resumed our travels. Members went to Zimbabwe, Mozambique, South Africa, Botswana, the Philippines, Lebanon, and Syria. The entire membership visited the PFLP in Lebanon in 1981, both to discuss politics and see their work and infrastructure in the Palestinian refugee camps and develop the feeling of common struggle.

The main objective with our studies was to be able to update and expand "the parasite state theory," and present it in a systematic and comprehensive way, which CWC had not been able to do. Appel was a Leninist. If there was a theoretical problem, his answer was, "Well, let's see what Lenin had to say."

Appel's analysis was a continuation of Lenin's concepts of "parasite state" and "labor aristocracy" in his writings on imperialism and opportunism in the European working class, in the contexts of the First World War and the split in the Second International. CWC adapted—so to speak—Lenin's concepts to the Scandinavian consumer state in the late sixties. Appel's parasite state theory was formulated in a long series of articles in 1967-69 written in polemical debate with Swedish and Danish left-wing groups, discussing the opportunism of the economic class struggle, the national chauvinist attitude of the working class, and the cooperation between capital and the working class in managing the capitalist welfare state. However, we also wanted to consolidate the "parasite state theory" in the economy of imperialism. Again, we turned to Lenin's book "Imperialism, the Highest Stage of Capitalism," and in particular, his concept of "super-profits"—extraordinarily high profits from colonial investments. We wanted to update Lenin's data from 1914 on foreign investments and profits and other factors related to imperialism, an exercise that had already been done by Varga and Mendelsohn in 1938.[23] We collected a huge amount of data and processed them into categories similar to Lenin's. We concluded that the profits from investments in the Third World alone were not sufficient to explain the difference in living standards between the imperialist countries and the Third World. However, our empirical studies also revealed that the ratios of wage levels between the imperialist center and former colonies had expanded from five to one before the Second World War to fifteen to one at the beginning of the 1970s. We also noted a substantial increase in trade based on an international division of labor exchanging raw materials and agricultural products from the Third World for industrial goods produced in the imperialist countries.

One should think that it would be obvious to couple these observations with "dependency theory," which had emerged in this period, but not so. The CWC looked for the answers within the body of work of Marx, Engels, Lenin, and Mao. There was skepticism toward the new academic Marxism. The relationship between struggles on the ground and academia is a complicated one. However, collaboration between academic "theorists" and "practitioners" would certainly benefit radical movements. On one hand, there is no radical theory without practical experience. Theoretical work cannot be separated from movements against capitalism and imperialism. It must respond to the questions posed by struggles on the ground. We cannot afford non-activist theory. On the other hand, there is no radical practice without theoretical reflection. We must evaluate the effects of our struggles and reflect on our experiences. We cannot afford anti-theoretical activism. Radical theory must contribute to radical practice. Its purpose is not just to understand things, but to change things. This requires the development of strategy and tactics.

CWC was not able to update its theory. It was limited by our own dogmatism, so to speak. However, on the individual level some of the members were beginning to read a huge amount of new political economy, which was published at the beginning of the 1970s. The Egyptian economist and historian Samir Amin had spoken of the rich countries forming the "center" and the

---

23 E. Varga and L. Mendelsohn (ed.) (1939), *New Data for V.I. Lenin's 'Imperialism, the Highest Stage of Capitalism'*. Moscow: Foreign Languages Publishing House.

poor and dependent countries the "periphery" of a global economic system that led to Third World poverty and underdevelopment. The American sociologist Immanuel Wallerstein had described the historical development of the world system and the division of poor and rich countries from the fifteenth century to the present. And Arghiri Emmanuel had presented the theory of "unequal exchange": rather than capital export and super-profits, unequal trade was the reason for the world being divided into rich and poor countries.

Emmanuel published his main work *Échange inégal* in 1969. It was translated into English in 1972, and reached the left-wing book shop in Copenhagen, where we got hold of it. There were several reasons why some of us were inspired by his work. His understanding of foreign trade and unequal exchange was a direct extension of Marx's theory of value. Marx had plans to investigate foreign trade more closely in a fourth volume of *Capital*, but never got to write it.[24] Emmanuel picked up this loose end. Another reason why Emmanuel appealed to us was his clarity on the political consequences of unequal exchange, namely the creation of a labor aristocracy. In 1974, a member of CWC visiting Paris went to Emmanuel's address to have a talk, but as he was not at home, he slipped some of our pamphlets in Emmanuel's mailbox. A week later, he got a letter from Emmanuel, regretting that he was not at home and that he was interested in developing contact and exchanging materials, stating that:

> I have found your efforts to clarify your position very remarkable. What I admire in particular is your courage, morally and intellectually. I know from my own experience how difficult it is to resist conformism. There are very few passages in your text that I would not sign [...] What impressed me most [...] was the remarkable way in which you clarify that the Marxist notion of the labor aristocracy does not inevitably mean a minority. If Lenin generally (even if not always) wrote about the labor aristocracy as a minority, it simply reflected historical reality. But there is nothing in the theories of Marx, Engels, Lenin, or any other classical Marxist that limits the 'aristocratization' of the proletariat to a certain percentage or minimum of a specific nation. I have written about this previously myself, but I now see that you stated this before I did.[25]

Actually, this was not true; Emmanuel was ahead of us. He introduced the notion of unequal exchange in his article 'Échange inégal et politique de développement' [Unequal Exchange and Development Politics] written together with Charles Bettelheim in 1962. In it, they asked the question: "Must we [...] enlarge Lenin's notion of the labor aristocracy, by saying that the

---

24 In the introduction to *A Contribution to the Critique of Political Economy*, Marx wrote: "I examine the system of bourgeois economy in the following order: capital, landed property, wage-labour; the State, foreign trade, world market." Marx, Karl (1977), 'Preface,' *A Contribution to the Critique of Political Economy*, MESW.

25 Letter from Arghiri Emmanuel (Mar. 15, 1974). Private correspondence. In French, my translation.

working classes of today's advanced countries constitute the labor aristocracy of the Earth?"[26]

However, due to the reasons mentioned above, the relations with Emmanuel and CWC were not developed in the following years. In 1978, we visited Emmanuel again and established closer contact. For us, the notion of unequal exchange provided the most accurate explanation of the economic foundation of the parasite state. We could now formulate a systematic and comprehensive theoretical basis for our anti-imperialist strategy and practice.

THE HISTORY OF THE BOOK

Unequal Exchange and the Prospects of Socialism was written in 1979-1981. It was a long process because it was written while we studied, and there were other tasks at hand. The idea was to summarize our economic analysis of global capitalism, outline its political consequences, and present a strategy for anti-imperialist practice in our part of the world.

The writing was a collective process. I wrote drafts, which were discussed in workshops, and then I rewrote the texts until the final manuscripts were accepted. The manuscript was translated into English, and a group of us went to Paris to discuss its contents with Emmanuel in 1982. None of us were academics in social science or economics. Rather, most of us were half- or full-time activists, working temporary jobs in order to make a living. However, we had extensive political schooling from CWC, which continued in M-CWG. We wanted to present the theory of unequal exchange in an accessible manner, showing the political implications of the value transfer and, most importantly, offering an anti-imperialist strategy based on our conclusions. We wanted to present the concept of unequal exchange as concretely as possible, by providing actual figures for the value transferred to the imperialist countries. We developed a method to calculate the size of unequal exchange. I spend days at the university library's statistical department, collating information on the numbers of workers in different countries, national wage levels, differences in productivity, and the dimensions and composition of world trade. We discussed the method, and the rest of our manuscript with Emmanuel, and he was kind enough to write a preface for the book.

As we could not find a publisher who would take on the book, we published the book ourselves in Danish in 1983 and in English in 1986. (We must have

---

26 Emmanuel, Arghiri and Bettelheim, Charles (1962), *Échange inégal et politique de développement, Problèmes de planification*, no. 2. Paris: Centre d'Étude de Planification Socialiste.

been busy with other things!) In 1987, we sent a copy to Samir Amin, who also was a great source of inspiration. He wrote back:

> I fully appreciate your work and do share most of it (yet I think you are too "severe" with the western working class) Anyway, I hope we shall have the opportunity to discuss this. I particularly appreciated your estimate of the transfer of value S-N inherent in in the price system. This is really a good piece.[27]

We tried to spread the book as best we could in the Third World, but were not very successful, and we did not receive much response at the time. However, in the last decade the book has been quoted in articles and books. I wonder how they got hold of it. In general, there has been a much better response to texts on unequal exchange and parasite state theory, than in the 80s where those kinds of ideas were totally marginalized.

★

Briefly, on the structure of the text: below is the original 1986 work *Unequal Exchange and the Prospects of Socialism*, with minor edits for clarity. This work referred to economic data of its contemporary era, which more or less expresses the same dynamics at work today, though of course the detailed numbers will have changed. Further analysis of the modern-day application of the analysis is contained in the epilogue, as well as in other texts.[28]

---

27 Letter from Samir Amin (Jan. 21, 1987). Private correspondence.

28 Such as Lauesen, Torkil (2024), *The Long Transition from Capitalism to Socialism*. Washington: Iskra Books. Also, a forthcoming work on Unequal Exchange in the 21st Century to be published by Iskra Books in late 2025.

Introduction

> But, if constructing the future and settling everything for all times are not our affair, it is all the more clear what we have to accomplish at present: I am referring to ruthless criticism of all that exists, ruthless both in the sense of not being afraid of the results it arrives at and in the sense of being just as little afraid of the conflict with the powers that be [...] In that case we do not confront the world in a doctrinaire way with a new principle: Here is the truth, kneel down before it! We develop new principles for the world out of the world's own principles. We do not say to the world: Cease your struggles, they are foolish; we will give you the true slogan of the struggle. We merely show the world what it is really fighting for, and consciousness is something that it has to acquire, even if it does not want to.
>
> —Karl Marx to Arnold Ruge (1843).

The Purpose of Theory is Practice

THE FUNCTION OF THEORY is to be the basis and guidance of our practical conduct. Without an analysis of reality, practice becomes erroneous or marked by accidental occurrences. Whereas a correct understanding of reality makes a rational and efficient action possible.

The basis of our view of the world is our experience, our practice, and our studies. The purpose of this book is to make clear our theoretical basis and thus strengthen our practice.

Therefore, a revolutionary theory should not only describe the world, but should identify the revolutionary classes and be framed so as to form the basis of a strategy for action and be a direction of what actually ought to be done.[1]

The theoretical and practical work and their interaction are the basis of the work of a revolutionary organization. Without practice, theory loses its sense, and without theory, practice loses its direction and becomes accidental.

Marxism—Dialectical Materialism

The preparation of a theoretical basis—and the consequential practice—must start from an analysis of reality, from a realization of what the world to be changed actually looks like and how it functions. Marx's theory with its materialist view and dialectical method applied to the concrete reality offers the best prerequisites of a realization of reality. Marx turned the study of society and its development into a science. Marxism is a method for the investigation of economic and social conditions which regards things as they are: constantly developing and constantly changing. The world has developed enormously since Marx and Lenin. Therefore, a fossilized and idealistic application of Marxism would prevent us from understanding capitalism as it appears today. Followers of Marxism must free themselves from dogmatism and wishful thinking and use the Marxist method when studying concrete reality.

The tendency to change Marxism into a religious dogma which should only be learned, remembered, and practiced, and from which indisputable truths can be inferred, is just as old as Marxism itself. Marx and Engels fought against this tendency, against those for whom "the materialist conception of history [...] serves as an excuse for not studying history."[2]

---

1 "Marxist philosophy holds that the most important problem does not lie in understanding the laws of the objective world and thus being able to explain it, but in applying the knowledge of these laws actively to change the world. From the Marxist viewpoint, theory is important, and its importance is fully expressed in Lenin's statement, 'Without revolutionary theory there can be no revolutionary movement.' But Marxism emphasizes the importance of theory precisely and only because it can guide action. If we have a correct theory but merely prate about it, pigeon-hole it and do not put it into practice, then that theory, however good, is of no significance. Knowledge begins with practice, and theoretical knowledge which is acquired through practice must then return to practice." Mao Zedong (1967), "On Practice," *Selected Readings from the Works of Mao Tse-tung*, p. 63. Peking: Foreign Languages Press.

2 Friedrich Engels to Conrad Schmidt (Aug. 5, 1890).

Analysis of the Economic Conditions is Fundamental

In the Marxist sense, an analysis of reality means first and foremost an analysis of the basic economic conditions, of the development of the productive forces, of the relations of production. Because these basic economic conditions determine social, class and political conditions.

> The materialist conception of history starts from the proposition that the production of the means to support human life and, next to production, the exchange of things produced, is the basis of all social structure; that in every society that has appeared in history, the manner in which wealth is distributed and society divided into classes or orders is dependent upon what is produced, how it is produced, and how the products are exchanged. From this point of view the final causes of all social changes and political revolutions are to be sought, not in men's brains, not in men's better insight into eternal truth and justice, but in changes in the modes of production and exchange. They are to be sought not in the philosophy, but in the economics of each particular epoch.[3]

However, this does not mean that the economic conditions are the only determining factors. Engels writes:

> According to the materialist conception of history, the ultimately determining element in history is the production and reproduction of real life. More than this neither Marx nor I have ever asserted. Hence if somebody twists this into saying that the economic element is the only determining one, he transforms that proposition into a meaningless, abstract, senseless phrase. The economic situation is the basis, but the various elements of the superstructure—political forms of the class struggle and its results, to wit: constitutions established by the victorious class after a successful battle, etc., juridical forms, and even the reflexes of all these actual struggles in the brains of the participants, political, juristic, philosophical theories, religious views and their further development into systems of dogmas, also exercise their influence upon the course of historical struggles and in many cases preponderate in determining their form. There is an interaction of all these elements in which, amid all the endless host of accidents (that is, of things and events whose inner interconnection is so remote or so impossible of proof that we can regard it as nonexistent, as negligible) the economic movement finally asserts itself as necessary. Otherwise the application of the theory to any period of history would be easier than the solution of a simple equation of the first degree. We make our history ourselves, but, in the first place, under very definite assumptions and conditions. Among these the economic ones are ultimately decisive. But the political ones, etc., and indeed even the traditions which haunt human minds also play a part, although not the decisive one.[4]

---

3   Engels, Friedrich, *Socialism: Utopian and Scientific*, MESW, p. 411. [**Ed. Note:** See Bibliography for full references].

4   Friedrich Engels to Joseph Bloch (Sep. 21, 1890), MESW, p. 417.

The Main Social Contradiction

Marx and Engels discovered that the cause of social development and social upheavals is the economic conditions, the contradiction between the development of the productive forces and the limits which the relations of production set to this development. In *A Contribution to the Critique of Political Economy* Marx writes:

> At a certain stage of their development, the material productive forces of society come in conflict with the existing relations of production, or—what is but a legal expression for the same thing—with the property relations within which they have been at work hitherto. From forms of development of the productive forces these relations turn into their fetters. Then begins an epoch of social revolution. With the change of the economic foundation the entire immense superstructure is more or less rapidly transformed. In considering such transformations a distinction should always be made between the material transformation of the economic conditions of production, which can be determined with the precision of natural science, and the legal, political, religious, aesthetic or philosophic—in short, ideological forms in which men become conscious of this conflict and fight it out. Just as our opinion of an individual is not based on what he thinks of himself, so can we not judge of such a period of transformation by its own consciousness; on the contrary, this consciousness must be explained rather from the contradictions of material life, from the existing conflict between the social productive forces and the relations of production.[5]

The Relationship Between Consciousness and Being

> The history of all hitherto existing society is the history of class struggles. Freeman and slave, patrician and plebeian, lord and serf, guildmaster and journeyman, in a word, oppressor and oppressed, stood in constant opposition to one another, carried on an uninterrupted, now hidden, now open fight, a fight that each time ended, either in a revolutionary re-constitution of society at large, or in the common ruin of the contending classes.[6]

The class struggle is the motive power of history. Man creates his own history. But what determines man's motive or rather the motive of the masses? What provokes the clashes of the struggling classes? The answer is: their conflicting economic interests.

About the relationship between being and consciousness Marx writes:

> In the social production of their life, men enter into definite relations that are indispensable and independent of their will, relations of production which correspond to a

---

5 Marx, Karl, op. cit., MESW, pp. 181-2.

6 Marx, Karl and Engels, Friedrich, *Manifesto of The Communist Party*, MESW, pp. 35-6.

definite stage of development of their material productive forces. The sum total of these relations of production constitutes the economic structure of society, the real foundation, on which rises a legal and political superstructure and to which correspond definite forms of social consciousness. The mode of production of material life conditions the social, political and intellectual life process in general. It is not the consciousness of men that determines their being, but, on the contrary, their social being that determines their consciousness.[7]

Of course, a change does not take place without being wanted. Without this desire, anger, and indignation it is not possible to organize the subjective forces of the revolution, who are to carry out the change. But it is important to maintain that revolutions do not primarily occur because people want them. Revolutions occur as a result of a necessity in the social development, a development which can be restrained or encouraged by the social classes, but not terminated. By this we do not mean that historical development is just one big mechanic, objective necessity, that the subjective forces of the revolution and the classes do not play any part in the development of history. On the contrary, it is through these that the objective necessity stands out.

Ultimately, the economic conditions force the oppressed into revolutionary action. Thus it is primarily the fact that they cannot live under the prevailing conditions which makes them revolt. Secondly, it is the fact that they do not want to. It is not possible to convince a class of the necessity of socialism if there is no economic background to this.

Thus it is not by chance that revolutionary upheavals have taken place in Russia, China, Cuba, Algeria, Southern Africa etc., and not in the United States or Western Europe. Neither is it accidental that today's desire for a change, for socialism, has gained much more ground in the Third World than in the United States and Western Europe. This is due to a fundamental difference in the objective economic conditions in the two parts of the world.

THE POPULATION OF THE WORLD IS DIVIDED INTO RICH AND POOR

The present economic world order is characterized by a division of the world population into rich and poor classes, mainly appearing as a division into rich and poor countries. This division is a consequence of the development of capitalism during the last one hundred years, when the growth of capitalism has been determined by this continuous polarization. The growth, wealth, and social welfare of the imperialist countries are inextricably bound up with the wretched

---

[7] Marx, Karl, 'Preface,' *A Contribution to the Critique of Political Economy*, MESW, p. 181.

6 Unequal Exchange and the Prospects of Socialism

poverty of the Third World. Imperialism constitutes these two aspects of the same economic system. The fact that, generally speaking, the capitalist world is divided into rich classes in the imperialist countries, and—a small privileged upper class apart—poor classes in the Third World, can hardly be explained away or denied. The historical facts and the material conditions of today's world speak for themselves.

In 1978 the World Bank quoted the gross national product (GNP) per capita of the 18 richest capitalist countries, which include Denmark, at \$8,070.[8] In the so-called medium income countries, the average gross national product per capita was \$1,250, and in the 38 poorest countries it was \$200. In other words, the GNP per capita of the richest countries is 6.5 times as high as that of the medium income countries, and 40 times as high as that of the poorest countries.[9]

The difference between the rich and the poor countries is worse than ever. The rich imperialist countries with only 25 percent of the total population of the world dispose of 83 percent of the GNP of the world. They consume 75 percent of all energy, 70 percent of all cereals, 92 percent of all industrial products, and use 89 percent of all education offered in the world.

The organisation Food and Agriculture of the UN (FAO) has made a conservative estimate that 450 million people of the underdeveloped countries suffer from serious under-nourishment, which means that they starve. Several hundred million other people in the Third World suffer from general under-nourishment and malnutrition. The per capita consumption of animal protein is 6 times as large in the industrialized countries as in the underdeveloped countries. The consumption of fat is 4.5 times larger, of cereals 2.3 times, and of milk 6 times larger.

UNESCO has made an estimate that in 1980 there were about 820 million illiterate people in the poor countries, which means three out of ten adults. This figure does not include those millions of children who do not attend school today and who will eventually join the masses of the illiterate population. The richest fifth part of the world, i.e. 20 countries with 21 percent of the total population of the world, spend 50 times more on education per capita than the poorest fifth part, i.e. 26 countries with about 23 percent of the total population of

---

8 Throughout this book, the \$ symbol indicates United States' dollars; and the term "billion" is used in its American sense, i.e. one billion = 1000 million (a European milliard).

9 The following figures and information come from a speech held by Fidel Castro at the Conference of The Inter-Parliamentary Union in Havana 15-23 September 1981 (quoted from *Granma*, Havana, 27 Sep. 1981), from *World Bank Atlas 1978*, Washington DC, 1979, and from *United Nations Statistical Yearbook 1978*, New York, 1979.

the world.

The health situation in the exploited countries also reflects the gulf between the rich and the poor countries. According to WHO, more than one thousand million people or 25 percent of the total population of the world live in conditions so poor that their lives are threatened. Seventy percent of the children in the underdeveloped countries suffer from infectious diseases and parasites. Infant mortality in the rich countries varies between 10 and 20 per 1000 live births. In Africa the figure is 150-200 per 1000. In Asia it is between 100 and 150 per 1000 and in South America between 30 and 170 per 1000 live births.

Of the more than 122 million children born annually in the Third World, 10 percent die before they reach the age of one year, and a further 4 percent before they are five years old. On a world scale, about 18 million children under five years of age die each year. Seventeen million of them, i.e. 95 percent, die in the underdeveloped countries. The risk of dying before adolescence is one in forty in the rich countries, one in four in Africa as a whole, and one in two in certain African countries. The expectation of life at birth is 72-74 years in the rich countries. In the poor countries, the average is 50 years but in certain parts of the world less than 40 years.

To sum up, the present situation of the poor countries can be described by the following figures (1980):

TABLE I.I

Undernourished (under the necessary energy and protein level, i.e. starving)	570 million
Adult illiterates	820 million
Totally without hospital facilities	1,500 million
Annual income under $90	1,300 million
Life expectancy under 60 years	1,700 million

The Consequences of the Present World Order

If the present is tragic, the future looks even worse. The total population of the world is estimated at about 4,400 million people, of whom 75 percent live in the underdeveloped countries. In the year 2000 the total population will reach about 6,400 millions. More than 90 percent of this increase in population will

8 Unequal Exchange and the Prospects of Socialism

occur in the poor countries, which means that 80 percent of the world's population—5,100 million—will be living in the poor part of the world in the year 2000. Four out of five will live in the underdeveloped countries.

Estimates made by the United Nations show that the GNP per capita in the year 2000 will be at a world average of about $2,311 (in 1975 dollars). This means a global increase of 53 percent compared with 1975. But the increase will not be equally distributed. The GNP per capita of the industrialized countries will increase to about $8,500, whereas the GNP per capita of the underdeveloped countries will remain at less than $590 on average. Thus in the year 2000, the average income per capita in the industrialized countries will be 14 times as high as in the underdeveloped countries. If we compare the GNP of the ten richest capitalist countries with that of the underdeveloped countries, the difference is of the order of 20. All this means that the gulf between the rich and the poor countries will become twice as wide during the next twenty years. In 1975, the average difference in the GNP per capita between rich and poor countries was about $4,000, in the year 2000 it will be about $8,000. The gulf which separates rich and poor today, and which seems so bottomless, will in only 18 years be twice as wide, if the present world order continues.

The profound economic, social, and political crises which the Third World is now experiencing, and which cannot be resolved within the imperialist world order, will inevitably result in profound revolutionary changes in the individual countries and in the relationship between the rich and the poor countries. The crisis in the Third World has resulted in a demand for socialism and for a world order which advances development in the exploited countries and reduces inequality in the world. This demand will gain strength during the coming years.

--------------------- ★ ---------------------

Below we shall deal with the historical background of this division of the world into rich and poor countries (classes). We shall describe how the rich imperialist countries exploit the poor countries, and how this has influenced economic development in the poor and in the rich countries, and we shall outline how this has affected the struggle for socialism on a global scale.

We have in our account concentrated on "unequal exchange" and its consequences, as we consider this to be the most important mode of imperialist exploitation. By the same token, world trade has become the main subject of our analysis. Consequently, the economies of the socialist countries will only be touched upon superficially, because their foreign trade is relatively small compared to that of the capitalist countries. In the global struggle against imperialism, and for socialism, socialist countries play an important role as counterweight against imperialism in the struggle of the oppressed masses in the poor countries. This role of the socialist countries in the world economy is a question of great importance, to which we will return in our future writings.

In the following we shall deal with the most important general lines. Undoubtedly, there are situations and exceptions which our representation does not cover. Thus, this is neither an adequate historical account nor any profound analysis of capitalism; it is rather an outline of some general features which we consider important for the understanding of the development and function of imperialism.

2

The Historical Background of Unequal Exchange

The Development of Capitalism in the Nineteenth Century

THE FIRST TENDENCIES towards a division of the world into a rich imperialist part and a poor exploited part can be seen in the second half of the nineteenth century. As early as at that time it seemed as if the capitalist mode of production was about to be played out as a progressive force. The capitalist world was shaken by ever more serious economic crises at ever shorter intervals. The social consequences of those crises made the specter of Communism haunt Europe.

However, imperialism and the consequential division of the world into rich and poor countries (classes) offered new conditions of growth for capitalism. The crisis was overcome and capitalism developed as never before. The specter of Communism was exorcized. Marx's and Engels' ideas about the potentialities of capitalism were turned upside down by this. Below we shall discuss in detail the contradictions which led to the capitalist crises—and what resolved them around the turn of the century.

Britain's Industrial Monopoly

The external precondition of Britain's growth as a capitalist country was a commercial empire which resulted in the foundation of a world-wide colonial empire. Britain became the center of world trade, and an industrial division of labor developed in relation to overseas countries. They supplied the raw material to British industry which in return supplied the finished products. Britain became the workshop of the world, and her industry expanded in an international vacuum created by the British navy. Thus the monopoly of the international market gave Britain a similar monopoly of industrial manufacture, a monopoly which Britain held during the first half of the nineteenth century.[1]

During this initial period British capitalism developed at the expense of handicraft nationally as well as internationally, which meant that British industrial goods were comparatively cheaper—British industry was able to sell all the goods that it could produce.

THE CONTRADICTION PRODUCTION—CONSUMPTION

Already in the 1840s capitalist Britain was marked by crises. These appeared as overproduction, which was a result of the contradiction production-consumption. This contradiction characterizes the capitalist mode of production. The capitalists produce only to increase their capital. In order to achieve the highest rate of profit possible the capitalists will always be forced to increase production, to introduce new technology and to throw an ever increasing number of articles into the market.

But the extent of the population's consumption is limited by the laws set by capitalist exploitation. On the one hand the capitalists fight to keep wages as low as possible to achieve the highest rate of profit possible. On the other hand wages represent a considerable part of the demand which is to yield the profit when the goods are sold.

Thus the capitalist mode of accumulation tends to ruin its own market. If the capitalists increase the wages, they will limit their own potential profit—and if the wages are lowered, the market will be limited. In both cases the capitalists will cease making investments. In the first case they will not have the capability, and in the second they will lack the incentive of a market able to buy. About this Engels writes:

> We have seen that the ever-increasing perfectibility of modern machinery is, by the anarchy of social production, turned into a compulsory law that forces the individual capitalist always to improve his machinery, always to increase its productive force. The bare

---

1 "The concentration of trade and manufacture in one country, England, developing irresistibly in the seventeenth century, gradually created for this country a relative world market, and thus a demand for the manufactured products of this country which could no longer be met by the industrial productive forces hitherto existing. This demand, outgrowing the productive forces, was the motive power which, by producing large-scale industry—the application of elemental forces to industrial ends, machinery and the most extensive division of labor—called into existence the third period of private property since the Middle Ages." Marx, Karl and Engels, Friedrich, *The German Ideology*, p. 72.

possibility of extending the field of production is transformed for him into a similar compulsory law. The enormous expansive force of modern industry, compared with which that of the gasses is mere child's play, appears to us now as a necessity for expansion, both qualitative and quantitative, that laughs at all resistance. Such resistance is offered by consumption, by sales, by the markets for the productive modern industry. But the capacity for extension, extensive and intensive, of the markets is primarily governed by quite different laws that work much less energetically. The extension of the markets cannot keep pace with the extension of production. The collision becomes inevitable, and as this cannot produce any real solution so long as it does not break in pieces the capitalist mode of production, the collisions become periodic [...] Capitalist production has begotten another "vicious circle."[2]

Marx & Engels On the Potentialities of Capitalism

As early as in the 1840s Britain was marked by such crises of overproduction. On the one hand the rapid accumulation in the first decades of the century meant an enormous increase in the capacity of the production apparatus. On the other hand the low wages meant a reduction of the domestic market. Internationally, French and American industry began to be competitive. Industry no longer competed with handicraft only. The competition among the capitalists themselves became the most important.

This initial period of the development of industrial capitalism resulted in a revolution of the productive forces and an enormous increase in productivity. The advance from spinning-wheel to spinning-machine, from hand-loom to power-loom, the invention of the steam engine, the introduction of the railways [...] increased productivity enormously. However, this increase in productivity did not in any way mean better conditions for the working class—on the contrary. During the whole period wages were near the physiological subsistence level.

Statistics from the first half of the nineteenth century are very scanty. By way of investigations on the consumption per capita of various consumer goods, E. J. Hobsbawm has studied the standard of living of the British working class and arrives at the following:

> From the later 1790s until the early 1840s, there is no evidence of any major rise in the per capita consumption of several foodstuffs, and in some instances evidence of a temporary fall which had not yet been completely made good by the middle 1840s. If the case for deterioration in this period can be established firmly, I suggest that it will be done on the basis of consumption data.
>
> Tea, sugar and tobacco, being wholly imported, furnish national consumption figures which may be divided by the estimated population to give a crude index of per capita

---

2   Engels, *Socialism*, MESW, p. 419.

consumption.

Table 2.1: Sugar Consumption per Capita

Decade	Annual Average
1800-09	19.12
1810-19	18.06
1820-29	17.83
1830-39	17.59
1840-49	18.45
1850-59	30.30
1860-69	53.90
1870-79	68.09

[...] Tea, sugar and tobacco indicate no marked rise in the standards of living, but beyond this little can be deduced from the crude series.

The case of meat is different. Here we possess [...] the Smithfield figures for London for the entire period [...] The Smithfield figures show that, while London's population index rose from 100 in 1801 to 202 in 1841, the number of beef cattle slaughtered rose only to 146, or sheep to 176 in the same period. The following table [2.2] gives the figures by decades:

Table 2.2: Decennial Index for London's Population: Beef and Sheep at Smithfield, 1801-51

Date	Population	Beef	Sheep
1801	100	100	100
1811	119	105	119
1821	144	113	135
1831	173	127	152
1841	203	146	176
1851	246	198	193

It will be seen that the increase in beef lagged behind that in population in all decades until the 1840s. Mutton also lagged—though less—except in the first decade. On the whole a per capita decline in London meat consumption up to the 1840s is thus almost certain [...]

About cereals and potatoes, the staple of the poor man's diet, we can also find out some things. The fundamental fact is that, as contemporaries already knew, wheat production and imports did not keep pace with the growth of population so that the amount of wheat available per capita fell steadily from the late eighteenth century until the 1850s, the amount of potatoes available rising at about the same rate.

On the basis of various case-studies, Hobsbawm also calculates unemployment during this same period at about 20 to 50 percent. He concludes that no basis exists for an improvement in the standard of living during this period, but rather a reduction, most pronounced from 1800-1815.

The contradiction between the still increasing production and the stagnant tendency in consumption resulted in a fall in the rate of profit—in crises of overproduction. Capitalism had only one way in which these crises could be avoided, and that was to find new markets for their goods and capital. Capitalism cannot be confined to one country; according to its very nature it must continuously expand. The *Manifesto of the Communist Party* says:

> The need of a constantly expanding market for its products chases the bourgeoisie over the whole surface of the globe. It must nestle everywhere, settle everywhere, establish connections everywhere [...] The bourgeoisie, by the rapid improvement of all instruments of production, by the immensely facilitated means of communications, draws all, even the most barbarian, nations into civilisation. The cheap prices of its commodities are the heavy artillery with which it batters down all Chinese walls, with which it forces the barbarians' intensely obstinate hatred of foreigners to capitulate. It compels all nations, on pain of extinction, to adopt the bourgeois mode of production; it compels them to introduce what it calls civilization into their midst, i.e., to become bourgeois themselves. In one word, it creates a world after its own image.[3]

Marx also describes how British capital had to seek outside Britain to find profitable openings for investments:

> The really disquieting feature for England [...] is this, that she is apparently at a loss to find at home a sufficient field of employment for her unwieldy capital; that she must consequently lend on an increasing scale, and similar, in this point, to Holland, Venice and Genoa, at the epoch of their decline, forge herself the weapons for her competitors.[4] She is forced, by giving large credits, to foster speculation in other countries in order to find a field of employment for her surplus capital; and thus to hazard her ac-

---

3   Marx and Engels, op. cit., MESW, pp. 38-9.

4   Marx writes in *Capital*: "Thus the villainies of the Venetian thieving system formed one of the secret bases of the capital-wealth of Holland to whom Venice in her decadence lent large sums of money. So also was it with Holland and England; By the beginning of the 18th century the Dutch manufactures were far outstripped. Holland had ceased to be the nation preponderant in commerce and industry. One of its main lines of business, therefore, from 1701-1776, is the lending out of enormous amounts of capital, especially to its great rival England. The same thing is going on to-day between England and the United States. A great deal of capital, which appears to-day in the United States without any certificate of birth, was yesterday, in England, the capitalized blood of children." Vol. I, p. 707.

16 Unequal Exchange and the Prospects of Socialism

quired wealth in order to augment and conserve it. By being obliged to give large credits to foreign manufacturing countries, such as the Continent of Europe, she forwards herself the means to her industrial rivals to compete with her for the raw produce, and thus is herself instrumental in enhancing the raw material of her own fabrics. The small margin of profit thus left to the British manufacturer, still reduced by the constant necessity for a country the very existence of which is bound up with the monopoly of forming the workshop of the world, constantly to undersell the rest of the world, is then compensated for by curtailing the wages of the laboring classes and creating home misery on a rapidly-enlarging scale. Such is the natural price paid by England for her commercial and industrial supremacy.[5]

Thus Marx regarded capitalist development as a centrifugal process. It was the contradictions of capitalism itself which caused this process. These contradictions were manifested by the decreasing possibilities of profitable investments in the highest developed, capitalist countries. At the same time more profitable investments could be made in the colonies and in the less developed countries. This situation led to capital exports. Marx believed that this would result in capitalism spreading all over the world. But he did not imagine that this would result in a "fixed" division of the world's highly developed imperialist center and an exploited and underdeveloped periphery. Marx thought that capital would flow out and make the rest of the world a reflected image of Britain and thus develop globally the same contradictions which threatened British capitalism.[6]

The country that is more developed industrially only shows, to the less developed, the image of its own future.[7]

Around 1830 Britain had carried through the initial stage of the industrial revolution. At that time continental Europe and the United States had hardly begun their industrial revolution. These countries did not become a periphery to Britain. On the contrary British capital contributed to a large extent to making them highly developed capitalist countries. The United States caught up with Britain a few decades later. Marx believed that the development in the colonies in Asia and Africa would be similar. When Britain had destroyed the original societies and introduced capitalism, these colonies would experience

---

5 Marx, Karl, 'British Commerce,' MECW, Vol. 15, p. 430.

6 Marx quotes H. Fawcett, professor of political economy, as follows: "The aggregate wealth which is annually saved in England, is divided into two portions; one portion is employed as capital to maintain our industry, and the other portion is exported to foreign countries [...] Only a portion, and perhaps, not a large portion of the wealth which is annually saved in this country, is invested in our own industry." Marx comments: "The greater part of the yearly accruing surplus-product, embezzled, because abstracted without return of an equivalent, from the English laborer, is thus used as capital, not in England, but in foreign countries." *Capital*, Vol. I, pp. 572-3.

7 Marx, Karl, *Capital*, Vol. I, p. 19.

a rapid development which would make them the reflected image of Britain. About Britain's role in India, Marx says:

> England has to fulfill a double mission in India, one destructive, the other regenerating—the annihilation of old Asiatic society, and the laying of the material foundations of Western society in Asia [...]
>
> I know that the English millocracy intend to endow India with railways with the exclusive view of extracting at diminished expenses the cotton and other raw materials for their manufactures. But when you have once introduced machinery into the locomotion of a country, which possesses iron and coals, you are unable to withhold it from its fabrication. You cannot maintain a net of railways over an immense country without introducing all those industrial processes necessary to meet the immediate and current wants of railway locomotion, and out of which there must grow the application of machinery to those branches of industry not immediately connected with railways. The railway system will therefore become, in India, truly the forerunner of modern industry.[8]

The opening of new markets in Africa and Asia, the capitalist exports to North and South America would put off the collapse of capitalism for a while. However, it would only be a short respite; the final result would merely be an even more intense accumulation which would lead to a new and more intensified crisis of overproduction.

Engels outlines the perspective of capitalist development in the following way:

> Even in quite barbarous lands the bourgeoisie is advancing. In Russia, industry is developing by leaps and bounds and is succeeding in converting even the boyars into bourgeois. Both in Russia and Poland serfdom is being restricted and the nobility thereby weakened in the interest of the bourgeoisie, and a class of free peasants is being created which the bourgeoisie everywhere needs [...] —In Hungary the feudal magnates are more and more changing into wholesale corn and wool merchants and cattle dealers, and consequently now appear in the Diet as bourgeois.—What of all the glorious advances of "civilisation" in such lands as Turkey, Egypt, Tunis, Persia, and other barbarous countries? They are nothing else but a preparation for the advent of a future bourgeoisie. In these countries the word of the prophet is being fulfilled: "Prepare ye the way of the Lord [...] Lift up your heads, 0 ye gates; and be ye lift up, ye everlasting doors; and the King of glory shall come in. Who is the King of glory?"—The bourgeois!
>
> Wherever we look, the bourgeoisie are making stupendous progress. They are holding their heads high, and haughtily challenge their enemies. They expect a decisive victory, and their hopes will not be disappointed. They intend to shape the whole world according to their standard, and, on a considerable portion of the earth's surface, they will succeed.
>
> We are no friends of the bourgeoisie. That is common knowledge. But this time we do not grudge the bourgeoisie their triumph. We can chuckle over the haughty looks which the bourgeois deign to bestow (especially in Germany) upon the apparently tiny band

---

8 Marx, *The Future Results of the British Rule in India*, MEOC, pp. 82,84.

of democrats and Communists. We have no objection if everywhere they force through their purposes.

Nay more. We cannot forbear an ironic smile when we observe the terrible earnestness, the pathetic enthusiasm with which the bourgeois strive to achieve their aims. They really believe that they are working on their own behalf! They are so shortsighted as to fancy that through their triumph the world will assume its final configuration. Yet nothing is more clear than that they are everywhere preparing the way for us, for the democrats and the Communists, than that they will at most win a few years of troubled enjoyment, only to be then immediately overthrown [...]

So just fight bravely on, most gracious masters of capital! We need you for the present; here and there we even need you as rulers. You have to clear the vestiges of the Middle Ages and of absolute monarchy out of our path; you have to annihilate patriarchalism; you have to carry out centralisation; you have to convert the more or less propertyless classes into genuine proletarians, into recruits for us, by your factories and your commercial relationships you must create for us the basis of the material means which the proletariat needs for the attainment of freedom. In recompense whereof you shall be allowed to rule for a short time. You shall be allowed to dictate your laws, to bask in the rays of the majesty you have created, to spread your banquets in the halls of kings, and to take the beautiful princess to wife—but do not forget that "The hangman stands at the door!"[9]

The New Manifestation of the Contradiction

Marx's and Engels' predictions regarding the development of the colonies and the early collapse of capitalism did not come true. Not that their analyses of capitalism at that time were wrong. At the middle of the nineteenth century, the capitalist system actually was on the verge of having exhausted its potentials. The crises arose at shorter and shorter intervals and assumed an increasingly serious character. The strength and fighting spirit of the proletariat grew accordingly. What Marx and Engels could not foresee was that the very fight of the proletariat for better conditions became the incentive behind a global change of the capitalist mode of accumulation, a change which meant a postponement of the collapse of capitalism. When aggravating crises seemed to bode its collapse, a development started which offered renewed growing power and life to capitalism, but based on transfer of values from abroad.

From the middle of the nineteenth century the conditions of the European proletariat began to change. For the first time in the history of capitalism, the capitalists had to pay wages above the mere subsistence level. This first tiny improvement was not primarily a result of the fight of the proletariat itself. The labor movement was politically weaker than before and Chartism had been im-

---

9 Engels, Friedrich, *Movements of 1847*, MECW, Vol. 6, pp. 527-9.

paired by cleavage and corruption.[10] These first improvements in wages and working conditions for the British proletariat were due to contradictions between the ruling classes.

As mentioned above, Britain had a virtual monopoly of industrial goods at the beginning of the nineteenth century. This monopoly resulted in extra profits. However, this profit did not primarily go to the industrial capitalists, and during the first part of the century it definitely did not result in higher real wages to the working class either. Paradoxically, the extra profits from the industrial monopoly had mainly gone to the class of landowners.

By virtue of their historically strong position in Parliament, the landowners had succeeded in introducing an embargo on the importation of corn and other agricultural products into Britain from 1804. This embargo meant that the landowners could maintain an artificially high level of prices for their products. The high prices meant that the capitalists had to pay the workers comparatively high nominal wages just to enable them to live above the breadline. However, wages were still subsistence wages, and no increase in real wages could be seen.

By this artificially high price of corn the landowners could secure a considerable part of the extra profits earned by the British industrial monopoly. So in the 1840s the industrial capitalists urged to have the Corn Laws repealed. Together with the working class they succeeded in repealing the laws in 1846. And the reopening of the importation of corn from Prussia especially and later from the United States did cause a fall in prices of bread and other food.

---

10 The Chartist movement was founded in 1836 by artisans and workers in London. It got its name from "The People's Charter," a number of demands for reforms in the parliamentary system with the purpose of strengthening the influence of the labor movement in Parliament. The movement was widely supported by the working class in the 1840s but without getting its demands for wider franchise satisfied. It died out in the 1850s.

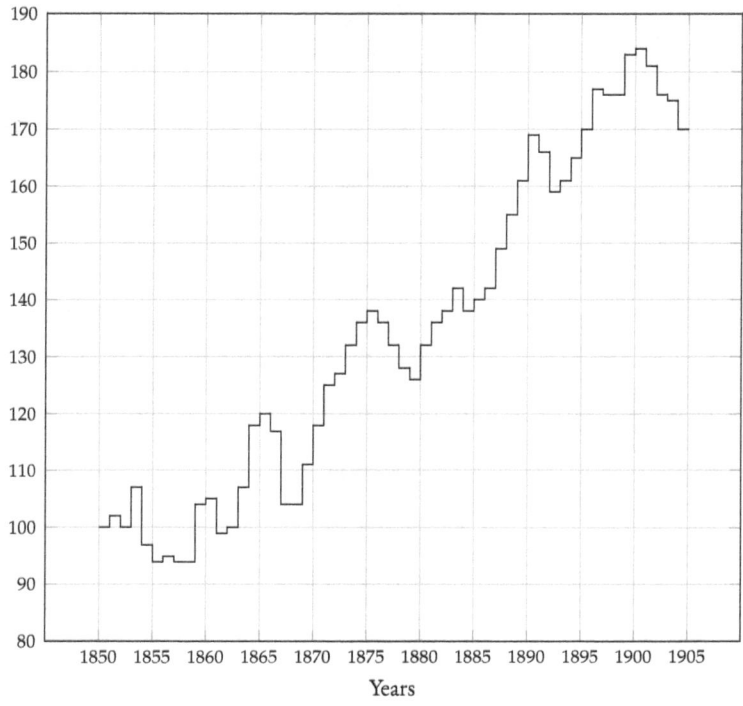

Figure I: Real Wages in Britain from 1850 to 1905[11]

Following the fall in corn prices, the industrial capitalists tried to decrease the nominal wages, but the working class was able to limit the decrease and thus to obtain an improvement in real wages. This tendency was further enhanced by the introduction of a ten-hour working-day, for which the working class had been fighting for 30 years. It was introduced shortly after the abrogation of the Corn Laws as the working class was unexpectedly supported by the landowners in Parliament, who thirsted for revenge on the industrial capitalists.

The extra profits of the British industrial monopoly and the internal fight between landowners and industrial capitalists thus meant that the wages of the British Working class were increased above the subsistence level at which they had so far been kept.

Towards the end of the century this tendency was further reinforced—now

---

11 Source: Jones, R.B., *Economic and Social History of Britain 1770-1977*, p. 170.

as a direct result of the struggle of the working class. The working class organized itself in powerful unions and became integrated into the bourgeois parliamentary democracy. Parts of the class succeeded in obtaining improved wages and working conditions and extended political and industrial rights. This increase in wages—which occurred first in Britain, later in France, Germany and the other West European countries—contributed to resolving the profound crises which capitalism experienced in the 1870s and 1880s in Europe. For the wage increases meant an expansion of the domestic market, growing market potentials and a solution to the crises of overproduction. This wage increase and the consequent market expansion took place without the rate of profit falling below the acceptable line for capital accumulation. The historical background to this was first the incorporation, i.e. the proletarization and exploitation, of an increasing number of people of the colonial areas into the capitalist system. Not only as markets for industrial products as had been the case before, but now to an increasing extent as laborers or workers in plantations, mines, and factories run by capitalists. But here wages were at a physical minimum—or below. This ruthless exploitation of colonial labor was the basis of bigger profits in the colonies compared with those "at home." Then the movement of capital within the individual colonial power and its colonies could gradually result in a tendency towards an equalization of the rate of profit. Money invested at home and money invested in the colonies yielded profits according to the amount of capital invested. The rate of profit did not depend on where the capital was invested or how much surplus labor it actually extorted from the workers. The fall in the rate of profit which could be expected as a result of the rising wages in Europe was equalized by the increase in surplus labor in the colonies. Surplus labor—extorted from the proletariat in the colonies—compensated for the fall in the rate of profit in the "mother countries." The compensation was seen by a tendency to an equalization of the rate of profit.

Globally, this was the beginning of a temporary solution to the contradiction production-consumption. On the one hand the capitalists took advantage of the increasing wages "at home" and the consequential improvement of the demand. On the other hand the low wages in colonial areas secured a high rate of profit.

The result was a gradual change of the capital flow within the global capitalist system. Instead of exporting capital, the highly developed capitalist countries—i.e. the imperialist countries—began to absorb capital from the colonies. Earlier, capital had tried to modify its tendencies towards crises by exporting surplus capital, but now things began to change. The imperialist countries could now—as a consequence of the expanding domestic market—find investments at home for their capital. Actually, there was not enough capital. Capital started to flow from the colonies to the imperialist countries. It is true that British capital exports increased strongly towards the end of the nineteenth century, but capital imports—the repatriation of profits—increased together with exports, so there was no question at all of capital exports in its proper sense. Therefore, during this epoch of classic imperialism British capital exports do not reflect a situation in which surplus capital in the domestic market cannot find profitable openings for investments.[12] Where capitalism had earlier tended to equalize the difference, in development between the highly developed industrialized countries and the colonies by means of net capital exports, a development now began which divided the world into developed and underdeveloped—into rich and poor countries. This division of the world became a historical necessity for continued expansion of the capitalist mode of production, and formed the basis of a new epoch in capitalist development. It created a framework which resulted in capitalism being able to develop the productive forces at renewed speed.

We would like to stress that this development or tendency starts at the end of the nineteenth century. At first, the improvements in wages and working conditions did not radically change the material conditions of the British working class. The increase in wages by no means applied to the entire class; they were confined to the skilled and better organized part of the industrial workers. Compared with today's standard of living in Europe even these workers' conditions were wretched. But compared to the general conditions during the first half of the century—and compared to the laborers and slaves in the colonies—improvements in wages, working conditions and political rights had certainly taken place. At the beginning of our century, widespread hunger and distress—as it can be seen in the Third World today—had disappeared in Britain and the other West European countries.

Generally speaking, the conditions of the working class have improved in these countries since at the end of the nineteenth century. Setbacks and crises have occurred, but they have been resolved within the framework of the system—and the solutions have led to a consolidation of the capitalist system in the rich countries.

Politically the new economic tendency immediately became of greater importance as it changed the conditions of the class struggle. The economic and political improvements which the capitalist class would not at any price grant during the first half of the century—and could not possibly grant at that time—it began to concede at the end of the century. But absolutely not voluntarily. The working class in Europe and in the United States won their economic and po-

---

12 See the article: Emmanuel, Arghiri (1972), "The White Settler Colonialism and the Myth of the Investing Imperialism." *New Left Review*, no. 73, May-June 1972.

litical improvements through hard industrial and political fights with the bourgeoisie. Earlier improvements of working class conditions questioned the very existence of capitalism. Now it became possible to obtain considerable improvements within the capitalist framework, because these improvements were paid for by the exploitation of the population in the colonies.

The difference in wages of the workers in the colonies and in the imperialist countries resulted in cheaper and cheaper products from the colonies, while products from the imperialist countries became increasingly expensive. In this way a new mode of imperialist exploitation arose: Unequal exchange—the exploitation of the poor countries through trade with the rich countries. The economic importance of unequal exchange has grown *pari passu* with the differences in wages between rich and poor countries. This method of exploitation becomes prevalent after the Second World War as a consequence of the very substantial wage increases in Western Europe and the United States. At the same time the decolonization meant an increased trade with the poor countries. This trade resulted in an intensified exploitation of these countries.

The Development of the United States of America from Colony to Advanced Capitalist Power

The rapid development of the United States illustrates well one of the most important factors for the development of capitalism—a large domestic market.

The development of the old European colonies was curbed by the change in the capitalist development, with the exception of the settler colonies in North America, Australia, and New Zealand. They broke away from European dominance and experienced a rapid development from relatively underdeveloped colonial societies to developed capitalist societies. This change took place in the course of less than one hundred years.

There were several reasons why the colonization of North America in the seventeenth century was so different from the colonization of South America a hundred years before. The Spaniards and the Portuguese came from feudal systems. They arrived in coats of mail to conquer and plunder the rich societies they met. After the first stage of plundering, they built up an economy based on large estates, characterized by feudalism where labor mainly consisted of slaves.

The colonists in North America were quite different. Most of them were people of humble means: in the first stage during the seventeenth and eighteenth century mainly proletarianized artisans and farmers. They were the result of economic and political revolutions in Europe. Civil wars and international conflicts in Europe had disrupted their old life. Often they were people who had been persecuted because of their political or religious conviction. They had often been fighting for liberal ideas and religious freedom, and were determined to keep and defend these ideas in their new country. A part of the ideological basis of the later American revolution can be found in this. The revolution resulted in the settlers breaking away from Britain.

The settlers went out to establish themselves as small farmers and artisans. They wanted land and they wanted to stay. In this way the settlers played a dual role in relation to the colonial powers. On the one hand they were the agents of these powers, the proper colonizers. They administered the colonies and suppressed wholeheartedly any resistance on the part of the colonized. On the other hand they were opposed to their earlier native country, to colonialism, because they wanted all the colonial plunder themselves. They competed with their "mother country" for the plunder from the exploitation of the colonized people and the riches of their country. Thus they were competitors of colonialism and later of imperialism. In that sense the settlers were an anticolonial and anti-imperialist element.

Thus the settlers lost their economic, political, and religious affiliation to the "mother country." From the point of view of the European trade capital they were of little use.[13] They did not produce any raw materials which could be sold in Europe. Neither did they buy European goods to any appreciable extent, since they produced their own necessities. The industrial capital in Britain found the settler colony to be useless and dangerous—dangerous because it might become a competitor. The contradiction between colony and colonial power was intensified when Britain introduced protectionist rules concerning North America at the beginning of the eighteenth century.

British mercantilism tried to maintain its monopoly of all trade to and from North American colonies. This resulted in a conflict as the Northern States produced many of the same products as the mother country. As regards fish and agricultural products New England was able to undersell Britain on the Caribbean market. This resulted in Britain losing millions of pounds because of lost trade and shipping. In return for their goods the North Americans received sugar, rum, tobacco, and other products from the islands, again without British participation. The British tried to the utmost of their power to stop this traffic by means of prohibitions and tariff legislation. However, this only changed the

---

13 The trade capital attached only little importance to the settler colonies, which for example can be seen from the fact that France chose to cede Canada after the defeat in the Anglo-French war, in North America 1752-9, when they had to choose between ceding Martinique or Canada.

trade into smuggling. British attempts to carry out the legislation and prevent the smuggling formed some of the basis of the American revolution.

British colonialism became a chain on the further development of the settler society. Gradually the settlers had had enough of British taxes and directives which disallowed their freedom. The taxes and the directives had two purposes: they should bring as much as possible back to Britain and they should retain the colony within the empire. The conflict between the "mother country" and the settlers was further deepened. Britain had to send troops off to try to suppress the insurrection. In 1776 the settlers declared British North America independent under the name of the United States of America. After a war which lasted until 1783 Britain had to recognize the independence of the United States of America.

It is characteristic of the United States that they changed into an almost "pure" settler state. All the earlier social structures and the majority of the Indigenous populations were eliminated. The settlers did not exploit the Indigenous Populations—they got rid of them. The Indigenous societies were annihilated to make room for an increasing number of land-hungry farmers.[14]

During the nineteenth century a new wave of settlers came to the United States. They were unemployed proletarians—created by the enormous growth of population and the increased introduction of machines into British industry. They constituted a part of the "industrial reserve army," emigrating especially from Ireland and England. They did not set out to earn profits for Europe, but to create a new life for themselves as farmers. This new wave of land-hungry emigrants caused an enormous geographical expansion of the United States.[15]

Before the peace with Britain in 1783, the United States covered only a stretch of coast between the Atlantic and the Appalachians. However, at the conclusion of peace with Britain, the United States obtained the enormous area between the Appalachians and the Mississippi River. Even this border was far from final. In the course of exactly 50 years (1803-53) the United States conquered an area the size of the whole of Western Europe. The settlers did not

---

14 **Ed. Note:** The original work did not mention the role of chattel slavery in North America and the Caribbean. For an investigation of the role of chattel slavery in North America and its political and economic significance, refer to the works of Gerald Horne such as *The Apocalypse of Settler Colonialism* (2018, Monthly Review Press, New York).

15 The majority of emigrants arrived during 1846-55, partly because of the pressure from the hard times in Europe, particularly in Ireland where unemployment and the potato blight, exacerbated by British Imperialism, caused hundreds of thousands of deaths, and partly because of the pull from the booming American economy. The United States' population grew from 4 million to 32 million between 1790 and 1860.

take it as a colony, but settled in the area and made it an integral part of the United States' economy. They built up and expanded the American capitalist society, bringing the United States' economic system and policy with them as they advanced towards the West and the South.

During the nineteenth century the United States' economic development was characterized by two factors: Firstly, there was plenty of relatively easily accessible and fertile soil. Secondly, there was not enough labor available. These two things were interdependent. Land was comparatively cheap and consequently labor was comparatively expensive. If the wages were not high enough, people could easily go to the west, where land was freely accessible and not encumbered with any duties, rates or other restrictions. The profitable conditions of agriculture thus set the lower limit of the price of labor. During the first half of the nineteenth century, wages in the United States were about twice the British price. During the second half of the nineteenth century wages in the United States were about 50 percent higher than they were in Europe, despite the fact that American labor was of lower quality than the European.[16] It was not skilled workers who emigrated to the United States; they could obtain comparatively high wages at home. The capitalist development of US agriculture and industry was thus strongly conditional on the following: The large areas of land, the lack of skilled labor, and the high wage level.

The lack of labor within American agriculture meant that labor-saving technology and machinery were introduced very early. This led to strongly increasing productivity. Iron and later steel plows were produced in new and better designs and sold in thousands in the United States.[17]

The most important invention within American agriculture during this period was the mechanical, horse-driven harvester.[18]

---

16 Adam Smith writes: "England is certainly, in the present times, a much richer country than any part of North America. The wages of labor, however, are much higher in North America than in any part of England." A. Smith, *The Wealth of Nations* (Edinburgh, 1814), bk I, ch. 8. Malthus estimated working-class wages in the United States at about 1 dollar per day, corresponding to 4 shillings. The British worker gets 2 shillings. This is also in accordance with statistical surveys on American history. (Malthus, *An Essay on the Principle of Population* (London, 1872), bk I, ch. 27. In *A Treatise on Political Economy* (London, 1821), J. B. Say calculates American wages to be three times as high as the French. (Book I, ch. 27). In 1874 American wages should be about 25-50 percent higher than the British, 40-70 percent higher than the Belgian and 100 percent higher than the equivalent French.

17 At the world exhibition in 1851 American plows proved to be much better than the European. Dudley Dillard, *Economic Development of the North Atlantic Community*, (New Jersey, 1967).

18 The harvester was invented in 1833 by Mc Cormick, an immigrant Scotsman, and produced in Chicago by the still existing International Harvester Company. (Dillard, op. cit.)

It was especially during harvest time that the lack of labor was felt, setting a limit to the area which the individual farmer dared sow. This problem was solved by the new harvester. The machine redoubled the productivity of the harvest process. By 1855 more than 10,000 harvesters were already in use in the United States. Mechanical threshers and sowing machines were introduced into US agriculture in the 1830s and also gained ground very quickly. The increased productivity meant larger units particularly on the East Coast. Small farmers who could not keep up with progress went bankrupt. Often they went westwards and started all over again. The increase in agricultural productivity by means of labor-saving machines was one of the prerequisites of the rapid industrialization of the United States. Even though agriculture employed an increasing number of people, they constituted a falling percentage of the total population. However, people employed within agriculture could supply themselves and those who were employed within other sectors of the economy. Furthermore, there was a surplus for an increasing exportation particularly to the European market. This development of agriculture meant that the farmer as a craftsman disappeared. Earlier the farmers had themselves produced almost everything they needed. It now became much more profitable for them to concentrate on agriculture. Home production could not compete with the factory-made goods either in price or in quality. Therefore, the farmers constituted a growing market with great purchasing power for both consumer goods and agricultural machinery.

At the beginning, British industry in particular benefitted from this new and enormous market for industrial products. However, this changed from the middle of the nineteenth century, mainly for two reasons: Firstly, the American state began to pursue a protectionist policy. Secondly, American industry itself became more and more competitive. Paradoxically, this was a result of the high wages and low quality of skilled labor. Because of the shortage of labor in the 1850s, wages in the United States were comparatively high. Therefore, it was often more profitable for the American capitalists to mechanize and thus save the expensive labor. As early as in 1840 the assembly line method was introduced in the slaughtering and meat packing industries, and this technology spread to other branches of industry.[19] An arms manufacturer, Eli Whitney, in-

---

19 In the slaughtering industry, centered on Cincinnati, a rudimentary form of assembly line was developed. Typically, the pig would hang on a hook and pass through the factory from worker to worker. One ripped up, one took out the heart, another cut out a specified piece of bacon etc., until all was salted and packed. These factories used the whole pig, producing raw leather, soap, candles, etc., from the waste products. The American industrialization had certain distinguishing features. One of the best descriptions of American industry in the 1850s is made by a group of British technicians who visited the United States at the time. They

troduced interchangeable standard components in armaments manufacturing. Before this, each single rifle was assembled from individually adapted components. It would be difficult for Whitney to find enough armorers to execute the order. He chose another solution. He introduced machines which worked with such accuracy that the components could be standardized. The components could thus be assembled immediately. Machines had superseded the accuracy of handwork.[20] Standardized components were also introduced into the manufacturing of locks, watches, sewing machines, typewriters, agricultural machinery, etc.

As compared to British industry, American industry was based on mass production, characterized by standardized components and assembly line technology. The price of American labor was an incentive to mechanization and to the introduction of labor-saving organization of the production. At the same time the size and growth of the American domestic market allowed for such mass production.[21] Other conditions contributed to the creation of the big homogeneous and continuous domestic market. The federation of the United States led to abolition of all restrictive tariff and duty barriers between the individual states. The American government developed the infrastructure. Transportation was improved by expansion of the networks of roads, railways, and canals. Furthermore a standard of coinage was introduced.

Thus the United States produced the same factors as Britain—comparatively high working class wages, and consequently a large home market. In this way the prerequisites of becoming an imperialist Great Power were established. As early as at the end of the nineteenth century the United States had developed a productive capacity which surpassed that of the British in most areas.

---

reported to the British Parliament, telling carefully about their observations. According to these reports American industry would be far more mechanized and standardized than the British. More patents were taken out in the US than in any other country during this period. Gunderson, Gerald, *A New Economic History of America*, p. 176.

20 In 1850 a British parliamentary commission visited Eli Whithey's arms factory. The American manufacturer took ten rifles, one from each of the years 1841-50, disassembled them, and mixed the components. Then he got hold of one of the factory workers, who assembled the rifles very quickly with a screw-driver. The Englishmen were "most impressed." A skilled British armorer would use many hours in order to fit the components into a working rifle. An American worker could assemble some fifty rifles in one day—a British worker about two. During those years the American arms industry was leading within the development of precision tools for metal-working—its know-how was used by other branches of industry. Gunderson, op. cit., p. 174.

21 The iron stove was one of the first mass produced consumer goods. Just between 1850 and '60, half a million stoves were produced in the United States. Gunderson, op. cit., p. 169.

The colonization of Asia and Africa by the European powers largely prevented American trade with these areas all up to the end of the Second World War. Instead, the United States developed an increasing trade with the Caribbean and Central and South America, initially in hard competition with Britain, but with increasing American dominance. The Caribbean and Central and South America became the "colonies" of the United States.

Summary

India never became a copy of Britain. But parts of continental Europe, and the settler states USA, Canada, Australia, and New Zealand did. At a very early time in their development, these countries had the same prerequisites as Britain. They had developed a large domestic market which attracted capital.

The rest of the colonies and South America did not follow this line. It was simply impossible for them to do so, since the exploitation and underdevelopment of these countries constituted the prerequisites for the growth of the rich countries.

The general law of capitalist accumulation states:

> Accumulation of wealth at one pole is, therefore, at the same time accumulation of misery, agony of toil, slavery, ignorance, brutality, mental degradation, at the opposite pole [...][22]

This law appeared with palpable distinctness during the first years of capitalism in Europe, when the accumulation mainly took place internally both in the "mother countries" and in the colonies. As the accumulation under imperialism became more and more international, so did the manifestation of this law. When imperialism grew in the economic sense, the division of the world into rich classes living mainly in rich countries and poor classes living in poor countries became increasingly clear.

In the following chapter we shall discuss in detail how the transfer of value from the poor, exploited countries to the rich imperialist countries is effected.

---

22 Marx, *Capital*, Vol. I, p. 604.

The Theory of Unequal Exchange

Introduction

As it has been explained in the previous chapter, it was the internal contradictions of the capitalist mode of production which led to the recurring and increasingly serious crises of overproduction during the last half of the nineteenth century. The contradiction between productive forces and relations of production showed itself as a disproportion between production and consumption, leading to overproduction. However, the contradiction changed its character around the turn of the 20th century. Capitalism showed a new international mode of accumulation which was reflected by a growing domestic market in Western Europe and the United States. The basis of this development was an intensified exploitation of the colonies and other poor countries. One country's exploitation of the other became a capitalist aspect of increasing importance, an aspect which is a characteristic of capitalism today.

An analysis of today's capitalist mode of accumulation must therefore be based on a global point of view. Today's capitalism is global and can therefore only be understood by means of a global analysis. Only then can we understand and explain the very different manifestations of capitalism in the rich and the poor countries. Danish welfare capitalism can only be understood through its connection with the exploitation of the "Third World" by the imperialist countries.

This global analysis of capitalism must be based on economic facts, because imperialism—which is the international form of the capitalist mode of production—is first and foremost an economic phenomenon characterized by the transfer of value from exploited countries to exploiting countries. The political, social, and cultural conditions are consequences of the imperialist economy. Other aspects are of course retroactive on the economy, but the economic forces are fundamental. Thus imperialism is not a policy which the imperialist countries can choose to pursue or to avoid. Ultimately, imperialist policy is a consequence of imperialist economy. An understanding of the political tendencies in the imperialist world must therefore be based on an understanding of its economic functions.

Marx himself never found time to work out a theory of the capitalist world market and international trade, even though it was part of his plan for the description of capitalism in *Capital*.[1] Since Marx, various people have dealt with imperialism but have not been able to work out a theory applying to the world market. A marxist theory of this phenomenon was not framed until the appearance of Arghiri Emmanuel's theory of 'unequal exchange.'[2] In this theory Emmanuel displays the mechanisms by means of which value is transferred from one country to another. His theory of unequal exchange is based on Marx's interpretation of the law of value. Therefore, we shall summarize below the part of Marx's theory which is necessary for understanding the theory of unequal exchange.

THE CAPITALIST MODE OF ACCUMULATION

The Commodity—The Value of the Commodity is a Social Relation. Marx starts his analysis of the capitalist mode of accumulation from an analysis of the commodity. A commodity has two properties: use-value and exchange-value. The use-value means that the commodity can satisfy physical or psychical human wants; the exchange-value is the quantitative relation in which various use-values are exchanged.

---

1 See the quote from 'Preface,' to *A Contribution to the Critique of Political Economy* cited in footnote 24 on p. xlvii.

2 Arghiri Emmanuel was born in Patras, Greece, in 1911. In 1942 he volunteered for the Greek Liberation Forces in the Middle East and was active in the April 1944 uprising against the Greek government-in-exile in Cairo. The uprising was crushed by British troops and Emmanuel was condemned to death by a Greek court-martial in Alexandria. He was granted amnesty at the end of 1945 and freed in March 1946. After the war he settled in Paris where he studied socialist planning. He received his doctorate in sociology from the Sorbonne. Until 1980 he was Director of Economic Studies at the University of Paris-VII. The theory of unequal exchange was advanced by Arghiri Emmanuel at the end of the 1960s and put forward in his book *L'echange inegal* in 1969, published in English in 1972 by Monthly Review Press (*Unequal Exchange, A Study of the Imperialist Trade*). Emmanuel has supported and developed his theory in a number of articles and further investigations. See Appendix: ' Works By Arghiri Emmanuel' on page 183.

A commodity is a product of human labor, made by an independent producer with the intention of exchanging it. Therefore, not all products of labor are commodities. If the product is exclusively made for the producer himself and is thus not exchanged, then it is no commodity, since it has only a use-value, and no exchange-value. Commodity production being production with a view to exchange, a product is considered a commodity because of its social properties, not because of its physical characteristics. Whether an object is a commodity cannot be definitely determined until it is put on the market to be exchanged.

The exchange relation between different commodities varies according to the circumstances under which the exchange occurs. It may for instance vary with time and place. Commodity exchange may thus immediately appear to be rather accidental. However, this is not the case. The exchange-value actually does reflect the common character of the commodities: the fact that they are products of human labor. The exchange-value is a manifestation of the value which the commodity has by virtue of being a product of human labor. What is actually compared at the commodity exchange is not the exchange-value itself, but the human labor inherent in the commodity. Thus commodity exchange is not a relation between objects or things. A commodity exchange reflects human relations between producers, i.e. social relations. This exchange of values appears as a relation between things, but it is a social relation.

Engels writes:

> Political economy begins with commodities, with the moment when products are exchanged, either by individuals or by primitive communities. The product being exchanged is a commodity. But it is a commodity only because of the thing, the product being linked with a relation between two persons or communities, the relation between producer and consumer, who at this stage are no longer united in the same person. Here is at once an example of a peculiar fact, which pervades the whole of economics and has produced serious confusion in the minds of bourgeois economists: economics is not concerned with things but with relations between persons, and in the final analysis between classes, these relations, however, are always bound to things and appear as things.[3]

To the dual character of the commodity corresponds a dual character of the labor. Use-value is based on actual labor: carpentry, forging, weaving etc., the use-value and the actual labor being of a qualitative nature. Exchange-value is based on abstract labor—on the consumption of human labor-power—which is of a quantitative nature. Thus abstract labor forms the basis of the value of the commodity which is compared to the value of other commodities when ex-

---

3 Engels, Friedrich, Marx, Karl, *A Contribution to the Critique of Political Economy*, MECW, Vol. 16, p. 476. See also: "As one of the earlier economists said, value is a relation between two persons; only he should have added: a relation concealed beneath a material wrapping." Lenin, V.I. (1964), "Karl Marx," *Collected Works*, Vol. 21, p. 60. Moscow: Progress Publishers.

changed.

Commodity Production—Generally Defined

Commodity production proper requires such a development of the social division of labor that an exchange of products is necessary. The individual producer expects that there is a social need for the produced use-values.

A commodity is thus a product of human labor, produced with the intention of being exchanged with other products of human labor. But it is not until the product is placed on the market that it can be seen whether the labor which was consumed in the production can be realized, i.e. whether it has a use-value to other people. So, society must consider the produced commodity to be necessary. There must be—either immediately after the production or some time in the future—a market able to buy it, otherwise the labor consumed has been wasted, from a social point of view, without creating any value.

Simple Commodity Production

The Producer Owns His Own Means of Production—The Commodity is Exchanged at Its Own Value. The social phenomenon which Marx calls simple commodity production belongs to a certain historical period before capitalism. The production of commodities is much older than capitalism. Commodity production existed in the slave society as well as in the feudal society. Early commodity production was characterized by the producer owning his own means of production, and his products. The producer, for instance a farmer or an artisan, thus acted alone in the production. At that time the exploitation of other people through wage labor was not yet pronounced. Labor power was not yet a commodity.

In a society with simple commodity production there is a tendency towards the commodities being exchanged at their value. This means that they are exchanged in accordance with the amount of abstract human labor contained in their production within the socially necessary labor-time—i.e. within the production-time required under normal conditions, with average degree of skill and intensity and with the technology normally used in the society in question. And, finally, society must regard the product as a necessity.

Commodity Production Under Developed Capitalism

Producer and Means of Production Separated—Commodities are Exchanged at the Prices of Production. In the case of simple commodity production the producer owns his own means of production. In the case of developed capitalism the producer owns neither the means of production nor the product. Thus the proletariat and the bourgeoisie came into existence. The arrival of these classes is discussed shortly below.

Primitive Accumulation

Marx and Engels write in the *Manifesto of the Communist Party*:

> We see then: the means of production and of exchange, on whose foundation the bourgeoisie built itself up, were generated in feudal society. At a certain stage in the development of these means of production and of exchange, the conditions under which feudal society produced and exchanged, the feudal organization of agriculture and manufacturing industry, in one word, the feudal relations of property became no longer compatible with the already developed productive forces; they became so many fetters. They had to be burst asunder; they were burst asunder.[4]

The disintegration of feudalism and the creation of the prerequisites of the capitalist mode of production Marx calls "primitive accumulation"—primitive because the birth of capitalism cannot be explained by the law of accumulation of the capitalist mode of production itself. The accumulation of the values which constituted the primitive capital was not a result of capitalist exploitation, wage labor, but a result of actual violence and open theft. The creation of the proletariat was not a consequence of capitalism but a consequence of the historical background of capitalism, of its basis.

In "The so-called primitive accumulation" (*Capital*, Vol. I, Part VIII), Marx goes thoroughly into the question of what primitive accumulation contains. He describes it as the process creating the basic conditions of capitalist production: On the one pole the creation of "free" propertyless laborers, unencumbered with the means of production; on the other pole the creation of the owners of money, means of production and means of subsistence, whose only aim it is to increase the sum of value they possess or—in short the capitalists. The original capitals were mostly a result of the exploitation of the colonial

---

4 Marx, op. cit., MESW, p. 40. Primitive accumulation was discussed (in Danish) in the magazine *Manifest*, nos. 4 and 7 (Copenhagen, 1979), in the series "The Division of the World into Two."

areas.

Marx writes:

> The discovery of gold and silver in America, the extirpation, enslavement and entombment in mines of the aboriginal population, the beginning of the conquest and looting of the East Indies, the turning of Africa into a warren for the commercial hunting of black-skins, signalized the rosy dawn of the era of capitalist production. These idyllic proceedings are the chief momenta of primitive accumulation. On their heels treads the commercial war of the European nations, with the globe for a theater [...]
>
> The different momenta of primitive accumulation distribute themselves now, more or less in chronological order, particularly over Spain, Portugal, Holland, France, and England. In England at the end of the 17th century, they arrive at a systematical combination, embracing the colonies, the national debt, the modern mode of taxation, and the protectionist system. These methods depend in part on brute force, e.g., the colonial system. But they all employ the power of the State, the concentrated and organized force of society, to hasten, hot-house fashion, the process of transformation of the feudal mode of production into the capitalist mode, and to shorten the transition. Force is the midwife of every old society pregnant with a new one. It is itself an economic power.[5]

As the primitive accumulation and the exploitation of the colonial areas were a condition of the break-through of capitalism, the creation of a proletariat was also a necessity. That means the existence of a class of "free" laborers, "free" in a double sense. Firstly, they must be able to sell their labor-power freely and not as slaves or bondsmen tied to a certain production. Secondly, they must be free from any rights of property to the means of production, and not work as the peasant or the artisan with their own means of production. They are to be free and idle on the market and thus forced to take part in the capitalist production as wage laborers to secure their subsistence. And so two basic classes arise under capitalism: the bourgeoisie and the proletariat; the capitalists with the capital, hence with the means of production, and the proletariat, deprived of this means of production, with only its labor-power to offer. Under capitalism, labor-power has thus also become a commodity.

LABOR-POWER—ITS VALUE AND PRICE

In several ways labor-power is not a common commodity. Its price, wages, is not fixed by economic laws to the same extent as the price of other commodities. Unlike the prices of other commodities, wages are fixed primarily by the class struggle in society. However, it is not only the class struggle which determines wages. Thus Marx distinguished between two elements in the case of

---

5 Marx, *Capital*, Vol. I, p. 703.

the determination of the value of labor-power. Partly the physical reproduction costs of labor-power and partly what he describes as the historical and moral element. The reproduction costs of labor-power means the price of the commodities which are necessary if the worker—and the working class as a whole—is to continue their work, their subsistence, and reproduction. It is a question of basic food, clothing, and housing. If the laborer is only paid a sum which covers the physical reproduction costs, it is described as subsistence wages.

All attempts to determine the price of labor-power from the physical reproduction-costs alone have hitherto failed. For wages to be determined by those circumstances a free labor-market would be necessary, and such a free market never existed, generally speaking, except perhaps for a short while immediately after the establishment of the capitalist system. The complex rules and regulations of the preceding feudal system, and the class struggle that was to follow, left very little room for any free labor-market.

Besides the prices of the purely physically determined means of subsistence, the value of the labor-power is determined by the "historical and moral element."

Marx says:

> On the other hand, the number and extent of his so-called necessary wants, as also the modes of satisfying them, are themselves the product of historical development, and depend therefore to a great extent on the degree of civilisation of a country, more particularly on the conditions under which, and consequently on the habits and degree of comfort in which, the class of free laborers has been formed. In contradistinction therefore to the case of other commodities, there enters into the determination of the value of labor-power a historical and moral element. Nevertheless, in a given country, at a given period, the average quantity of the means of subsistence necessary for the laborer is practically known.[6]

The factors which determine the value and price of labor-power—namely the class struggle and the reproduction costs—interact during the course of development. In the same way, a dialectic relationship exists between the value of labor-power and the price of labor-power, i.e. wages. The value of labor-power is thus in itself indirectly determined by the wages. Even though the value also determines the wages, the wages retroact on the value, as the working class gets the possibility of including more commodities in its reproduction when it obtains higher wages through the class struggle. When the higher wages have existed for some time, this price of labor-power becomes equivalent to the value of labor-power.

Thus "the historical and moral element"—which means the class struggle

---

6 Ibid., p. 168.

and its entire historical and economic basis—determines to a high degree the wage-level under capitalism. However, the historical and moral element is also influenced by earlier wage-levels.

If we assume that wages fluctuate around the value of labor-power, this means that the value of labor-power differs throughout the world. Where comparatively high wages are paid, the value of labor-power is at a comparatively high level. Conversely, the value of labor-power is at a comparatively low level where comparatively low wages are paid. Consequently the value of labor-power is at a high level in the wealthy imperialist countries and at a low level in the exploited countries in the Third World. Throughout a long historical period, a high wage level in the rich countries has resulted in a high level of reproduction costs. Reproduction costs have in these countries included many consumer goods of various kinds and are consequently an expression of a high value. The low wage level in the Third World means reproduction costs at a low level and thus it reflects a low value. The reproduction costs in the Third World include mainly physical subsistence goods. If we define the value of labor-power in this strictly theoretical way from a national point of view, it is because: It is a fact that the price level of the commodity labor-power differs very much in the world.

Therefore, there is no moral evaluation contained in the concept of value in this connection. It is a strictly economic definition. That labor-power is paid according to its value has nothing to do with fairness.

Of course the use-value of labor-power—the ability to create value—is not influenced by these differences in the value of the actual labor-power. Labor performed with the same qualifications is equally productive no matter where the labor is performed and no matter what value the actual labor-power has. Why should a docker in Esbjerg in Denmark create more value than a docker in Bombay in India just because the Danish docker's wages are 50 times higher? With the same qualifications and the same intensity; the value of their work must be the same no matter what the value of their labor-power might be.

Thus the size of the wages is dependent on the relative strength between the classes and on the position of the country in the world. Consequently, the market for labor-power differs from the normal commodity market. There are norms, rules, laws, and union regulations as to the length of the working day, working conditions, overtime, minimum wages, piece rates etc. There are comparatively fixed limits to the variability of wages within one country. These limits do not immediately reflect economic laws, but rather political conditions. The internationally different course of the class struggle has created considerable differences in wages internationally. However, within the individual country—particularly the imperialist countries—there is a tendency towards an equalization of the wage level. This national tendency towards equalization is partly due to the comparatively high degree of, labor mobility within the countries and partly to political interventions.[7]

A similar tendency cannot be seen internationally. On the contrary, the differences in wages between the imperialist countries and the exploited countries have increased. The price for the commodity labor-power has not followed the general tendency towards the setting of one world market price. Wages vary relatively little within a given period but very much from place to place. There are subsistence wages in the Third World and comparatively high wages in the imperialist countries. On the other hand, the price of most commodities varies enormously from time to time but comparatively little from place to place in the world. For example the price of copper or wheat may vary considerably from month to month or even from day to day, but geographically the price varies only little. At a specified time there is a world market price. The opposite applies in the case of wages.

Emmanuel writes:

> From remotest antiquity to the beginning of the 19th century, the wage has, in real terms, hardly varied in any country; from the beginning of the 19th century up to the present it has, in certain countries, moved slowly and steadily upwards. Such a constancy in certain periods or certain countries, such an evenness and duration of a one-dimensional movement in certain other periods and other countries, are contrary to the endogenous economic determinations which are plastic and multiform. An extra-economic (institution) vector alone can generate them.
>
> At any rate, on the international plane, the multiplicity of wage rates is inconsistent with the existence of a market since the essential function of the market is precisely to secure one price for each item. Now in the case of wages, this disparity continues without the slightest attenuation, even when, here or there and in certain epochs, the labor-factor enjoys a relatively important mobility. Neither the great immigration of Europeans into the United States during the 19th century and the beginning of the 20th, nor the contemporary considerable immigration of North Africans, Portuguese, Greeks, etc., into the developed countries of Western Europe after the last war, have given rise to the slightest tendency towards the equalization of wages between the countries of origin and the host countries.
>
> [...] There is no relevance between the conjunctural fluctuations of employment in different countries and the comparative rates of wages in these same countries. For example: during the 1929-34 crisis, unemployment in the United States was 36.47% of the active population against 13.42% in France and only 7% in Italy. Yet the American wage remained, during the worst of the crisis, two to three times that in France and three to four times that in Italy.

---

7   In the countries of the Third World a national difference in wages is found to a greater extent than in the imperialist countries. See for example: Dandekar, V. M. (Jan. 12, 1980), "Bourgeois Politics of the Working Class," *Economic and Political Weekly*, Vol. XV.

> We can conclude that the determination of wages is more a political than an economic process. Its variations reflect the fluctuations of the relations of power between social classes. This extra-economic institutional determination makes possible a lasting gap between the price and value of labor power.
>
> However, these two magnitudes continue to be connected to each other in a dialectical interaction. A wage greater than the value of labor power, if it prevails for a long time, ends by driving upwards this value itself, since the extra consumption which it allows ends by being transformed into vital needs—what Marx calls a second nature—and, hence, by being incorporated into the real cost of reproduction of the labor force.[8]

Wage labor must be regarded as it is: a social relation in which classes fight for their interests—i.e. the struggle for the division of the social product into wages to the laborers and profit to the capitalists. Thus wages constitute a part of the social product and their size reflects the relative strength between the classes and the economic basis on which the class struggle takes place.[9]

Productivity and Wages

One of the most popular explanations of the international differences in wages is that they are based on corresponding differences in productivity. There are even people who claim that the workers in the developed, imperialist countries—because of their high degree of productivity—are more exploited than the proletariat in the Third World.

Their argumentation can be summed up as follows: Generally, the rate of productivity in the imperialist countries is much higher than in the Third World. This high rate of productivity results in a fall in the value of the commodities which form part of the laborers' consumption. Consequently, the necessary labor-time decreases—i.e. the time required for the production of the commodities necessary for the reproduction of labor power—in proportion to the surplus labor. The high wages which can buy many commodities, do not reflect a higher value but only a higher rate of productivity. The increasing wages have not even been able to keep pace with the increasing productivity. Surplus labor accounts for an increasing part of the working day in proportion to the necessary labor. Thus the working class in the imperialist countries enjoys an increasing standard of living while it is exploited more and more at the same time. However, in the Third World the rate of productivity is lower for the products included in the

---

8   Emmanuel, Arghiri, *Unequal Exchange Revisited*, pp. 49-50.

9   Thus the value of the commodity—labor power—appears as a social relation, namely the class struggle, and in this way all the material covers which enclose "normal" commodities have been peeled off.

consumption of the working class. This means that the necessary labor-time accounts for a larger part of the total labor-time than in the imperialist countries.

Thus, in spite of the wretched conditions, the labor power in the Third World is less exploited than the labor-power in the imperialist countries. This is due to the difference in the rate of productivity in the world. A high rate of productivity means high wages, a low rate of productivity means low wages.

In this chapter we shall deal with the above assertion from a theoretic point of view. (In Chapter 4 we shall deal with it empirically.)

A Marxist definition of productivity must strictly distinguish productivity from the terms intensity and profitability. These three terms are often mixed up. The bourgeois economists mostly focus on "output per laborer" measured by the quantity of commodities produced or by the quantity of profit created. Whether an increased "output per laborer" is due to increased price on the products, newer, more efficient technology or harder wear of the labor-power is not so important to them. Also many Marxists confuse intensity (the rate of wearing out the labor-power) and productivity (the efficiency of the machines). by defining productivity as "number of produced commodities per unit of time." They are unable to distinguish between the results of new technology or of harder wear of the labor-power.

To make it possible to distinguish the influence of the different components, we will define the terms as follows:

Profitability is the proportion between the market price and the price of production of a given commodity. An increasing market price or a decreasing price of production results in higher profitability.

Intensity is the rate of consumption of the labor-power. Higher intensity means faster wearing out of the laborers, and more produced commodities per unit of time by the same means of production. (The exploitation of women workers in South Korea is an example of high intensity and fast wearing out of labor power.)

Productivity is determined by the efficiency of the technological facilities and by the organization of the production. Improving the technology and/or the organization, keeping intensity the same, results in a production of more commodities per unit of time.

Both increased intensity and increased productivity results in creation of more use-value per unit of time. But only increased intensity creates more value per unit of time. Increased productivity just means the production of a greater quantity of commodities containing the same value.

In his analysis of piece rates and piece payment (*Capital*, Vol. I, ch. 19), Marx shows how the apparent connection between productivity and wages is false, since piece rates are a concealed form of time wages. If the piece rate for one unit in a certain enterprise is for example $4—and the average wage for the labor in question is $40 per day,—the piece rate only reflects that the capitalist has calculated that an average worker is able to produce 10 units per day. The worker who is able to produce 12 units with the same machinery, tools, etc. and who gets $48—does not work more productively but more intensively and therefore demands higher reproduction costs. If new and more productive machinery suddenly made it possible for the average laborer to produce 20 units instead of 10, this would not result in a twofold increase of the day's wages.

This thought is absurd under capitalist relations of production. What would happen is that the piece rate would be reduced twofold. The wages are not the price for the result of the labor, but the price for the labor-power.

Engels writes in a letter to Lafargue:

> [...] in what respect the wage worker gains an advantage in seeing his productivity increase, when the product of that productivity does not belong to him and when his wage is not determined by the productivity of the machine.[10]

Improvements in productivity are a result of improved technology of the capitalist production apparatus. A gain which is a result of improvements in productivity goes to the capitalist as profit, perhaps surplus profit, for a short period. A profit in which the laborer has no claim to share under capitalist relations of production. The value and payment of the labor-power do not depend on whether the laborer operates an expensive, highly productive plant or a screwdriver. No matter how big the difference in productivity is, it cannot be a result of the labor-power in itself. In the case of an equal amount of used labor-power—i.e. an equal wear of muscles and nerves and equal education and qualifications—an unequal result can only be explained by other factors, i.e. the quality of the means of production which is paid through profit. The assertion that the wages of agricultural workers are determined by the fertility of the soil, and the wages of the industrial workers by the size and quality of the machinery is not only absurd, but has nothing to do with reality. In a capitalist society, the product of the soil or of the machinery belongs to the landowner or the industrial capitalist. Only in the case of independent producers, who own their land and tools, is there a connection between the productivity and the wages of the labor.

---

10 Friedrich Engels to Paul Lafargue (May 11, 1889), *Frederick Engels-Paul and Laura Lafargue: Correspondence*, Vol. I, p. 233.

The productivity of the laborers' work does not influence his wages. However, Marx believes that an increased productivity in the sectors which are included in the determination of the value of the labor-power may have an influence—in a downward direction. But if we assume it to be in an upward direction it is difficult to understand why the working class in the Third World does not benefit from the productivity increases to the same extent.

> [...] one could not see why the same quantity of labor of the same qualification, incorporating the same learning and training should be paid ten times more or less according to whether it is supplied some miles on this or the other side of the American-Mexican border and according to whether the name of the vendor is John or Fernandez. Of all monopolies, this one, grounded on a passport or a birth certificate, seems to me the most "un-ethical."[11]

The commodities which represent the reproduction costs of the working class do more or less cost the same all over the world. Generally speaking, the costs of maintaining a living standard as a Danish worker are the same in Denmark, Tanzania, Brazil, or Hong Kong. The price for one kilo of wheat, one kilo of meat, one watch, or a transistor radio varies by 10, 20 or 50 percent from country to country. However, the wages are 5, 10, 20 or 50 times higher in the imperialist countries.

If there were a connection between productivity and wages in an enterprise, it would mean that the laborer and the capitalist would find it in their common interest to improve productivity. The capitalist would do better in the competition and the laborer would obtain a wage increase. Marx attacked this point of view. The capitalist does not buy the labor but the labor-power. The labor-power is not paid according to the result of the labor. A surplus arising from a productivity increase belongs to the capitalist.[12]

Historically, the connection between productivity increases and wages has not been to the laborers' advantage. This is one of Marx's conclusions. He dealt very thoroughly with the relation between the development of the productive forces, the productivity increase, and the effect of it on the standard of living of

---

11 Emmanuel, Arghiri, *Unequal Exchange Summary*, p. 25.

12 The assertion that workers and capitalists should have the same basic economic interests in the development of the means of production owned by the capitalists has divided and still divides the socialist movement into a reformist and a revolutionary line. Marx, Engels, and Lenin were heavily against the view that workers and capitalists have a common economic advantage of the development of the means of production, whereas Bernstein, Kautsky, and the entire Social Democratic movement maintained this view. Today a considerable part of the left wing maintains this Social Democratic view in a covered up version by linking productivity and wages, so that improvements in productivity do automatically lead to wage increases—i.e., the working class and the capitalists have a common interest in the development of the means of production. A view identical to the reformist view.

the working class at his time. He describes how the accumulation of capital, the expansion of productive forces, and the productivity increase creates the industrial reserve army, decreasing wages and decreasing the standard of living.

> The greater the social wealth, the functioning capital, the extent and energy of its growth, and, therefore, also the absolute mass of the proletariat and the productiveness of its labor, the greater is the industrial reserve army. The same causes which develop the expansive power of capital, develop also the labor power at its disposal [...] The more extensive [...] the industrial reserve army, the greater is the official pauperism. This is the absolute general law of capitalist accumulation.[13]

In the same connection, Marx gives some concrete examples of this. During the period 1846-66—in which the productive forces advanced considerably in Britain—the standard of living decreased.[14] Thus, according to Marx there is no internal, regular connection between development of productivity and the standard of living which create wage increases. Actually, the considerable increase in productivity which took place from the breakthrough of industrial capitalism at the end of the eighteenth century, did not at all mean wage increases or improved standard of living for the working class. The first period 1790-1845 meant a direct decrease in the standard of living. Not until the abolition of the Corn Laws in 1846 did the working class obtain its earlier standard of living.[15] The incipient wage increases in the 1870s were not based on productivity increases either, but were a result of the formation of a new economic world order—imperialism.

We conclude that the alleged economic connection between productivity increases and wage increases is wrong. What determines the wages is the class struggle and the possibilities of wage variation which the international position of the national economies can offer.[16]

---

13 Marx, *Capital*, Vol. I, p. 603.

14 Similar tendencies can be seen today in the Third World. The industrialization of Brazil in the second half of the 1960s and in the 1970s did not result in an increase in the standard of living of the working class, on the contrary. A clear indicator of this is the increasing rate of infant mortality in the industrial centers. Whereas it was falling until the middle of the 1960s, it began to rise in 1965. Frank, A.G. (1981), *Crisis in the Third World*, p. 166. London.

15 In several places Marx refers to this fall in real wages during the initial period of capitalism. From 1742-52 to 1800-8 the weekly wages increased from 6 to 11 s., but at the same time the price for one quarter of wheat increased from 30 s. to 86 s. 8 d. Thus the purchasing power of the wages fell from 102 points to 60 points. (Marx, *Theories of Surplus Value*, Part II, p. 584.)

16 The connection between productivity and wage increases in today's Western Europe is political—based on class struggles. The unions demand a share in the profits which are a result of the ever increasing rise in productivity.

The Use-Value of Labor-Power

To the capitalist the commodity labor-power has one quality which is different from the qualities of all other commodities. It can be used for the production of commodities, the value of which is higher than the value of the components used in the production. In order to use the labor-power, the capitalist must possess the means of production.

The Circulation of Capital

The capitalist invests partly in buildings, machinery, raw material etc., in short, the production apparatus. This part of the capital is called constant capital, because it does not differ in value during the accumulation. Another part is invested by the capitalist in labor-power. This part of the capital is called variable capital, because it forms the basis of the creation of new value in the production. Thus the commodities which the capitalist acquires by investments are divided into two main parts which both are equally vital: variable capital and constant capital.[17]

The circulation of capital consists of a production of and a trade in commodities. These two aspects of the circulation are interdependent: no production without trade, and no trade without production.

The first stage in the circulation of industrial capital is the trade in commodities, when the capitalist buys labor-power and the means of production. The next stage, the production—which is the basis of the increase in value—is the consumption of the purchased commodities, those being the labor-power, the raw materials, and a partial consumption of the means of production. This

---

17 "That part of capital, then, which is represented by the means of production, by the raw material, auxiliary material and the instruments of labor, does not, in the process of production, undergo any quantitative alteration of value. I therefore call it the constant part of capital, or, more shortly, constant capital. On the other hand, that part of capital, represented by labor-power, does, in the process of production, undergo an alteration of value. It both reproduces the equivalent of its own value, and also produces an excess, a surplus-value, which may itself vary, may be more or less according to circumstances. This part of capital is continually being transformed from a constant into a variable magnitude. I therefore call it the variable part of capital, or shortly, variable capital. The same elements of capital which, from the point of view of the labor-process, present themselves respectively as the objective and subjective factors, as means of production and labor-power, present themselves, from the point of view of the process of creating surplus-value, as constant and variable capital." Marx, *Capital*, Vol. I, p. 202.

is the production of commodities which the capitalist assumes that they can sell at a higher price than the amount of the original investment.

The value of the labor-power and the value created by the laborer during the working process are two different quantities. The created value, the increase in value, consists of the value which exceeds the value of the labor-power. Or in other words: the value which exceeds the "time" when the laborer has performed a piece of work corresponding to the work necessary to produce the commodities which the laborer buys for his wages. Only the living labor, labor-power, can be the source of created value. The means of production, which the capitalist bought to start his production, change their shape (for example from leather to shoes), but their value does not change. They maintain their value, which is transferred to the finished commodities to the same extent as the means of production are used during the production.

The following stage is again in the trade in commodities where the appropriation of the value takes place. In order to make it possible for the capitalist to secure all of the created value, it is important that the finished commodities can be sold at their value. This means the total capital outlay for variable and constant capital plus the surplus value. If they succeed, the capitalist has increased the original capital by the surplus value. It can be used productively—i.e. for a new, expanded circulation—or unproductively, for consumption.

The total circulation of capital appears as follows:

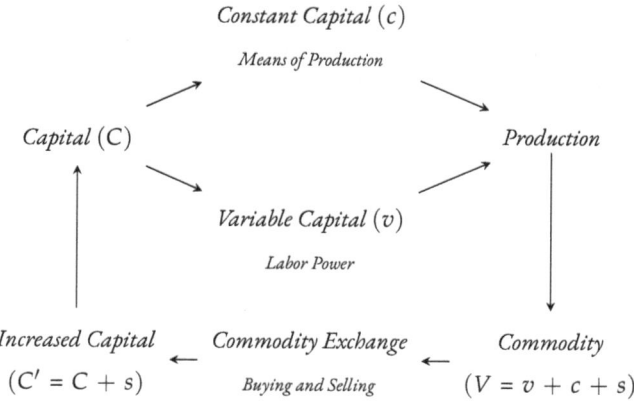

FIGURE II

Thus the circulation of capital, the course of capitalist accumulation, consists of a production (where the material goods are created) and of a trade in commodities (where the commodities are distributed and appropriated by the classes). These two elements form a whole.[18] Therefore, a correct understanding of capitalist accumulation is only possible if all its elements are analyzed, their connection and mutual influence.

Surplus Value

The surplus value is the value created by the laborer exceeding the value of his own labor-power. Theoretically, the working-day in a capitalist enterprise can be divided into two parts: the necessary labor-time when the laborer reproduces the value of his own labor-power, and the surplus labor-time when the surplus value is created.[19]

The Rate of Surplus Value

The rate of surplus value is the ratio of surplus labor to the necessary labor. Expressed in terms of value, it is the ratio of the value of labor-power to the surplus value or the ratio of variable capital to surplus value:

---

18 "The conversion of a sum of money into means of production and labor-power, is the first step taken by the quantum of value that is going to function as capital. This conversion takes place in the market, within the sphere of circulation. The second step, the process of production, is complete as soon as the means of production have been converted into commodities whose value exceeds that of their component parts, and, therefore, contains the capital originally advanced, plus a surplus-value. These commodities must then be thrown into circulation. They must be sold, their value realized in money, this money afresh converted into capital, and so over and over again. This circular movement, in which the same phases are continually gone through in succession, forms the circulation of capital." Marx, *Capital*, Vol. I, p. 529.

19 "The working-day is thus not a constant, but a variable quantity. One of its parts, certainly, is determined by the working-time required for the reproduction of the labor-power of the laborer himself. But its total amount varies with the duration of the surplus-labor. The working-day is, therefore, determinable, but is, per se, indeterminate. [...] Besides these purely physical limitations, the extension of the working-day encounters moral ones. The laborer needs time for satisfying his intellectual and social wants, the extent and number of which are conditioned by the general state of social advancement. The variation of the working-day fluctuates, therefore, within physical and social bounds. But these limiting conditions are of a very elastic nature, and allow the greatest latitude. So we find working-days of 8, 10, 12, 14, 16, 18 hours, i.e., of the most different lengths. [...] Hence is it that in the history of capitalist production, the determination of what is a working-day, presents itself as the result of a struggle, a struggle between collective capital, i.e., the class of capitalists, and collective labor, i.e., the working-class." Marx, *Capital*, Vol. I, pp. 223, 225.

$$\text{Rate of Surplus Value} = \frac{\text{Surplus Value}}{\text{Variable Capital}} \qquad \left(s' = \frac{s}{v}\right)$$

Figure III

Thus the rate of surplus value reflects the rate of exploitation of the labor-power. The constant capital does not influence the value which is created. Whether it forms a large or a small part of the production does not influence the rate of surplus value.

Within the frontiers of a country, there is a tendency towards an equalization of the rate of surplus value in the various spheres of production, caused by the movements of the labor-power, which will seek employment where the rate of exploitation is lowest.

Marx writes:

> This (the equalization of the rate of exploitation) would assume competition among laborers and equalization through their continual migration from one sphere of production to another.

Marx meant that this tendency to equalization made itself felt in the developed capitalist countries:

> We see at a glance that, in our capitalist society, a given portion of human labor is, in accordance with the varying demand, at one time supplied in the form of tailoring, at another in the form of weaving. This change may possibly not take place without friction, but it must take place.[20]

Cost-Price

The individual capitalist is not interested in surplus value and the rate of surplus value. They are not interested in knowing how much surplus value they force from the laborer, but they are interested in how much profit the total amount of invested capital yields.

---

20 Quoted from Dandekar, V.M. (Jan. 12 1980), "Bourgeois Politics of the Working Class," *Economic and Political Weekly*, Vol. XV, no. 2. See also: "Capitalist society is characterized by a degree of labor mobility much greater than prevailed in any previous form of society. Not only do workers change their jobs relatively frequently, but also the stream of new workers entering the labor market is quickly diverted from declining to rising occupations. [...] This is a conclusion which commands universal assent in the modern world, it flows from such common facts of experience that no one would think of denying it." Sweezy, P.M. (1956), *The Theory of Capitalist Development*, pp. 30-32. New York: Monthly Review Press.

$$\text{Rate of Profit} = \frac{\text{Surplus Value}}{\text{Aggregate Capital}} \qquad \left(p' = \frac{s}{C}\right)$$

FIGURE IV

Therefore, what actually interests the capitalist is the production costs of the finished commodities—their cost-price.

> The value of every commodity produced in the capitalist way is represented in the formula: V=c+v+s. If we subtract surplus-values from this value of the product there remains a bare equivalent or a substitute value in goods, for the capital-value c+v expended in the elements of production [...] This portion of the value of the commodity, which replaces the price of the consumed means of production and labor-power, only replaces what the commodity costs the capitalist himself. For him it, therefore, represents the cost-price of the commodity.[21]

How this cost-price is distributed between constant and variable capital does not interest the capitalist. To him the profit is the yield of the aggregate capital.

In its assumed capacity of offspring of the aggregate advanced capital, surplus value takes the converted form of profit.[22]

THE RATE OF PROFIT

The ratio of the surplus value to the aggregate advanced capital is defined as the rate of profit:

Theoretically, the rate of profit of the individual capitalist depends therefore partly on the rate of surplus value and partly on the ratio of the constant capital to the variable capital. An increase or fall in the rate of surplus value results in a similar tendency for the rate of profit. The proportion of constant to variable capital is also defined as the organic composition of capital. This proportion of values is based on the technical composition of labor-power and means of production, respectively, in the given line of industry. Capital has a low organic composition if the variable capital forms a large part of the aggregate capital. Conversely, capital has a high organic composition if the constant capital forms a large part.[23]

---

21 Marx, *Capital*, Vol. III, p. 25-6.

22 Ibid., p. 36.

23 Thus the petrochemical industries with a very large share of constant capital have a high organic composition, whereas the textile industries with much more variable capital have a low

50 Unequal Exchange and the Prospects of Socialism

In the following example, in which the same rate of surplus value and the same turnover time are used,[24] it is shown how the organic composition of capital affects the rate of profit. The higher the organic composition, the lower the rate of profit, and the lower the organic composition, the higher the rate of profit.[25]

TABLE 3.1[26]

	Aggregate Capitals $C = c + v$	Rate of Surplus Value $\frac{s}{v}$	Surplus Value s	Value of Product $V = c + v + s$	Rate of Profit $p' = \frac{s}{C}$
I	$80c + 20v$	100%	20	120	20%
II	$70c + 30v$	100%	30	130	30%
III	$60c + 40v$	100%	40	140	40%
IV	$85c + 15v$	100%	15	115	15%
V	$95c + 5v$	100%	5	105	5%

The Creation of an Average Rate of Profit Between the Branches of Production

From table 3.1 it can be seen how equally big capitals with different organic composition obtain different surplus values, which theoretically result in very different rates of profit from equally big capitals. However, this tendency cannot be seen in reality. If it could be seen, it would mean that the capital would flow to the branches of production with a low organic composition—where the variable capital is a comparatively large amount of the aggregate capital—and away from branches of production with a high organic composition where

---

organic composition.

24 The turnover time influences the rate of profit. The turnover time is the period from the investment of the capital to the return of investments and profit. A capital which turns over twice a year has an annual rate of profit which is twice as high as the annual rate of profit of a capital which only turns over once a year—other things being equal.

25 We stress that these differences in the rates of profit as a result of the different organic composition of the capital is purely a theoretical phenomenon—in the real world an equalization takes place—more about that later.

26 Source: Marx, *Capital*, Vol. III, p. 155.

$$\genfrac{}{}{}{}{Price\ of}{Production} = Cost\text{-}Price + \genfrac{}{}{}{}{Total\ Used}{Capital} \times \genfrac{}{}{}{}{Average\ Rate}{of\ Profit}$$

Figure V

the constant capital constitutes a comparatively large part. However, this is not the case. The capital does not particularly seek branches of production with a low organic composition. We know from the real world that substantial differences in the average rates of profit for the various lines of industry do not exist—apart from transitory, accidental differences which equalize each other in the long term. They cannot exist without abolishing the capitalist system. Therefore, the question is how and why this equalization takes place.

The average rate of profit is formed by the capitalists' continuous search for higher rates of profit. If a heavy demand for the commodities of a certain line of industry arises, the price for these commodities will increase and consequently the rate of profit within that sector will increase. This will result in capital flowing to that sector to obtain a share of the higher rate of profit. This leads to an increased production of the commodities of the sector which again leads to a saturation of the social wants, perhaps to overproduction, and thus to a fall in prices, which means a lower rate of profit—and consequently a flight of capital from the sector. Thus the difference in the rates of profit from one line of industry to the other is the basis of continuous capital movements and consequently of a tendency towards an equalization of the rates of profit. Thus the competition between the capitals tends towards equalizing the rates of profit of the various lines of industry to an average rate of profit so that equally big capitals yield equally big profits, no matter where the investment is made, and no matter how the capital is distributed between constant and variable capital. Then the average profit can be defined as the profit which, according to the general rate of profit, goes to a capital of a given size no matter how the organic composition is.

This means that the original commodity values are turned into prices of production. In other words: the price of production of a commodity is equal to its cost-price plus the share of the annual average profit of the aggregate capital invested (not merely consumed) in its production (in accordance with the conditions of turnover).

The price of production must not be confused with the market price.[27] It

---

27 The market price is the price at which a commodity is actually sold on the market. The fluctuations of the market price around the price of production are regulated by supply and demand.

is a coincidence if they are identical. During the historical period of simple commodity production, the commodity prices fluctuated around the commodity value. But under developed capitalism the price of production forms the center of the fluctuation for the current market prices. Thus the price of production for the individual commodity is not the same as the value of the individual commodity. But the total sum of the prices of production will equal the sum of the commodity values—just as the sum of the profits will equal the total surplus value.

Let us see how the formation of an average rate of profit influences table 3.1. In table 3.2, each aggregate capital is still 100, the rate of surplus value is constant: 100%. We assume that the whole capital turns over in one circulation. The new thing in table 3.2 is the formation of the average rate of profit:

$$\frac{20\% + 30\% + 40\% + 15\% + 5\%}{5} = 22\%.$$

> Taken together, the commodities are sold at 2+7+17=26 above, and 8+18=26 below their value, so that the deviations of price from value balance out one another through the uniform distribution of surplus-value, or through addition of the average profit of 22 per 100 units of advanced capital to the respective cost-prices of the commodities I to V [...] The prices obtained as the average of the various rates of profit in the different spheres of production, added to the cost-prices of the different spheres of production, constitute the prices of production. They have as their prerequisite the existence of a general rate of profit, and this again, presupposes that the rates of profit in every individual sphere of production taken by itself have previously been reduced to just as many average rates. These particular rates of profit = s/C in every sphere of production, and must [...] be deduced out of the values of the commodities. Without such deduction the general rate of profit (and consequently the price of production of commodities) remains a vague and senseless conception. Hence, the price of production of a commodity is equal to its cost-price plus the profit allotted to it in percent, in accordance with the general rate of profit, or, in other words, to its cost-price plus the average profit.[28]

---

28 Marx, *Capital*, Vol. III, p. 157.

TABLE 3.2[29]

	Total Capital C	Surplus Value s	Value V	Average Rate of Profit p'	Price of Production PP	Deviation of Price of Production from Value PP − V
I	80c + 20v	20	120	22%	122	+2
II	70c + 30v	30	130	22%	122	−8
III	60c + 40v	40	140	22%	122	−18
IV	85c + 15v	15	115	22%	122	+7
V	95c + 5v	5	105	22%	122	+17

As can be seen from the table, the organic composition of the various capitals varies widely. This means that each of them employs very different quantities of human labor. Thus the basis of different quantities of surplus value within the various lines of production is formed. However, the surplus value does not necessarily fall to the line of production where it was created. By means of the equalization of the rate of profit there is a transfer of value from one line of production, which is below average, as to organic composition, to the lines of production which are above.

This transfer of value is of no interest to the capitalists. They do not observe it. The individual capitalist does not care how high the rate of surplus value is in the enterprise or line of production in question. The capitalist is interested in the profit, and because of the equalization of the rate of profit, it is evenly distributed between all capitals, no matter how organic the composition is.

This transfer of value is called "unequal exchange" by some economists.[30] However, there is nothing "unequal" about this transfer, as it is a condition of the actual function of capitalism. This equalization of the rate of profit makes it profitable for the capitalist to continuously improve his production apparatus—indeed it forces him to do so in order to survive the competition. Thus capital-

---

29 Table 3.2 is identical to the one in *Capital*, Vol. III, p. 157. However, Marx has divided the constant capital c into fixed and flowing parts in order to prove that this does not have any consequence. Therefore, it has been omitted here in order not to complicate the matter unnecessarily.

30 Marx did not consider the transfer of value because of different organic composition as something unequal. This was first done by Otto Bauer at the beginning of this century. Bauer's definition of "unequal exchange" has nothing to do with the definition made by A. Emmanuel.

ism gets the dynamics, the capability to improve the productive forces. If we imagine that the commodities were sold at their value instead of at a price which fluctuates around the price of production, it would lead to a stop in investments, in mechanization and in productions of a highly organic composition, whereas labor-intensive productions with much variable capital and consequently with much surplus value would gain ground. Chemical industries would die out and wood-carving would flourish.

The Conditions for an Equalization of the Rate of Profit Nationally

Marx describes these in Capital:

> Now, if the commodities are sold at their values, then, as we have shown, very different rates of profit arise in the various spheres of production, depending on the different organic composition of the masses of capital invested in them. But capital withdraws from a sphere with a low rate of profit and invades others, which yield a higher profit. Through this incessant outflow and influx, or, briefly, through its distribution among the various spheres, which depends on how the rate of profit falls here and rises there, it creates such a ratio of supply to demand that the average profit in the various spheres of production becomes the same, and values are, therefore, converted into prices of production. Capital succeeds in this equalization, to a greater or lesser degree, depending on the extent of capitalist development in the given nation; i.e., to the extent the conditions in the country in question are adapted for the capitalist mode of production [...].
>
> The incessant equilibration of constant divergences is accomplished so much more quickly, 1) the more mobile the capital, i.e., the more easily it can be shifted from one sphere and from one place to another, 2) the more quickly labor-power can be transferred from one sphere to another and from one production locality to another. The first condition implies complete freedom of trade within the society and the removal of all monopolies with the exception of the natural ones, those, that is, which naturally arise out of the capitalist mode of production [**Ed. Note:** i.e.: the capitalist monopoly of capital, and the labor monopoly of labor-power.] [...]—The second condition implies the abolition of all laws preventing the laborers from transferring from one sphere of production to another and from one local center of production to another; indifference of the laborer to the nature of his labor; the greatest possible reduction of labor in all spheres of production to simple labor; the elimination of all vocational prejudices among laborers; and last but not least, a subjugation of the laborer to the capitalist mode of production.[31]

---

31 Marx, *Capital*, Vol. III, pp. 195-6. It is not a prerequisite of the equalization of the rate of profit that the rate of surplus value has been equalized. Marx did not deal with the mobility of the labor force as a prerequisite of an equalization of the rate of surplus value, but as a prerequisite of the labor force being able to follow the movements of the capital from line to line and from place to place and by this secure the possibilities of capital movements.

Summary

Thus, under developed capitalism, there is sufficient mobility of the labor-force within the frontiers of the individual country for a tendency towards an equalization of the rate of surplus value. Similarly, there is sufficient mobility of capital for a tendency towards an equalization of the rate of profit. This results in the fact that the exchange relationship between the commodities—their market price—no longer fluctuates around the value but around the price of production.

Now the question is, How is it internationally? Is the mobility of the labor-force sufficient for an equalization of the rate of surplus value—i.e. of the rate of exploitation? Is the mobility of the capital between the countries sufficient for an equalization of the rate of profit and thus for the creation of prices of production? In short the question is, how does the capitalist world market function?

The World Market

As far as the rate of surplus value is concerned, we feel absolutely convinced that no equalization has taken place internationally. The mobility of the labor-force between the countries has not been sufficient to produce anything at all like a tendency towards this. The development has been the opposite.

The industrial and parliamentary struggle, which was carried on by the working class in the imperialist countries at the end of the last century, led to an increasing wage level on the basis of the exploitation of the rest of the countries in the world. On the other hand this exploitation of the poor countries meant that they had no possibility of a similar development; on the contrary, during the twentieth century this situation resulted in an increasing disparity in wage levels between the developed and the underdeveloped countries, or, in other words, in a high rate of surplus value in the poor countries and in a lower in the rich countries.

As far as the rate of profit is concerned, we believe that the international mobility of capital—particularly after the Second World War and the decolonization—has been sufficient to produce a tendency towards equalization, and thus sufficient for the determination of prices of production at an international level. Thus the prerequisites[32] for the determination of the prices on the world market are:

---

32 In Chapter 4, we shall go into details concerning the validity of these two prerequisites.

1. Wages

Unequal payment of labor-power. Internationally, the class struggle has been fought on an unequal economic basis which has resulted in the wage levels and consequently the rates of surplus value varying enormously between the imperialist countries and the exploited countries.

2. Profit

Equal payment of the capital. The mobility of capital is sufficient to produce a tendency towards an international equalization of the rate of profit.

Unequal Exchange Between Countries

Let us see what these prerequisites lead to in Marx's tables of prices of production:

We suppose two countries A and B. Firstly, we suppose that the rate of surplus value and the rate of profit in the two countries are equal. This means that the mobility of the labor-force and the capital is sufficient for an equalization (table 3.3).

The organic composition of the production in the countries A and B is the same (c and v is 100 in both countries). This has been done to make "other things equal"—to eliminate the possibility that a higher organic composition should be the cause of any transfers of value. This means that in this case the value and price of production coincide.

The equal organic composition in no way indicates that this is a question of a production of identical commodities, because then the wage increase in country A would mean that A's commodities would be outstripped by country B's lower prices. The characteristic feature of the trade between the imperialist countries and the exploited countries is namely that they exchange different commodities.

Finally, we suppose that the entire capital turns over at the same speed in both countries.

In table 3.3, the rate of surplus value and the rate of profit between the two countries have been equalized. Thus the exchange relationship between the two countries is equal.

In table 3.4, a 50 percent increase in wages has been introduced in country A, resulting in a lower rate of surplus value—a lower degree of exploitation. This affects the exchange relationship between the two countries.

TABLE 3.3

Country	Constant Capital	Variable Capital	Surplus Value	Cost Price	Value	Rate of Profit	Average Rate of Profit	Price of Prod.
	c	v	s	$c + v$	$c + v + s$	$\frac{s}{c}$	p'	$(c + v) + p' \times C$
A	100	100	100	200	300	50%	50%	300
B	100	100	100	200	300	50%	50%	300
					= 600			= 600

TABLE 3.4

Country	Constant Capital	Variable Capital	Surplus Value	Cost Price	Value	Rate of Profit	Average Rate of Profit	Price of Prod.
	c	v	s	$c + v$	$c + v + s$	$\frac{s}{c}$	p'	$(c + v) + p' \times C$
A	100	150	50	250	300	20%	33.33%	333.33
B	100	100	100	200	300	50%	33.33%	266.67
					= 600			= 600

Equal quantities of labor-power are used in the two countries. It is only the price for the labor-power which is not the same and, therefore, the value of the production in the two countries is the same. The rate of surplus value (??) is different in the two countries. But the rate of profit is the same. Because the price for labor-power is different, we get different prices of production even though there is the same quantity of human labor and the same quantities of value in the two countries.

Whereas the commodities in table 3.3 were equally exchanged by 300 to 300, the wage increase of 50 percent in table 3.4 (which is moderate compared to the real differences) results in an unequal exchange: 333 1/3 and 266 2/3 respectively. Country B is missing 300—66 2/3 = 33 1/3 as compared to equal exchange. And country A gains 33 1/3—300 = 33 1/3. In the case of a complete exchange of commodities between country A and country B, country A would gain 33 1/3 + 33 1/3 = 66 2/3. At the same time the wage increase in country A means that the overall average rate of profit falls from 50 percent to 33 1/3 percent.

In this way, value is transferred from countries with a low wage level to countries with a high wage level. Through the international commodity and capital markets, the rich imperialist countries benefit from trade with the poor countries by means of unequal exchange.

The colonial form of imperialism at the end of the nineteenth century gave rise both to higher wages in the developed countries and to extra profits. But the mobility of capital, which also was a result of imperialism, tended soon to equalize the differences in the rates of profit between the investments in the colonies and in the imperialist countries. The working classes of the imperialist countries succeeded through parliamentary and industrial struggles not only in maintaining but also in increasing the comparatively high wage level they had obtained compared to that of the proletariat in the exploited countries.

The efficient industrial struggle of the American and West European working classes and the simultaneous brutal suppression of the same political and industrial struggle in the Third World, has resulted in differences in wages of 10 to 20 times. The increasing international mobility of capital, particularly after the Second World War, has resulted in a tendency towards an equalization of the rate of profit. In general, capital invested in the Third World does not yield higher profits than capital invested in the imperialist countries. Therefore, the international differences in wages are felt in the prices. Commodities from the Third World are cheaper, and when the two groups of countries exchange commodities, value is transferred from the poor exploited countries to the rich imperialist countries.

On Exploitation Between Countries

In the last analysis, exploitation is an appropriation of other people's labor. This is true whether it is one person's exploitation of another person or one country's exploitation of another. The products of human labor are commodities or services and, therefore, the appropriation of human labor is the appropriation of these commodities and services. Consequently, all exploitation between countries is ultimately based on an unequal exchange of commodities and services.[33]

---

33 This also applies to financial operations such as capital exports, repatriation of profits, etc. In the last resort the money, which is transferred in the case of such operations, represents a claim for commodities from the country in question. Capital export from Britain is the exportation

This may either be reflected by a deficit in the balance of trade, which means that the imperialist country imports more commodities than it exports according to current world market prices, or the inequality may be found in the actual price formation. We believe the latter to be correct.

Emmanuel says:

> To simplify still further: one country can only gain something at the expense of another by taking more goods than it provides or by buying the goods it obtains too cheaply and selling those it provides at too high a price.[34]

During a long period and generally speaking, the imports of the Third World from the imperialist countries exceed their exports measured in world market prices. The countries of the Third World have to take loans continuously to cover this import surplus.[35] Thus the transfer of value from the Third World is not based on an export surplus to the rich countries measured in world market prices. The transfer of value takes place on the basis of an inequality of market prices as one of the price-determining elements contains an inequality—namely the wages.

The international mobility of capital and the consequential tendency towards an equalization of the rate of profit prevents the low wages in the poor countries from resulting in generally higher rates of profit of capitals invested in these countries. The national and international competition between capitalists means that the low wages do not result in higher profits but in lower prices. The low wages lead to low prices, and thus the consumers benefit from this, whether they are capitalists or wage-laborers. The consumers are first and foremost the population of the imperialist countries. Table 3.5 shows how the imperialist countries account for around 3/4 of the exports of the poor countries.

---

of British pounds which return sooner or later as a claim for British commodities.

34 Emmanuel, *Unequal Exchange Revisited*, p. 56. During most of the nineteenth century there was a considerable deficit of the British balance of trade, which was possible because of the position of Britain as an economic, political, and military Great Power.

35 In 1981 the total debt of the Third World was more than $500 billion according to official figures. (This amount corresponds to the total annual military expenses of the world.)

TABLE 3.5: DISTRIBUTION OF DEVELOPING COUNTRIES' EXPORTS[36]

Export to	1972	1973	1974	1975	1976	1977
Industrial Countries	74.3%	74%	75.2%	73.3%	73.5%	72.9%
Developing Countries	21.1%	21.3%	21.3%	22.7%	22.5%	23%
Socialist Countries	4.6%	4.7%	3.5%	4.0%	4.0%	4.1%

ON EXPLOITATION

Capitalist exploitation is not exclusively and in isolation connected to production or to the concrete relationship between capital and labor. Under developed capitalism, the exploitation must be seen in relation to the circulation of capital as a whole—i.e. both in relation to production and to the trade in commodities.

Under developed capitalism, value is transferred from undertakings of low productivity to undertakings of high productivity within one line of industry. Value is transferred from lines of industry with a low organic composition to lines with a high organic composition. Finance and trade capital can appropriate value without even being directly attached to the productive sphere. Value is transferred from countries with a low wage level to countries with a high wage level. All these transfers of value—conditions of exploitation—can only be understood, if the capitalist circulation is considered as a whole and not only on the basis of production. The basis of the surplus value—the surplus labor—is created in production, the appropriation and distribution of the surplus value take place in the trade in commodities.

The fact that, technically, a person takes part in production as a wage-laborer does not necessarily mean that he or she is exploited and that he or she cannot exploit other people. Wage-labor is a *sine qua non* of capitalist exploitation but it is not enough. The exploitation depends on the actual ratio between the "necessary labor" (the wages) and the "surplus labor" (the surplus value). Thus, if you can secure more value for your wages than you have created, you are not being exploited but you are exploiting.

In principle there is nothing new about this. In *Grundrisse*, pp. 434-43, Marx deals with the fact that through the determination of prices of production and a national average rate of profit, laborers could benefit from other laborers' products being sold below their value to the extent that these products were part

---

36 Source: International trade 1975/76 and 1977/78, GATT, Geneva 1976 and 1978.

of their consumption. However, when he wrote *Grundrisse* in 1857-8, Marx did not regard this as something important. He writes:

> As regards the other workers, the case is entirely the same; they gain from the depreciated commodity only in relation (1) as they consume it; (2) relative to the size of their wage, which is determined by necessary labor. If the depreciated commodity were, e.g. grain—one of the stuffs of life—then first its producer, the farmer, and following him all other capitalists, would make the discovery that the worker's necessary wage is no longer the necessary wage; but stands above its level; hence it is brought down [...]³⁷

Engels did not doubt the possibility of the British' proletariat exploiting the colonial proletariat.

> [...] the English proletariat is actually becoming more and more bourgeois, so that this most bourgeois of all nations is apparently aiming ultimately at the possession of a bourgeois aristocracy and a bourgeois proletariat alongside the bourgeoisie. For a nation which exploits the whole world this is of course to a certain extent justifiable.³⁸

And in a letter to Kautsky he wrote:

> You ask me what the English workers think about colonial policy. Well, exactly the same as they think about politics in general: the same as the bourgeois think. There is no workers' party here, you see, there are only Conservatives and Liberal-Radicals, and the workers gaily share the feast of England's monopoly of the world market and the colonies.³⁹

Thus the fact that wages of a certain size can contain more value than the labor performed in order to get the wages is not something new.⁴⁰

It is a question of quantity whether it applies in the case of a managing director with an annual salary of $100,000, or in the case of an assistant manager with a salary of $25,000—or if it already applies to the skilled worker earning $15,000. It is a question of calculations, not of principles.

SOUTH AFRICA—A CONCRETE EXAMPLE

A working class (labor aristocracy) may very well share in the exploitation of a proletariat. In order to illustrate this we shall look at a concrete example: the participation of the white working class in the exploitation of the black prole-

---

37 Marx, Karl, *Grundrisse*, p. 439. Depreciated, i.e. the price of production is lower than the value of the product.

38 Friedrich Engels to Karl Marx (Oct. 7, 1858), MESC, p. 110.

39 Friedrich Engels to Karl Kautsky (Sep. 12, 1882), MESW, p. 678.

40 Such a production may very well be profitable to the capital. From the point of view of the individual capitalist, value and surplus value is of no interest. What is important is the price of production or rather the market price and the rate of profit, and to the individual capitalist the rate of profit has no connection with the actual substance of surplus value.

tariat in South Africa. In his article "The White Working Class in South Africa" (*New Left Review*, no. 82, Dec. 1973), Robert Davis describes the basis of the high standard of living and racist ideology of this class, which can be explained by its participation in the economic exploitation of the black working class in South Africa.

Robert Davis writes:

> For it is clear that a section of the labor-force will tend to become most fully tied to the bourgeoisie when it benefits from the extraction of surplus value, in other words when it participates in the exploitation of the majority of the working class. Tables [3.6] and [3.7] below represents an attempt to show that it is true of the white mining, industrial, and construction workers in South Africa.
>
> From table [3.6] it is clear that the average white mining wage (and even the basic white rate) have been, for the whole period in question, consistently above what we have called the "average allowable wage with no surplus content," very roughly an indication of the average wage each worker would receive if there were no exploitation.

TABLE 3.6: ROUGH INDICATION OF WHITE MINERS' SHARE IN SURPLUS PRODUCED IN THE MINING SECTOR (CURRENT PRICES AT TIME OF ORIGINAL PUBLICATION)

	1911	1920	1930	1940	1950	1961	1970	1972
Total Market Value of Sales (R million)	95,358	136,664	118,570	259,090	393,314	893,281	1,563,375	1,942,344
Depreciation (C)	28,030	35,686	35,470	71,834	142,726	341,216	615,046	632,739
Wages (V)	37,634	46,068	40,446	75,322	139,224	293,259	488,100	570,757
Surplus (S)	29,694	54,910	42,654	111,934	111,364	258,806	460,229	738,848
Average Allowable Annual Wage with No Surplus Content $\left(\frac{S+V}{\text{Labour Force}}\right)$	R222	R345	R242	R377	R507	R826	R1,347	R1,963
Average White Wage	R560	R819	R648	R911	R1,594	R2,501	R4,074	R5,098
Surplus Content of Average White Wage	R338	R525	R406	R534	R1,087	R1,675	R2,727	R3,125
Basic Grade White Rates (Selected Years)		R624*	R520*				R3,036	
Average Black Wage	R62	R64	R59	R69	R110	R159	R235	R302
Rate of Exploitation of Black Labor $\left(\frac{S}{\text{Total Black Wages}}, \%\right)$	181%	331%	232%	365%	240%	278%	316%	415%

*Lowest Grade

Since the "average allowable wage with no surplus-content" represents an average free of employers' exploitation, roughly speaking any group of workers who receive an average wage above this level trust either be contributing more labor power than the average, or else be receiving this higher wage at the expense of fellow workers, through some (workplace or national) political arrangement.

That the first possibility does not apply to white mineworkers is borne out by the following facts. In the gold mines the ratio of white wages to black wages in 1911 was 11.7:1, while by 1966 the gap had increased to 17.6:1. But between 1920 and 1965 the productivity of black gold miners rose from an annual rate of 222 tons of ore mined per man to 417 tons, per man—an increase of 188 percent.[41] The productivity of the whole labor force had meanwhile increased from an annual rate of 39 fine oz. of gold per man to 51 oz. per man over the same period.[42] This represents an increase of 157 percent. The black increase in productivity was therefore above the total average increase in productivity, and we therefore also conclude that the average white miner's increase in productivity must have been rather less than that of his black colleague.

TABLE 3.7: ROUGH INDICATION OF WHITE MANUFACTURING AND CONSTRUCTIONS WORKERS' SHARE IN SURPLUS IN THOSE SECTORS (SELECTED YEARS, CURRENT PRICES AT TIME OF ORIGINAL PUBLICATION)

	1960	1961	1965	1968	1969
Gross Value of Manufacturing and Construction Output (R million)	1,292	1,373	2,241	2,827	3,236
Depreciation (Approximately at National Average) (C)	110	137	179	226	259
Wages (V)	652	695	1,228	1,613	1,675
Surplus (S)	530	541	834	988	1,302

---

41 **R. Davis' note:** Figures for the wages gap calculated by Francis Wilson, and for productivity by T. F. Muller, chairman of the mining house Federale Mynbou. Both quoted in Bunting, *The Rise of the South African Reich* (London, 1969).

42 **R. Davis' note:** Calculated from the figures given in the 1920 Union of South Africa Yearbook and in the 1969 State of South Africa Yearbook.

TABLE 3.7 (CONTINUED)

Average Allowable Annual Wage with No Surplus Content $\left(\frac{S+V}{Labour\ Force}\right)$	R1,483	R1,555	R1,854	R1,862	R2,002
Average White Wage	R1,870	R1,901	R2,727	R2,955	R3,095
Surplus Content of Average White Wage	R387	R346	R873	R1,093	R1,093
Average Black Wage	R389	R451	R582	R643	R576
Rate of Exploitation of Black Labor $\left(\frac{S}{Total\ Black\ Wages},\%\right)$	241%	213%	171%	141%	195%

In other words whilst black miners had increased their relative contribution of labor value, their relative income position had declined. So, indeed, did their real income: for the average black miner received less in real terms in 1966 (R71 at 1938 prices) than in 1911 (R72 at 1938 prices)[43] The reverse, of course, applies to the white miner. On productivity grounds, therefore, the differentials should have become smaller not larger. Increased productivity thus cannot account for the white miners higher than "allowable wage with no surplus content."

Of course, the explanation for this state of affairs is political. Black wages are kept low by the laws against effective political and trade union organization, by the color bar and by the migratory labor system—all official instruments of State policy. Black workers are therefore victims of a super-exploitation, which has tended to increase rather than to diminish (as the table shows). Since the average white wage is a significant amount above the "surplus free wage," and since it is not based on higher productivity, the inescapable conclusion is that the white mine workers benefit from surplus value created by blacks; in other words they indirectly share in the exploitation of blacks, via their political support for the State and the economic privileges they receive from it in return. If

---

43 **R. Davis' note:** Bunting, op. cit., p. 513. For a graphic recent description by an American observer of a typical work process in a South African mine, see J. Hoaglund, *South Africa: Civilisations in Conflict* (London, 1973), pp. 196-7: "I watched two mine workers [...] 3,500 feet down a mine shaft [...] 50 miles west of Johannesburg. Willie, the white miner, crouched inside a four-foot high pit, or stope as it is called by the miners. He had already marked the face of the rock wall for drilling. A black laborer, known to the company not by name but by an identity number, sat on the floor of the pit, his arms and legs wrapped around a jack-hammer drill. As Willie dropped his hand as a signal the black laborer started to drill. [...] At the end of the eight hour shift, Willie would insert explosive charges into the hundred holes being drilled in the rock face, and the blasting of a part of the gold and ore would begin. Willie [...] earned about R300 a month. The black laborer (technically miner is a rank that only whites can hold in South Africa) made R20 a month. The work they did is not all that different, a mining supervisor [...] conceded in response to a question. Then why the large gap in pay? 'Because Willie's skin is white,' the (supervisor) replied matter-of-factly. 'It is the most valuable commodity you can have in South Africa. It is more valuable than this yellow stuff we blast out of the earth.'"

we look at similar figures for industry and construction, we see the same pattern repeated for fundamentally the same reasons.

In industry and construction, as well as in mining, the white worker has visibly benefited from political privilege, and if the same analysis were applied to other sectors of the economy, doubtless the same trend would appear. What can then be said, without fear of contradiction, is that since the white wage is high by virtue of political privilege, if this privilege were to disappear, the white wage would be reduced. This would be so in any type of society that replaced it: neo-colonial, independent (if such thing is possible) native capitalist, or socialist. In a socialist society, unless exceptionally high productivity were proven (not, as we have seen, true of the South African white worker), a worker's income would tend to be close to the "allowable wage with no surplus content" (this income would, of course, consist partly of collectively consumed items and there would be some contribution for new investments). The average white South African worker would therefore stand to lose at least one-third to two-thirds of his current income by the introduction of a socialist society, and must on economic grounds therefore be judged likely to oppose either phase of the "two-stage" freedom struggle, as envisaged by classical Stalinist Strategy.

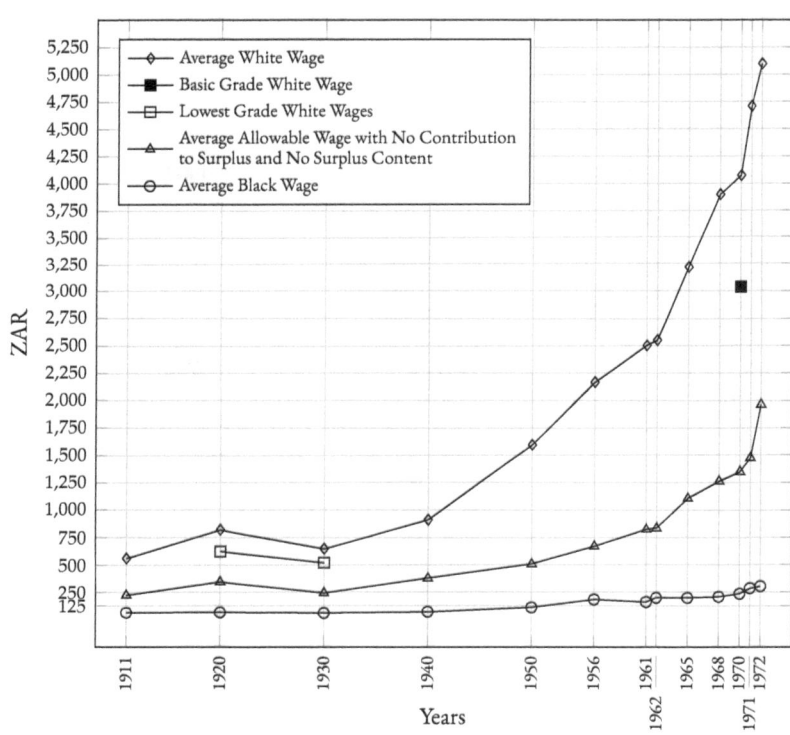

FIGURE VI: MINING WAGES

The Theory of Unequal Exchange 67

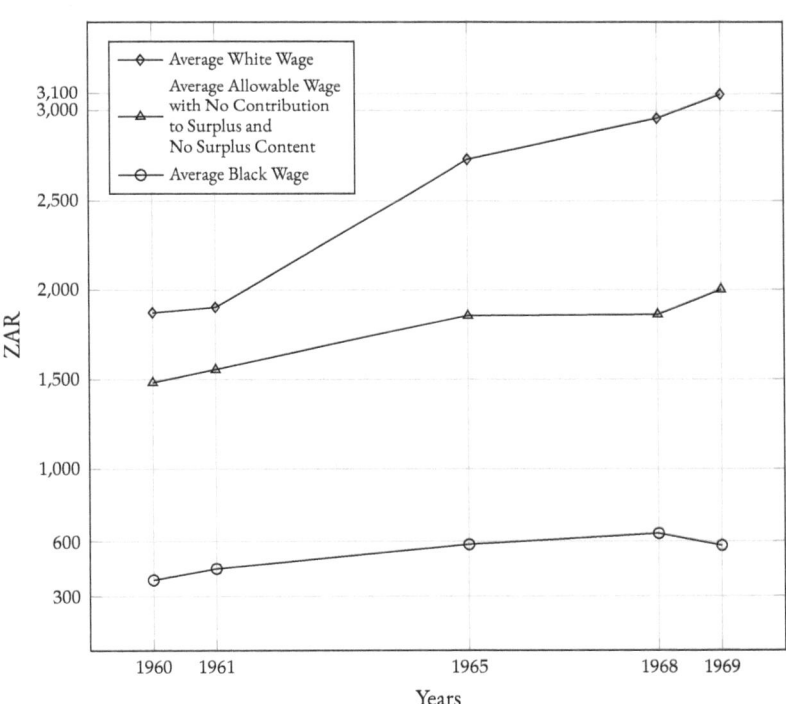

Figure VII: Manufacturing and Construction Wages

Global Inequality

Emmanuel has made a similar but global calculation:

> In 1973, the average annual wage in the USA amounted to around 10,500 U.S. dollars. The population of the entire capitalist world at that time was about 2 billion six hundred millions, and there was a little over a billion economically active. To pay all these economically active people on an American scale would require close to 11,000 billions US $. However, the total national income of these countries in 1973 amounted to only $2,700 billion.[44]

Based on the same method of calculation, we have tried to compare the national income of various countries to the total wages if the workers were paid the average Danish wage, of the year concerned.

TABLE 3.8: DANISH WAGES 1973-1977 (USD)

Year	No. of Wage Labourers	Total Money Income	Annual Average Wage
1973	2,426,000	$14,824,006,000	$6,110
1975	2,365,000	$20,168,339,000	$8,527
1977	2,578,000	$26,035,410,000	$10,409

The following table shows that India's national income should have been 29 times as big as it was in 1975 to have paid the Indian workers according to the Danish level of wages (and in this calculation profits to capitalists or any appropriation of capital for repairs or new investments are not allowed).

---

44 Emmanuel, Arghiri, *The Socialist Project*, p. 70.

TABLE 3.9

Country	Year	(I) National Income at Factor Costs	(II) Number of Economically Active	(III) Total Wages If All Workers Got Danish Average Wages	(IV) Cols III/I Ratio
India	1975	69,217,858,000	239,372,000*	2,041,125,000,000	29
Indonesia	1975	27,233,743,000	52,240,000*	445,450,480,000	16
South Korea	1975	16,665,289,000	12,340,000	105,223,180,000	6
	1977	27,833,057,000	13,440,000	139,896,960,000	5
Pakistan	1973	7,419,091,000	26,482,000*	161,866,120,000	23
Philippines	1975	12,158,455,000	14,517,000	123,786,450,000	10
Sri Lanka	1975	2,672,500,900	5,404,000*	46,079,908,000	23

* = Number of economically active is estimated at 40% of the population.

This means that even if the entire capitalist class was expropriated, that is if all profits were paid out as wages, and even if no money at all were put aside for investments and maintenance, each laborer could only get an average pay of $2,500, which is no more than a quarter of the average American wages.

In the same article Emmanuel continues:

This means that the United States can be the United States and Sweden can be Sweden only because others, that is the 2 billion inhabitants of the Third World, are not.

This also means that every material equalization from the top down is excluded. If by some miracle, a socialist and fraternal system, regardless of its type or model, were introduced tomorrow morning the world over, and if it wanted to integrate, to homogenize mankind by equalizing living standards, then to do this it would not only have to expropriate the capitalists of the entire world, but also dispossess large sections of the working class of the industrialized countries, of the amount of surplus value these sections appropriate today. It seems this is reason enough for these working classes not to desire this "socialist and fraternal" system and to express their opposition by either openly integrating into the existing system, as in the United States of America or the Federal Republic of Germany, or by advocating national paths to socialism, as in France or Italy.[45]

Thus, under developed capitalism—imperialism—the appropriation of other people's abstract labor does not only take place in the relationship be-

---

45 Ibid., p. 71.

tween capitalists and laborers. The high wage level of the population as a whole in the rich countries means that also the laborers are able to appropriate the surplus value created in the poor countries so that the laborers are able to appropriate more value than they create themselves. This is a characteristic of the position of the working class in eastern Europe and North America today.

4

The Validity of the Prerequisites of Unequal Exchange

Introduction

FROM THE END of World War II and until the Oil Crisis in 1973, when the recession began to be felt, capitalism had existed almost without crises in the imperialist countries. The period was characterized by an increase in prosperity for the majority of the population of these countries as never seen before. The working class achieved its lot by increasing real wages. Cars, refrigerators, television sets, stereo sets, and other electronic equipment became necessities. Travel, weekend cottages, bungalows, yachts etc. became obtainable objects for a large number of the workers in the imperialist countries. The youth became large-scale consumers of clothes, music, and fashions. Guaranteed minimum wages, unemployment insurance, sickness insurance, social relief programs, etc., removed the possibility of potentially lethal poverty in the case of unemployment, and sickness. Capitalism received a "human face" in Western Europe and North America.

The main working class parties, the 'Social Democrats,' came into power in most West European countries without changing the imperialist character of these states. The national interests of the imperialist countries included both the working class and the bourgeoisie. The prosperity of the countries became the prosperity of all classes so that the population of the rich countries constitutes the upper class of today's world. In other parts of the world capitalism did not mean prosperity but economic, social, and political crisis. To the exploited countries in Asia, Africa and Latin America capitalism means gross exploitation, plundering of natural riches, oppression of elementary human and democratic rights, and wretched poverty. The high wages in the rich countries determine and are determined by the fact that a majority of the population of the world live in poverty and wretchedness and receive wages which hardly cover their mere physical reproduction cost. The effective industrial struggles of the North American and Western European working classes together with the brutal suppression of the political and industrial struggles in the Third World have resulted in large differences in wages in the world.

Conversely, the international mobility of capital, which has grown particularly after World War II, has resulted in a tendency towards a global equalization of the rate of profit. In general, capital invested in the Third World does not yield considerably higher rates of profit than capital invested in the imperialist countries. Therefore, the international differences in wages can be felt in the prices. Commodities from low-wage countries are cheap and commodities from high-wage countries are expensive. When the two groups of countries exchange commodities, value is transferred from the low-wage countries to the high-wage countries. This is the fundamental thesis of the theory of unequal exchange, which is based on two prerequisites:

1. WAGES

Unequal payment of the labor-power. Internationally, the class struggle has been fought on an unequal economic basis, which has led to the wage level and consequently the rate of surplus value varying enormously.

2. PROFIT

Equal payment of the capital. The mobility of capital is sufficient to produce a tendency towards an international equalization of the rate of profit.

Below we shall deal with the validity of these two prerequisites, and in this chapter we shall include concrete economic facts.

VARIATION IN WAGES IN A DIVIDED WORLD

Introduction. Under capitalism, labor-power is a special commodity. Special because the price of the commodity, the wages, does not primarily reflect economic rules but political conditions. The wage level reflects the strength of the working class in relation to the bourgeoisie and depends on the economic framework which the society in question has provided for wage-variation.

Wages form part of the social product. Thus, apart from being the price for labor-power, wages constitute an important and basic element in the distribution of social production. Wages and profit are two parts of a connected whole, two parts of social production. The distribution of this production is determined by the struggle of the classes.

The price of labor-power is determined by moral and historical elements, just as the market for labor-power is full of norms, rules, and regulations. These reflect the relative strengths between the classes. They result in a tendency towards an equalization of the wage-level within the individual countries, particularly within the imperialist countries. This also means that the rate of exploitation is equalized. The tendency towards an equalization of the national wages is partly due to the comparatively high mobility of the labor-power within the country and partly to political intervention.

Internationally, a similar tendency has not been seen, on the contrary. Historically, there has been a tendency towards a growing gulf between the wages in the poor countries and the wages in the rich countries. Today the differences in wages are bigger than ever. There is not one world market price for labor-power as is the case with the majority of other commodities. There are many prices. However, the main tendency is that wages are divided into two kinds: subsistence wages to the proletariat in the exploited countries and comparatively high wages to the workers in the imperialist countries in North America, Northern Europe, Japan, Australia, etc. This tendency not only continues but is becoming more prominent.

From the break-through of capitalism and until the middle of the nineteenth century, there were only limited differences in wages internationally. Subsistence wages were prevailing, as they had been for centuries to the extent that wage-labor had existed. The variations which could be seen reflected climatic and other natural conditions, which made life easier or more difficult. In their theories, the classical economists Adam Smith and David Ricardo presupposed constant and equal wages. To them and their contemporaries wages were closely identified with the subsistence level. And studies of the conditions of wages and prices during the first ten years of the nineteenth century do show a close relation between wages and the price of bread. Expenses for bread alone amounted to about 50 percent of the wages for a working-class family. (The studies have been quoted by Emmanuel, *Unequal Exchange*, pp. 49-50.) As mentioned above, it was the industrial struggle in Britain in the 1860s which made the wages increase slowly. The concrete differences in wages which have occurred in the world since then will be discussed below.

The Concrete Variations in Wages

A global study of wages by Cairnes in 1874 comes to the following results: wages in the United States were 25-50 percent higher than in Britain, 48-70 percent higher than in Belgium, and about 100 percent higher than in France.[1] If we consider countries such as India and China, American wages were about 4-5 times as high. During the one hundred years which have passed since then, this tendency has become much more emphasized. Today the differences in wages between the imperialist countries and the exploited countries are not 4-5 times but 10-20-30 times. Table 4.1 gives an outline of the time rates in the industries of a number of selected countries, which are characteristic of both the imperialist countries and the exploited countries. The figures in the table correspond to the wage level in the sectors which in the countries in question produce for the world market.

As it appears in table 4.1, there are considerable international wage variations in the case of industrial workers. In the case of agricultural workers the wage differences are even more pronounced, as it appears from the table, since agricultural workers in the Third World receive wages which are lower than the industrial workers of the countries in question. This applies especially to the exporting plantations which produce coffee, cocoa, tobacco, tea, rubber, peanuts, bananas, cotton, and similar commodities, which are mainly consumed by the population of the imperialist countries and by the middle and upper classes of the exploited countries. Agricultural workers in the Third World are paid about 30 times less than the workers of the richest countries.

It is evident that a table like this is vitiated by errors and uncertainty, but other studies[2] and our own experiences from travels in the Third World confirm the main results of the investigation.

If we use the figures in table 4.1 and weigh them with the number of industrial workers in the countries in question, the average figure representing the wages of the industrial workers appears:

Imperialist countries: about $5.60 per hour

Exploited countries: about $0.46 per hour

As it has been impossible to find reliable figures for the number of agricul-

---

1 Quoted by Emmanuel, op. cit., p. 46.

2 See for example: Frank (1981), *Crisis In the Third World*, pp. 179-182 or Fröbel, Heinrichs, Kreye (1980), *The New International Division of Labour*, p. 361.

tural workers in most countries and, as many of the wage figures for agricultural workers do not represent the real remuneration, we have chosen to estimate on the basis of the figures available the ratio of the number of industrial workers to agricultural workers and the ratio of the wages in industry to agriculture, and have reached the following result:

The ratio of the number of industrial workers to agricultural workers:

Imperialist countries: 18:1

Exploited countries: 1.3:1

The ratio of the wages of the industrial to the agricultural workers:

Imperialist countries: 1.4:1

Exploited countries: 2:1

Thus the average wages of both industrial and agricultural workers can be calculated:

Imperialist countries: $5.50 per hour

Exploited countries: $0.36 per hour

Thus wages are, in general, 15 times higher in the imperialist countries than in the exploited countries.

In the following, we shall use this ratio of the wages in the imperialist countries to the exploited countries (15:1) in our calculations, well aware that this method of calculation is not the safest. Several things indicate that the difference in wages is bigger in real life. The wages which are actually paid in the poor countries, are often lower than the ones stated. This is due to sheer evasion of agreements and legislation on the part of the employers.[3] Furthermore, the

---

3 Ibid., p. 353. "The following examples illustrate in detail the wages actually paid in the free production zones and world market factories. In Hong Kong in 1974 the daily rates in the garment industry were US $3.15; in the electronics industry US $2.36 for female workers, in the plastic industry US $2.56 for female workers and in the toy industry US $3.34. In 1976 in the Export Processing Zone in Bombay unskilled workers were paid an average of US $25 per month (including fringe benefits), semi-skilled workers US $33, and skilled workers US $50. In 1974 in Malaysia in the electronics industry semi-skilled workers were earning US $1.45-1.75 per day. In 1975 in the Export Processing Zone of Bataan in the Philippines wages averaged US $36 per month. The daily wage for unskilled workers was US $1.20, for semi-skilled workers it was US $1.48-1.77, and skilled workers were receiving US $1.772.22. In 1976 in the electronics industry in South Korea wages came to roughly US $1.50 per day for foremen and toolmakers. In Thailand at the end of 1974 unskilled workers in world market factories were paid US $1.00 per day. In Nicaragua in 1975 world market factories in the electronics industry were paying unskilled/semi-skilled workers US $0.27 per hour; skilled workers were getting US $0.90 per hour. In Costa Rica export-processing industry unskilled/semi-skilled workers were paid US $3.14-3.35 per day, skilled workers an average of US $4.31 per day. In 1974 in the Dominican Republic wages in the free production zones were US $0.25-0.40 per

statistics often only apply to organized laborers. In the Third World many laborers are not organized and they get even lower wages than the organized members of their own class. In many imperialist countries the employer pays insurance, pensions, etc., which are not paid directly to the workers. These amounts ought to appear as part of the wages. Thus it would perhaps be much nearer reality, if we estimated a wage difference of between 15 to 25 times, instead of the 15 times which we have chosen as our basis of calculation.

TABLE 4.1: HOURLY WAGES (USD)[4]

Country	Industry		Agriculture			
	Year	Wage	Year	Wage	Paid in Cash	Part. Paid in Kind[a]
Africa						
Egypt	1973	0.22	—	—		
Kenya	1978	0.94	1977	0.23[b]	✓	✓
Nigeria	1978	0.44	1975	0.30[c]	✓	
Tanzania	1974	0.45	1974	0.26		✓
Zambia	1976	0.75	1976	0.33	✓	
Ghana	1970	0.40	—	—		
Latin America						
Argentina	1977	0.22	1977	0.18 (U)		
Bolivia	1977	0.61[c]	—	—		
Brazil	1976	1.23	—	—		
Colombia	1978	0.65	—	—		
Chile	1978	0.60	1978	0.22[c]	✓	
Ecuador	1977	0.75	—	—		
Mexico	1976	0.97	1978	0.49[c]		✓*

hour for unskilled and semi-skilled workers. The lowest wages were paid in the Export Processing Zone in Mauritius. In 1975 unskilled female workers were paid US $0.70 per day and semi-skilled female workers US $0.88 per day." Fröbel, Heinrichs, Kreye, op. cit., pp. 351-2.

TABLE 4.1 (CONTINUED)

Asia						
Bangladesh	1977	0.14 (S)[c]	1977	0.09 (S)[c]	✓	
Burma	1977	0.17	—	—		
Hong Kong	1978	0.70[c]	—	—		
India	1977	0.22	1977	0.18[c]		✓
Japan	1978	6.79	1976	1.67 (M) 1.33 (W)		✓
Pakistan	1975	0.19	1978	0.12	✓	
Philippines	1975	0.25	1975	0.11[b]	✓	
Singapore	1978	0.79	—	—		
Sri Lanka	1978	0.21	1978	0.07		✓
South Korea	1979	1.06	1978	0.86 (M)[c] 0.65 (W)[c]		✓
Turkey	1977	0.84	1977	0.80		✓**
Europe						
Denmark	1978	8.76	1978	6.51	✓	
Spain	1976	1.99	1978	1.43	✓	
France	1978	4.18	1976	2.10[b]	✓	✓
West Germany	1978	6.42	1978	3.98 (M)[c] 3.02 (W)[c]		✓
Greece	1978	1.85	—	—		
Italy	1977	3.07	—	—		
Switzerland	1979	7.23	1978	7.07 (M) 5.19 (W)	✓***	
Sweden	1978	7.52	1978	6.10 (M) 5.49 (W)	✓	✓
Great Britain	1978	3.97 (M) 2.74 (W)	1977	2.68 (M) 2.15 (W)	✓	

TABLE 4.1 (CONTINUED)

Oceania						
New Zealand	1979	4.29	1978	2.61^c	✓	
Australia	1978	5.88 (M) 4.69 (W)	—	—	✓	
North America						
Canada	1979	6.34	1978	3.17^c	✓	
USA	1979	6.66	1978	3.07^{bc}	✓	✓

M = Men   W = Women   S = Skilled   U = Unskilled

* = Day-laborers   ** = Fishermen   *** = Woodmen

a = Some of the wages are paid in kind. The statistics show only the amount paid in cash.

b = Besides the wages stated, free meals and free lodgings are granted.

c = The amounts shows the wages agreed to through collective bargaining. It is usually the minimum wage. In the exploited countries this figure will almost correspond to the actual wages or it may be just above.

Working Conditions

The wages paid to the industrial and agricultural workers in the exploited countries are often not enough to cover the physical, reproduction costs of the labor-power. The wages in these countries are often simply not high enough to keep the working force alive. This is evident when the wages are compared with the prices of basic foodstuffs. If the laborer does not get any kind of supplement from his family who work on subsistence farms, the consequence will be an extremely rapid attrition and change of labor-power. A rate of change of 5-7 percent each month and of 50-100 percent annually is not abnormal within industries and plantations in the Third World.[5] Within the electronics industries of Asia, e.g. in Hong Kong, Singapore, Malaysia, and Taiwan, young female laborers are preferred. They have no family life, domestic work or child minding to take care of besides their work and are therefore able to work harder and longer

---

4   Source: The figures have been calculated on the basis of various UN and ILO statistics as well as on the basis of Fröbel, Heinrichs, Kreye, op. cit., p. 351.

5   Fröbel, Heinrichs, Kreye, op. cit., pp. 529-30.

hours, up to sixty hours weekly. They do not participate in the maintenance of the family and are therefore paid low wages. After 3-4 years of back-breaking work at the microscopes they are worn down. Their sight and nerves can no longer comply with the demand of the production for speed and accuracy and they are fired—or as it is called "encouraged to retire and marry." New and fresh labor-power is employed.[6] Fröbel, Heinrichs and Kreye have looked into the working hours in the Third World:

> In most of the countries where free production zones and world market factories are in operation the standard working week is forty-eight hours. The difference between this figure and the standard working week of forty to forty-four hours in the traditional industrialized countries is only a partial reflection of the real prolongation of the working day in the new production sites in the developing countries. The high number of weeks worked in the year, the large amount of overtime and the low number of days off serve to prolong the total annual working time still further, so that the labor-force in some world market factories works up to 50% more hours per year than the traditional industrial countries. For example, working hours in manufacturing industry in Hong Kong often amount to more than sixty hours per week.(a) In the world market factories in South Korea the usual working week of the factory worker is sixty hours.(b) Total productive hours per year amounts to approximately 2800, compared with 1860 on the average in Federal Germany.(c) Workers in South Korean industry are required to work seven days, eighty-four hour weeks—i.e. a twelve hour shift each day without rest days.(d) In Thai manufacturing industry a nine hour working day with only one day off per month is often required.(e)[7]

When the authors lay stress on a working week of 60 hours it is not an unique example. "There is no legal restriction of the working day for men over the age of 18 years," as advertised by Hong Kong Trade Development Council. In 1968, 52 percent of all workers in Hong Kong worked 10 hours a day or more. 58 percent of the labor-force worked 7 days a week. According to a survey made in 1971, 171,439 out of 700,000 industrial workers worked 75 hours a week or more. Of these 13,792 worked 105 hours or more a week, which corresponds to 15 hours a day. The same year 36,000 children worked illegally in Hong Kong.[8] Conditions have not improved since then, on the contrary. These conditions can be compared to the worst Manchester capitalism in Britain in the 1830s.

---

6 Frank, op. cit., p. 164.

7 Op. cit., pp. 353-5. Notes from Fröbel, Heinrichs, Kreye: (a) "There is no legal restriction on the hours of work for men over the age of 18 years. Consequently many men work ten hours a day with a rest period of one to two hours, although tree-shift working, enabling machinery to be used 24 hours a day, is common [...] Women and young persons aged 16 and 17 may work eight hours a day plus two hours overtime up to an aggregate of 300 hours overtime per year. Working hours for these persons is limited to 48 hours per week." Trade Development Council; *Industrial Investment in Hong Kong*, p. 25.

8 Frank, op. cit., p. 169. This book contains several atrocious examples from Brazil and South Korea among other countries.

Productivity and Wages

The Myth of the Low Productivity in the Exploited Countries. One of the most popular explanations of the international wage differences is that they are based on similar differences in productivity. This explanation is also used as an objection against the theory of unequal exchange. As established in Chapter 3, this explanation is theoretically wrong because the extra profits temporarily yielded by productivity increases fall first and foremost to the capitalist. The fact that increases in productivity are used by the unions of the imperialist countries as an argument for higher wages in the case of collective bargaining does not mean that productivity increases are an economic factor which regularly pushes up wages. Whether the working class succeeds in benefitting from productivity increases does not depend on the actual increases but on the relative strength of the working class and the capitalist class. The wages are not the price for the results of the work but the price for the labor-power.

However, the view that the productivity of the export sectors in the Third World is lower is wrong. The enterprises in the Third World are not generally characterized by low productivity. Often one finds a rate of productivity which corresponds to that of the imperialist countries—if they can be compared at all. The same technology is used. Samir Amin, who has been dealing with this, writes:

> [...] the exports of the Third World are not, in the main, made up of agricultural products coming from backward sectors with low productivity. Out of an overall total of exports from the underdeveloped countries of the order of $35 billion (in 1966), the ultramodern capitalist sector (oil, mining, and primary processing of minerals, modern plantations—like those of United Fruit in Central America, or Unilever in Africa and Malaya) provides at least three-quarters, or $26 billion [...]
>
> As regards the other exports of the Third World, provided by the backward sectors, with low productivity (agricultural produce supplied by peasantries of the traditional type), is the situation less clear? Here the differences in the reward of labor (the term "wage" is out of the place in this context) are accompanied by a lower productivity. How much lower? It is all the harder to say because the products involved are, as a rule, not comparable: tea, coffee, cocoa are produced only in the periphery. It can be safely suggested, however, that rewards are proportionately much lower in the periphery than are productive activities. An African peasant obtains, for example, in return for 100 days of very hard work every year, a supply of imported manufactured goods the value of which amounts to barely twenty days of simple labor of a European skilled worker.[9]

The really low rate of productivity can be found on the subsistence farms in the agricultural areas, the development of which is blocked by the unequal

---

9   Amin, Samir, *Unequal Development*, p. 143.

development, which again is a consequence of the unequal wage level. But this part of the economy of the Third World does not influence the exportation to the imperialist countries. A large number of studies of individual enterprises and analyses of various industries show that the rate of productivity—defined as output per head—is by and large the same in the world market industries in the Third World and in the rich countries. The multinational company Philips has concluded—based on surveys in 1970 and 1978 into the enterprises of the company in Europe, Japan, Australia, and in the Third World—that the productivity (measured as produced units per laborer) is more or less the same in these areas.[10] On the basis of a number of studies, Deutsche Entwicklungsgesellschaft concludes that the rate of productivity of the industries in the exploited countries which have turned their production towards the world market is only a little lower than the rate of similar industries in Western Europe. In light of the longer working hours in the Third World, the workers have a much higher rate of performance than the workers of Western Europe.[11] According to studies made by The United States Tariff Commission, the rate of productivity of workers in American-owned enterprises outside the United States is by and large the same as the rate of productivity of workers within the same lines of industry in the United States. According to these studies, the workers in the clothing industry of the exploited countries produce just as many units per hour as their American colleagues do. Certain studies even conclude that the rate of productivity of the industries in the exploited countries is higher than that of the imperialist countries. So Baerresen concludes in a report that the productivity in American-owned enterprises in Mexico in certain cases is considerably higher than it is in similar enterprises in the United States. For example in the case of the electronics industries, the Mexican rate of productivity was 10-25 percent higher than it was in the United States. According to Baerresen, American managers in Mexico report that South Korean labor-power is a further 10-40 percent more productive than the Mexican labor-power. The American managers have also worked for American firms in South Korea. Managers in the United States and Western Germany, who were the heads of Malayan textile and electronics enterprises, unanimously stressed after a few months of production that the rate of productivity in Malaya was the same as at home. Another American study by R. W. Moxon concludes that as far as the electronics industry is concerned the rate of productivity is generally higher in the exploited countries than in the United States.[12]

---

10 *Le Nouveau Journal* (1979), 18/4. Paris.

11 These studies and the following are quoted from Fröbel, Heinrichs, Kreye, p. 356.

12 "The great majority of American electronics companies with off-shore plants have been very satisfied with the results obtained, and have continued to expand their offshore operations.

It should be stressed that in these studies the definition of productivity is the number of units produced per laborer within a given time unit. As the rate of productivity turns out to be the same or higher in the exploited countries, it is often due to a much higher labor intensity in the Third World. Very often many of the manual operations are mechanized or automatized in the imperialist countries. This means that the laborers in the Third World have to work much more intensively to achieve the same rate of productivity. If the working processes have not been mechanized, in this part of the world, it is only due to the wages being so low that it would not be of any advantage to the capitalists to mechanize.

In the exploited countries the rate of productivity is often much higher within mining and plantations than in the imperialist countries. This is first and foremost due to natural (geologic, climatic etc.) prerequisites, although this does not change the situation. The actual differences in productivity cannot be explained away, whatever the reason is for their existence. As the world looks today, it would be extremely costly for the imperialist countries, both as far as labor hours and money are concerned, to produce most of the "exotic" products within for example mining and plantations.[13]

Productivity and Wages—Final Remarks

Productivity increases are primarily for the benefit of the capitalists and should be looked upon as a part of the mutual competition of the capitalists. Productivity increases are not affected because the capitalists "want" them, but because they are constantly forced to improve the productive forces. The capitalists who produce at the quickest speed and at the lowest price do best in the competition. And, therefore, they try to limit the production costs of which the wages make up a considerable part. It is a fact that improved relations of production in the form of lower wages can be felt in the prices. The consequence is—as has already been stressed above—that value is transferred from the exploited countries to the imperialist countries. But it also means that the industries in the Third World outstrip industries in the imperialist countries to the extent that the same commodities are produced. This tendency can be seen very clearly within shipbuilding, textile manufacturing, and certain electronics industries where, in

---

They have generally a low-cost source of workers who are more productive than those in the United States, and have been able to manufacture products of the required quality." Richard W. Moxon, *Offshore Production in Less Developed Countries*, p. 61, quoted from Fröbel, Heinrichs, Kreye, p. 356.

13 See Emmanuel, *Unequal Exchange Revisited*, p. 33.

particular, South East Asian low-wage industries outstrip the high-wage industries of the Western World, which often survive only by means of political intervention, government subsidies etc. The rapid growth of the South East Asian industries and the crises in the corresponding industries in the Western World should be sufficient proof that there is a strong connection between wages and prices. High wages mean expensive commodities: low wages mean inexpensive commodities. It is just as evident that this applies to all exporting economies in the Third World, even though it is most evident within the industries where the low-wage companies do best in the competition. Many economists of various political views refuse to recognize these realities. On the western economists' hypocrisy and dual attitude to this problem, Emmanuel writes:

> When it is a question of importing coffee or bananas, which the rich countries do not themselves produce, and the low prices of which can consequently be only to the advantage of the purchasing countries, then any notion of artificially increasing prices is repudiated in the name of the sound principles of economic rationalism, and no allusion to the low wages of the producers is allowed, since, in accordance with these same sound principles, these wages are not the cause of prices but their effect. When, however, by chance the poor countries decide to export products such as Indian cotton goods or Japanese transistors, which are already included in the production of a traditional branch of industry in the rich countries, then all these principles are cheerfully forgotten, and, it is discovered that it is only proper that the rich country should make up by means of artificial tariff barriers for the equally artificial difference in wages; thus brusquely and brazenly admitting that wages are not the effect of prices but their cause.[14]

It is often called "social dumping" when low-wage industries by means of child labor etc., combined with modern technology, crush the industries of the rich countries.

The factors of price formation are related to the unequal exchange by Emmanuel, who goes thoroughly into the matter:

> But if this conjunction causes the prices of Indian cotton goods and Japanese ships to be abnormally low, why are the prices of bananas and coffee not also abnormally low, since wages in these branches are just as exotic and productivity is undoubtedly higher than in the West? (Has anyone ever thought what it would cost to grow bananas or coffee in Flanders or the Rhineland?)
>
> "Unfair competition by means of low wages," "pauperized labor," "social dumping," etc., are expressions of which present-day writing on economic matters is full, while pure economics goes on imperturbably teaching that wages depend on prices, and not the other way round.
>
> In the days when wages varied from one country to another only as 1 to 2, or even 1 to 3 or 1 to 4, it was perhaps legitimate to suppose that fluctuations on the commodity market could be the underlying cause of these variations. When, however, wages vary at the rate of 1 to 20.or 1 to 30, and vary only in space, while possessing extreme rigidity in

---

14 Emmanuel, *Unequal Exchange,* pp. 69-70.

time (in which only a slow and linear trend is to be observed, with hardly any variation), we are indeed compelled to recognize that they probably vary in accordance with laws peculiar to themselves and that, consequently, they really are the independent variable of the system.[15]

Conclusion

We cannot but conclude that the first assumption, which we made a condition of the validity of the theory of unequal exchange, is in accordance with reality. Unequal pay of the labor-force does exist. Internationally, the class struggle has been fought on an unequal economic basis, which has resulted in the wage level and thus the rate of surplus value being at least 15 times higher in the imperialist countries than in the exploited countries.

Equalization of the Rate of Profit

The other condition of the validity of the theory of unequal exchange—namely an equal return on capital wherever it is invested—depends on the mobility of capital. In this connection mobility means that the capital has the possibility of moving. Thus it is not necessary that the capital actually moves in order to be characterized as capital with sufficient mobility for creating an equalization of the rate of profit. If there are no stimuli attracting capital and it does not move, it cannot be concluded that it is immobile. The international mobility of capital depends on the political barriers set by the various countries to capital imports and exports.

The establishment and the following extension of the colonial system at the end of the nineteenth century and the beginning of the twentieth century increased the trade and the international movement of capital between the imperialist and the exploited countries. Usually, these capital movements took place within the individual colonial empires. But at the time Britain made comparatively big investments in North and South America which were outside her empire. However, it was difficult for the individual colonial powers to invest in the empire of other powers, and the United States, which had no colonies, was restrained by the colonial system.

The decolonization, the establishment of the OECD,[16] and the political de-

---

15 Ibid., pp. 70-71.

16 The Organization for Economic Cooperation and Development was founded in 1961 by the

velopment after World War II meant greater freedom to the capital movements in the capitalist world both between the imperialist powers and between these and the exploited countries. These improved possibilities of international mobility of capital meant increased competition between the capitals, as capital flow towards branches and areas where the rate of profit is high, and away from branches and areas where the rate of profit is comparatively low. These continuous changes in the rates of profit of various branches and areas result in capital movements which again result in an equalization of the rate of profit to an international average. This average forms the axis around which the rate of profit varies continuously. However, the tendency towards an equalization of the rate of profit does not exclude the existence of "super-profits" in some sectors at the same time as an equalization takes place in the other sectors.[17]

Statistics on international rates of profit are rather problematic. Partly because the information on which the statistics are based is unreliable, as tax and book-keeping conditions may lead to the rates of profit quoted not being in accordance with the "real" rates. Partly because detailed information is seldom found in the statistics as to how the rates of profit quoted have been calculated. However, the available statistics—although vitiated by uncertain factors—mainly confirm the assumption that the rate of profit is equalized internationally.

R. A. Lehfeldt, who has looked into British rates of profit during the years 1898-1910, declares that the return on colonial securities was 0.2 percent higher than the return on British securities of the same time.[18] The return on foreign securities was 1 percent higher than that on British securities.[19] "R. P. Dutt compares the respective rates of profit in Britain and in the British colonies. He finds, for the year 1951, differences in gross profit ranging from 34 to 47 percent. If,

---

imperialist countries in Europe together with the USA and Canada. Since then Japan and Australia have joined. The aim of OECD is to develop the capitalist economies of the member-countries by removing obstacles from world trade, among other things by opening up trade with the former colonial areas.

17 Karl Marx writes on this: "Nothing would be altered if capitals in certain spheres of production would not, for some reason, be subject to the process of equalization. The average profit would then be computed on that portion of the social capital which enters the equalization process." *Capital*, Vol. III, p. 174.

18 The majority of foreign investments made during the first ten years of this century were in the shape of securities, loans secured on government bonds, bills of exchange etc., whereas the majority of today's foreign investments are made as direct investments, i.e. in plants or in buying up industries, which ensure the investor the supervision of operations.

19 FEIS, Europe: The World's Banker, quoted from Emmanuel, *Unequal Exchange Revisited*, p. 51

says John Strachey, he had taken 1950 instead of 1951, he would have found, instead, the figures 25 and 29 percent."[20]

One of the critics of Emmanuel, Klaus Busch, has published a table (4.2) to reject the theory of unequal exchange. If the petroleum and mining industries are omitted, the table actually shows that the rate of profit does not vary materially between the exploited ("underdeveloped") countries, and the imperialist ("developed") countries. There is complete agreement between the rates of profit of the individual sectors in both groups of countries as regards, both the American-owned industries and the British-owned industries in which the mining sectors are also included. The high rate of profit of US-owned oil companies in the exploited countries and the corresponding very low rate of the same companies in the imperialist countries could rather be an indication of a bookkeeping transfer of profit to the exploited countries for tax reasons, than a matter of, actual variations in the rates of profit.

TABLE 4.2: RETURN ON DIRECT CAPITAL INVESTMENTS IN DEVELOPING COUNTRIES AND DEVELOPED COUNTRIES MADE BY THE UNITED STATES, GREAT BRITAIN AND WEST GERMANY[21]

Sector(s)	Period	Return on Investment in	
		Developing Countries	Developed Countries
United States			
	1951-70	11.2%	11.7%
Manufacturing Industry	1951-60	11.6%	13.9%
	1961-70	11.0%	11.0%
	1951-70	10.2%	11.6%
Other Industry	1951-60	11.1%	11.8%
	1961-70	9.6%	11.5%
	1951-70	27.7%	3.8%
Petroleum	1951-60	29.3%	6.5%
	1961-70	26.9%	2.8%

20 R. Palme Dutt, *Crisis of Britain and the British Empire*, and Strachey, *End of Empire*, quoted from Emmanuel, *Unequal Exchange*, p. 43. "Strachey is right: the year 1951 is not representative. It was the year of the Korean War boom, with a flare-up in prices of primary products and an inflation of the profits of colonial enterprises." Op. cit., p. 97.

The Validity of the Prerequisites of Unequal Exchange 87

TABLE 4.2 (CONTINUED)

	1951-70	16.8%	11.2%
Mining	1951-60	13.5%	11.1%
	1961-70	18.9%	11.2%
Great Britain			
All Sectors exc. Petroleum	1961-69	10.4%	10.0%
West Germany			
All Sectors	1965-69	6.3%	

As far as the figures are correct, they can in no way reject the fact that the rate of profit is equalized internationally, especially because extremely high profits may occur periodically in certain sectors (as for example mining) without influencing the general tendency of equalization. Thus these specific sectors do not participate in the equalization.

TABLE 4.3: AMERICAN DIRECT INVESTMENT IN MANUFACTURING INDUSTRY. MOVEMENT OF THE RATE OF PROFIT[22]

Year	Canada	Latin America	Europe
1960	8.2%	9.9%	12.8%
1961	5.2%	10%	12.4%
1962	8.6%	8.7%	10.1%
1963	9.0%	7.7%	11.1%
1964	9.1%	9.6%	11.8%
1965	8.7%	9.8%	11.3%
1966	8.1%	10.3%	9.6%
1967	7.5%	7.5%	8.6%
1968	7.9%	10.2%	9.6%

It appears that, with the exception of Canada which enjoys preferential conditions due

---

21 Source: K. Busch in *Problemen des Klassenkampfes*, no. 8-9, Deutsches Institut für Wirtschaftsforschung: Wochenbericht, 22/72, Berlin 1972, pp. 199-202.

22 Table 4.3 and the comment to it is quoted from Emmanuel, *Unequal Exchange Revisited*, p. 52. Source: *Documentation Française*, 15 March 1971.

to neighborhood, language and other links, the two other groups, Latin America and Europe, the one under- or semi-developed, the other developed, show a remarkable convergence with or even a slight superiority to Europe, which runs counter to what the supporters of the non-equalization thesis want to prove.[23]

The tendency towards an equalization of the rate of profit does not necessarily mean that the rate of profit is the same in all countries. Capital invested in the exploited countries often yields a few percent more ("danger money"). The social unrest in the Third World, the threat of a possible nationalization etc., cause the investing capitals to demand a higher rate of return if they are to invest abroad, If, for example, the rate of profit is 10 percent in the United States, it may be 15 percent in Thailand, and 20 percent in Namibia or El Salvador. However, this does not prevent an equalization in the long view.

About the studies of the tendency towards an equalization of the rate of profit Emmanuel concludes:

> If the physical mobility of labor, even when now and then it becomes quite important, is not—as we have seen—sufficient to bring about the equalization of wages, generally a marginal mobility of capital on the international plane is indeed quite sufficient—experience shows—to generate a clear tendency towards the equalization of its rate of remuneration. The economists who deny this tendency generally base their position on logical inferences, while all those who have undertaken empirical investigations are unanimous in acknowledging the fact that there are no meaningful differences in the rates of profit between developed and under-developed countries.[24]

Capital Movements

The variations in the rates of profit in the world can be studied in an indirect way by looking at the capital movements, as capital moves towards the highest rate of return. Table 4.4 shows the distribution of the investments of the imperialist countries.

---

23 Op. cit., p. 52.

24 Ibid., p. 50.

TABLE 4.4: STOCK OF DIRECT INVESTMENT ABROAD OF DEVELOPED MARKET ECONOMIES, 1967-75[25]

Year	Total Value ($ Billion)	Return on Investment in Developing Countries	Return on Investment in Developed Countries
1967	105	69%	31%
1971	158	72%	28%
1975	259	74%	26%

Thus in 1975 three quarters of the total investments of the imperialist countries were directed towards the same imperialist countries. Only one quarter was invested in the exploited countries, and their relative share even seems to decrease. The reason why investments are scarce in the Third World is not a lack of social need for capital investments nor unfavorable terms on the part of the governments of these countries. On the contrary, most countries in the Third World are very interested in receiving foreign investments. This applies both to the countries of a capitalist outlook and the regimes of more or less planned economy. Many countries and groups of countries in the Third World even lay down conditions of capital investment which are more favorable than those of the imperialist countries. They try to attract capital, for instance, by establishing free trade and tax free areas. The reasons why the imperialist countries attract by far the largest part of the total world investments, and the reasons why the Third World is not capable of attracting more capital than it actually does, are that the imperialist countries have an enormous domestic market, whereas the exploited countries have a very limited one.

Thus the limits of the world market offer possibilities of investing only a little more than 25 percent in the exploited countries and about 75 percent in the imperialist countries. If higher rates of profit existed in the Third World in general, capital would flow to that part of the world, and the total investments would grow faster in the exploited countries than in the imperialist countries. That is not the case. Profits created in the Third World even flow to the imperialist countries to a certain extent, instead of being reinvested in the exploited countries. The share of the total investments in the Third World decreases.

Emmanuel quotes a Cuban study with approval:

> [...] the best proof that the rate of profit in the underdeveloped countries is not particu-

---

25 Source: UN, *Transnational Corporations in World Development*, New York, 1977

larly high is provided by the investment in the developed countries of a large part of the capital held by the national bourgeoisies of the backward countries.[26]

The latest example of capital exports to the imperialist countries is the oil billions of the Arab countries, which to a great extent return to the United States and Europe as investments in industries and as hot money. Of course, this applies particularly to the OPEC countries with a capitalist economy such as Saudi Arabia, Kuwait, and the United Arab Emirates. In 1980 the OPEC countries had invested $343 billion in the United States and Western Europe, and investments in the imperialist countries by OPEC are estimated to reach more than $1,000 billion in 1985.

We can establish that the differences in the rate of profit are much smaller than the wage differences, and whereas the wage differences follow the national borders, there is no indication of the rates of profit doing the same.

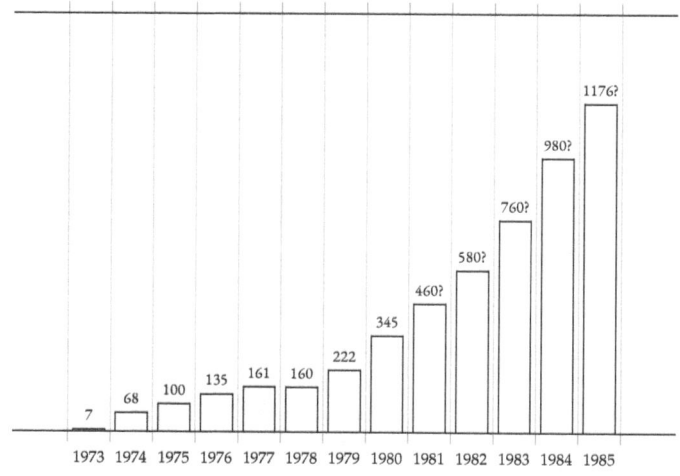

FIGURE VIII: VALUE OF OPEC HOLDINGS IN THE WEST (USD BILLION)

This figure was estimated by the British magazine Business Week in 1981, before the recent fall in crude oil prices.

Investigations by J. Dunning show on the contrary that the rate of profit

---

26 Emmanuel, *Unequal Exchange*, p. 44.

can be higher for years in high-wage imperialist countries compared to most low-wage exploited countries.[27] The low wages in the exploited countries do not result in particularly high rates of profit. In general, we can state that the tendency towards an equal return on capital, no matter where it is invested, can be seen at an international level.

TABLE 4.5: YEARLY ANNUAL AVERAGE RATE OF PROFIT ON INVESTED BRITISH CAPITAL

Imperialist Country	1955-64	1960-65
North America	—	6.6
United States	6	8.9
Canada	10	5.1
Western Europe	—	6.5
Belgium & Luxembourg	—	1.8
France	14	3.6
Federal Republic of Germany	1	16.2
Italy	7	−0.1
Holland	—	6.2
Denmark	11	2.5
Switzerland	—	11.9
Others	—	6.8
Average	—	7.1

---

27 Transient changes in profits due to short term price movements have deliberately been omitted from the discussion, as these do not affect the long term tendencies.

Exploited Country	1955-64	1960-65
Latin America	—	7.7
Argentina	15	7.7
Brazil	11	12.9
Commonwealth	—	12.9
Australia	8	6.6
New Zealand	—	6.4
South Africa	5	12.1
India	9	7.7
Malaysia	2	15.9
Jamaica	7	6.2
Ghana	3	12.3
Nigeria	13	4.3
Average	—	9.0

Conclusion

Thus we conclude that the conditions of an exploitation of the low-wage countries of the Third World through unequal exchange are present. On the basis of the enormous differences in wages which exist between the imperialist countries and the exploited countries, and through an international equalization of the rate of profit, values can be transferred from the poor exploited countries to the rich imperialist countries because of the low prices of products from the exploited countries and the high prices of products from the imperialist countries.

The Size of the Unequal Exchange

In the end one country can only exploit another country by importing commodities of a total value which is higher than the value of the exported commodities. This may take place by simple plundering as was the case during early colonialism. Or it may take place by having a constant trade deficit as Britain had during the last century. Finally, it may take place through a distortion of the actual prices at which the commodities are sold, which is the case today between the imperialist countries and the exploited countries. The imperialist countries sell

---

27 Source: Dunning J. (1970), *Studies in International Investment*, pp. 57, 94. London. The two time periods cannot be compared.

The Validity of the Prerequisites of Unequal Exchange 93

their commodities at prices which are too high compared to the value, and the exploited countries sell at prices which are too low.

The size of this transfer of value is difficult to calculate precisely. In the following we would like to give just an impression of the size in question. Below we shall consider world trade in a more concrete way in order to estimate the size of the unequal exchange. Table 4.6 shows the development of world trade from 1948-82 between the imperialist countries, the exploited countries, and the centrally planned economies both in absolute figures (i.e. in prices) and in percentages.

TABLE 4.6: WORLD TRADE BY REGION, 1948-1982[28]

Export From	Year	World Total	Export To					
			Developed Market Economies		Developing Market Economies		Centrally Planned Economies	
			Total	%	Total	%	Total	%
Developed Market Economies	1948	36.5	23.7	65%	11.3	31%	1.5	4%
	1956	68.4	45.9	67%	19	28%	1.7	2%
	1965	128	95.3	74%	25.9	20%	5.2	4%
	1970	224.2	172.5	77%	41.4	18%	8.9	4%
	1975	577.2	402	70%	138	24%	33.8	6%
	1980	1,260.6	894	71%	293.4	23%	61.2	5%
	1982	1,161.2	802.9	69%	289.6	25%	53	5%
Developing Market Economies	1948	17.3	11.8	68%	5.0	29%	0.5	3%
	1956	24.9	18.3	73%	5.9	24%	0.8	3%
	1965	35.9	25.6	71%	7.4	21%	2.6	7%
	1970	54.9	39.8	72%	10.9	20%	3.4	6%
	1975	209.4	146.7	70%	49	23%	10.1	5%
	1980	558.5	391.5	70%	138.9	25%	20.5	4%
	1982	486.5	312.2	64%	145.6	30%	23.7	5%

TABLE 4.6 (CONTINUED)

	1948	3.7	1.5	41%	0.4	11%	1.7	46%
	1956	10.1	2	20%	0.9	9%	7.2	71%
Centrally	1965	21.8	4.7	22%	3.3	15%	13.8	63%
Planned	1970	32.8	7.8	24%	5.1	16%	19.9	61%
Economies	1975	84.6	23.1	27%	13.3	16%	47.6	56%
	1980	175.1	56.4	32%	31.6	18%	85.5	49%
	1982	189	58.5	31%	41.5	22%	88.9	47%

Let us look at the importance of Third World exports to the imperialist countries. From table 4.7 it appears that the imports of the imperialist countries from the Third World amount to about one quarter of the total imports, calculated on the basis of the current world market prices. Furthermore, if this figure is compared to the national product of the imperialist countries, imports from the Third World amount to about 4-6 percent. The fact that imports from the exploited countries make up a relatively small part compared to the trade between the imperialist countries, and an even smaller part compared to the national product of these countries in terms of world market prices, could induce one to believe that the importance of trade with the Third World and thus of the unequal exchange was comparatively small. But nothing could be more wrong. Rather, the opposite conclusion should be drawn. Because the unequal exchange is, indeed, based on the disproportionately low prices of commodities from the Third World, which result in disproportionately low trade figures. The lower the wages are, the lower the prices and the lower the trade figures. The argument that the comparatively small trade with the Third World should show the inferior importance of the unequal exchange, indicates that the theory of unequal exchange has been misunderstood.

---

28 FOB (Free on board) prices: The prices at the frontier of the exporting country—excluding international transport and insurance charges. Source: UN, Statistical Yearbook, 1978 and 1981, UN, Monthly Bulletin of Statistics no. 5, May 1984.—UN statistics place People's Republic of China, Mongolian PR, PDR of Korea, and Vietnam, in the group of centrally planned economies together with the East European countries and the USSR. Cuba, Angola, and Mozambique are placed in the group of developing countries with a market economy.

TABLE 4.7: EXPORTS TO DEVELOPED MARKET ECONOMIES[29]

Year	Total	From Developed Market Economies		From Developing Market Economies		From Centrally Planned Economies	
		Total	%	Total	%	Total	%
1965	125.6	95.3	76%	25.6	20%	4.7	4%
1970	220.7	172.5	78%	39.8	18%	7.8	4%
1975	571.9	402	70%	146.7	26%	23.1	4%
1980	1,341.9	894	67%	391.5	29%	56.4	4%
1982	1,173.5	802.9	68%	312.2	27%	58.4	5%

TABLE 4.8: EXPORTS TO DEVELOPING MARKET ECONOMIES[30]

Year	Total	From Developed Market Economies		From Developing Market Economies		From Centrally Planned Economies	
		Total	%	Total	%	Total	%
1965	36.6	25.9	70%	7.4	20%	3.3	9%
1970	57.3	41.4	72%	10.9	19%	5.1	9%
1975	200.3	138	69%	49.0	25%	13.3	7%
1980	464	293.4	63%	138.9	30%	31.6	7%
1982	476.7	289.6	61%	145.6	31%	41.5	9%

It is far more interesting and more significant to look at the distribution of the exports of the Third World. From table 4.6 it appears that about 70 percent of the exports of the Third World are exported to the imperialist countries. The internal trade between the countries of the Third World amounts only to 25-30 percent. Furthermore, this trade is relatively less important for the transfer of value between the countries, as they have more or less the same wage level. Ex-

---

29 FOB (Free on board) prices. Source: UN, Statistical Yearbook 1981, and UN, Monthly Bulletin of Statistics no. 5, May 1984.

30 FOB (Free on board) prices. Source: UN, op. cit.

ports to the socialist countries—the centrally planned economies—amount to about 5 percent only. Thus the imperialist countries import by far the majority of the cheap commodities from the Third World, and in this way they benefit from the unequal exchange and exploit the Third World.

From table 4.8 it appears that 60-70 percent of Third World imports comes from the imperialist countries. Some 20-30 percent is internal trade between the exploited countries, and 7-9 percent is imported from the planned economies. Thus both as regards exports from the Third World and as regards imports to the Third World, the imperialist countries are predominant, whereas the "socialist countries"—the centrally planned economies keep to themselves to a much larger extent.

The internal trade between the imperialist countries accounts for a considerable part of total world trade in terms of world market prices. In 1982 total world trade amounted to $1,836.6 billion, out of which inter-imperialist trade amounted to $802.9 billion. However, this trade is of less direct importance in comparison with international transfers of value between the imperialist countries and the exploited countries, because the wage differences between the imperialist countries are relatively small compared to the global wage differences.[31] However, inter-imperialist trade is of importance to the distribution of the values from the exploited countries, which take place by trade in further processed commodities.

The contents of inter-imperialist trade also differ from trade between the imperialist countries and the Third World. Inter-imperialist trade is to a large extent an exchange of the same products, whereas trade with the Third World is based on the exchange of different products. Denmark sells Bang & Olufsen and buys Philips, Sony, and Grundig. West Germans buy Volvo, Fiat, Toyota, and Citroën and sell VW, Mercedes, and BMW. The exchange of a large number of industrial products, machines, and consumer goods has only one function, namely to extend the choice as regards shape and color.

The case of trade between the imperialist countries and the Third World is different. The Third World exports commodities which to a large extent form the material basis of the production of the industrialized countries. In return, imperialist countries sell a large number of industrial products to the Third World. To the extent that the countries in the Third World start lines of industry which have so far only existed in the industrialized countries, they are very

---

31 To the extent that there are differences in wages, it is also a question of unequal exchange. It applies for instance to the Danish trade with Greece and Portugal, whose wage level is about one fifth of the Danish.

competitive, as we have stressed before.

TABLE 4.9: EEC Dependence on Raw Materials from Developing Countries (in 1972)[32]

Industry	Materials	EEC Import Dependence	Developing Countries' Share of EEC Import	Developing Countries' Share of World Export
Exhaustable Raw Materials				
Industrial Raw Materials	Copper	100%	60%	44%
	Tin	86%	85%	77%
	Iron	75%	55%	42%
	Bauxite	83%	50%	88%
	Phosphate	99%	63%	43%
	Manganese	100%	45%	51%
	Tungsten	95%	43%	50%
Energy Raw Materials	Uranium	75%	—	15%
	Petroleum	98%	98%	45%
	Natural Gas	3%	100%	5%
	Coal	11%	1%	10%
Reproducible Raw Materials				
Tropical Products	Coffee	100%	99%	97%
	Cocoa	100%	97%	98%
	Tea	100%	80%	84%
	Bananas	100%	100%	95%
	Spices	100%	100%	90%

TABLE 4.9 (CONTINUED)

Industrial Raw Materials	Timber	50%	29%	43%
	Leather	—	23%	23%
	Rubber	100%	100%	98%
	Cotton	—	60%	57%
	Wool	—	12%	13%
	Jute	100%	98%	95%
	Sisal	100%	100%	97%
Agricultural Products	Meat	—	35%	20%
	Oilseeds	100%	—	43%
	Fruit	—	45%	25%
	Sugar	—	99%	73%
	Corn	—	25%	10%
	Rice	—	55%	40%
	Tobacco	—	24%	21%

Table 4.9 shows the qualitative dependence of the EEC on trade with the Third World. It is difficult to make exact calculations of the size of the unequal exchange. Partly because the information on wages and on the size of the laborforce is subject to some uncertainty. Partly because it is difficult to estimate the wage-share of the price of the product. Therefore, the following estimate is only meant as an illustration of an approximate size. The calculations have been made on the basis of 1980 figures:

According to table 4.6 the exports of the exploited countries to the imperialist countries amount to:

$391.5 billion

The exports of the imperialist countries to the exploited countries:

$293.4 billion

Assuming that wages amount to 20 percent of the price of the products from imperialist countries and 15 percent of the price of the products from ex-

---

32 Source: EEC commission.

ploited countries, the wage-share amounts to:

Of exports from exploited countries: $58.7 billion

Of exports from imperialist countries: $58.7 billion

According to the International Labour Organization[33] there are about 400 million people engaged in active employment in the imperialist part of the world—and about 800 million people engaged in active employment in the non-"socialist" part of the Third World.

If we assume that wages in the imperialist countries are 15 times higher than wages in the exploited countries, we can fix the wages in the exploited countries at 1 and the wages in the imperialist countries at 15. Thus we can calculate an average wage-factor.

Laborers of imperialist countries:

400 mill. at factor 15 = 6000 million

Laborers of exploited countries:

800 mill. at factor 1 = 800 million

Total number:

1200 mill. at average factor = 6800 million

Average wage factor: $\frac{6800}{1200} = 5.7$

The factor 5.7 reflects the global average wages. Paid by means of these average wages the wage-share of the exports would be:

Of exports from the exploited countries:

$\frac{58.7 \text{ billion} \times 5.7}{1} = \$334.7 \text{ billion}$

Of exports from the imperialist countries:

$\frac{58.7 \text{ billion} \times 5.7}{15} = \$22.3 \text{ billion}$

The wage share is now again added to the remaining production costs, and the following prices of exports appear:

Exports from exploited countries:

391.5 × 85% + 334.7 = $667.5 billion

Exports from imperialist countries:

293.4 × 80% + 22.3 = $257.0 billion

---

33 ILO (1974), *International Labour Review*, Vol. 109, no. 5-6, pp. 422-429.

Compared to this hypothetical situation of equal wage the gain of the imperialist countries from unequal exchange amounts to:

From low import prices:

667.5 − 391.5 = $276.0 billion

From high export prices:

293.4 − 257.0 = $36.4 billion

Total gain in 1980: $312.4 billion

By way of comparison it may be mentioned that in 1980 the GNP of the USA was $2,573 billion.

The amount of the repatriated profits of the multinationals from investments in the Third World during the period 1970-78 was about $100.2 billion.[34] This means that by way of unequal exchange, the amount of value which is transferred in one year is 3 times bigger than the amount of profits from the investments of the imperialist countries in eight years.

Therefore, we conclude that in spite of relatively many uncertainties in these figures show that the unequal exchange is by far the most important kind of exploitation in the relationship between the poor and the rich countries. The big differences in standard of living existing in today's world can only be explained by unequal exchange.

The increases in oil prices since 1973 and the ensuing recession in the economy of the Western World have given a hint of the size and significance of this transfer of value to the well-being of the imperialist world economy. The increases in oil prices were not a result of wage increases within the oil extracting industries, but a consequence of government taxation. However, the immediate effect was the same to the oil consumers: the price of oil increased. The increases in oil prices have upset the economies of the imperialist countries more than any other event since the Second World War, although the effect of the price rises has been limited by the return of a considerable part of the oil incomes of the Arab countries to the United States, Japan, and Western Europe by way of investments in industries and bank deposits.

On the importance of unequal exchange Emmanuel writes:

> I do not claim that unequal exchange explains by itself the entire difference between the standards of living of the rich countries and the poor ones, even though, if we base ourselves on certain statistical data that are available, however fragmentary and arguable these may be, we arrive at a loss in double factorial terms (if not in terms of trade) that

---

34 Castro, Fidel (Sept. 27, 1981), "Speech at the Conference of the Inter-Parliamentary Union in Havana, 15-23 September 1981," *Granma*.

The Validity of the Prerequisites of Unequal Exchange 101

is enormous in relation to the poverty of the underdeveloped countries while being far from negligible in relation to the wealth of the advanced countries. Even if we agree that unequal exchange is only one of the mechanisms whereby value is transferred from one group of countries to another, and that its direct effects account for only part of the difference in standards of living, I think it is possible to state that unequal exchange is the elementary transfer mechanism, and that, as such, it enables the advanced countries to begin and regularly to give new impetus to that unevenness of development that sets in motion all the other mechanisms of exploitation and fully explains the way that wealth is distributed.[35]

Though we have tried above to put the theory of unequal exchange into figures, we must stress the importance of not focusing exclusively on the quantity expressed in these figures. Whether unequal exchange amounts to 250, or 350, or 1000 billion dollars a year, the qualitative aspect is even more important. Unequal exchange is the indispensable prerequisite of the function of the imperialist system, and has been the indispensable prerequisite of the development of the imperialist countries to the level of today. Unequal exchange secures the necessary supply of value which prevents the imperialist countries from entering an insoluble contradiction between the development of the productive forces and the private ownership of the means of production. If this supply of value to the imperialist countries from unequal exchange did not exist, then the high wages of these countries would not result in the solution of the inborn overproduction crises, which is a characteristic of capitalism.

So, unequal exchange constitutes not only a yearly transfer of about 300 billion dollars, but constitutes exactly the indispensable condition, which keeps overdeveloped capitalism alive.

---

35 Emmanuel, *Unequal Exchange*, p. 265. For this phenomenon we use the name "unequal development," which means the process according to which the world is divided into rich imperialist countries and poor exploited countries—a fact which continuously reproduces itself. This division is reflected by the rich countries developing the productive forces at a tearing speed and the poor countries developing the productive forces at a much slower speed. Thus the cleavage between the imperialist countries and the Third World continuously grows. The historical basis of unequal development is colonialism and the other direct and often violent kinds of exploitation of the Third World. However, unequal development was first fully established after the establishment of the exploitation by unequal exchange.

5

The Possibilities of Socialism in a Divided World

On Productive Forces and Relations of Production

According to the materialist conception of history, production and exchange of commodities are the basis of the social order. Therefore, social changes and political revolutions are in the last resort due to changes in the modes of production and exchange and not to the political ideas of the classes.

> [...] the final causes of all social changes [...] are to be sought not in the philosophy, but in the economics of each particular epoch. The growing perception that existing social institutions are unreasonable and unjust, "that reason has become unreason and right wrong," is only proof that in the modes of production and exchange changes have silently taken place with which the social order, adapted to earlier economic conditions, is no longer in keeping. From this it also follows that the means of getting rid of the incongruities that have been brought to light must also be present, in a more or less developed condition, within the changed modes of production themselves. These means are not to be invented by deduction from fundamental principles but are to be discovered in the stubborn facts of the existing system of production.[1]

Thus, it is not ideas in people's heads or wretchedness and exploitation which form the basis of social changes. It is the lack of potentialities within the existing relations of production which bring about the revolutionary changes. Instead of promoting development, the relations of production have become a chain to development. As the chain is tightened, an economic, social, and political crisis arises, and the consciousness that a change is necessary grows out of this crisis.[2]

---

1 Engels, *Socialism*, MESW, pp. 411-12.

2 Lenin described the revolutionary situation as follows: "To the Marxist it is indisputable that a revolution is impossible without a revolutionary situation; furthermore, it is not every revolutionary situation that leads to revolution. What, generally speaking, are the symptoms of a

The class struggle must be considered in the light of the economic and material conditions and not as an independent, isolated motive power in history. Therefore, our evaluation of the possibilities of socialism in the world is primarily based on the tendencies of economic development.

The Possibilities of Socialism in the Imperialist Countries

The perspectives of socialism in the imperialist countries cannot be analyzed separately, as the position of the working class is closely related to the development of capitalism in the whole world. The possibility of a socialist development in the imperialist countries must therefore be considered in relation to the development of the imperialist system. The development of the working class in these countries—from being an exploited proletariat to becoming a class appropriating more value than it produces—is the most important material reason why the working class does not develop in socialist direction. It is the preferential position of the class internationally which determines its political attitude. *Pari passu* with the wage increases of the working class in the imperialist countries, trade between the exploited countries and the imperialist countries became characterized by unequal exchange. This led to an unequal development and a more profound division of the world into rich and poor countries. However, the wage increases not only meant a rise in consumption in the imperialist countries and a growing exploitation of the Third World. The changed conditions of the working class meant that it had an objective interest in the capitalist system continuing its international accumulation, paid by the proletariat in the Third World. A result of this development is the consumer society which emerged at

---

revolutionary situation? We shall certainly not be mistaken if we indicate the following three major symptoms: (1) when it is impossible for the ruling classes to maintain their rule without any change; when there is a crisis, in one form or another, among the 'upper classes,' a crisis in the policy of the ruling class, leading to a fissure through which the discontent and indignation of the oppressed classes burst forth. For a revolution to take place, it is usually insufficient for 'the lower classes not to want' to live in the old way, it is also necessary that 'the upper classes should be unable' to live in the old way; (2) when the suffering and want of the oppressed classes have grown more acute than usual; (3) when, as a consequence of the above causes there is a considerable increase in the activity of the masses, who uncomplainingly allow themselves to be robbed in 'peace time,' but, in turbulent times, are drawn both by all the circumstances of the crisis and by the 'upper classes' themselves into independent historical action.

"Without these objective changes, which are independent of the will, not only of individual groups and parties but even of individual classes, a revolution, as a general rule, is impossible. The totality of all these objective changes is called a revolutionary situation." (*The Collapse of the Second International*, LCW, Vol. 21, pp. 213-214.)

the end of the 50s in Europe and somewhat earlier in the United States.³ Thus the consumption of the Danish population is considerably bigger than the consumption of the whole population in North Africa. Put together, the domestic market of Denmark and Sweden is larger than that of Africa excluding South Africa. If Norway is included, the population of the whole of Scandinavia consumes more than the population of the whole of Africa. The domestic markets of West Germany and France are bigger than that of the entire non-communist Third World. And the United States alone, i.e. 6 percent of the population of the world, consumes more than 40 percent of the total production of the world.

The imperialist countries, which make up about 20-25 percent of the population of the world, consume about 70 percent of the total amount of energy produced in the form of coal, petroleum, uranium, and electric power, and 75 percent of the copper and aluminum production. The two thirds of the population of the world who live in Asia, Africa and Latin America consume only about 12 percent of the raw material in the world, in spite of the fact that about half of the raw material in the world is produced in these countries.⁴

The consumer society in the wealthy areas of the world offers perfect conditions for capitalism. It means mass production and mass consumption. Under these circumstances capitalism has shown its highest rates of growth. In the 1960s and the greater part of the 1970s the working class of the imperialist countries experienced an ability to consume never experienced by any working class before. In general, the imperialist countries started to contain only classes which

---

3   The American consumer society came into existence as early as in the 1920s, a development which Europe did not reach until at the end of the 1950s. The 1920s in the United States were characterized by an enormous increase in consumption. House building increased rapidly, totally new lines of industry were founded—producing automobiles, airplanes and durable consumer goods. The production of durable consumer goods increased twice as rapidly as the production of non-durables. In the United States in the 1920s, private cars gained ground to an extent unknown in Europe until the 1960s. Henry Ford began a mass production of cars and a large-scale and modern marketing. In 1920 the United States produced 83 percent of all cars in the world. There were 20 times as many cars on the American roads as in the second greatest car nation, Canada. From 1909 until 1927 15 million cars of the Ford model T were produced, a record which was not beaten, until in the middle of the 1970s by the "Beetle" of the Volkswagen factories. In connection with the car industries, oil, rubber, and glass industries were established. The Crash of 1929 meant a temporary halt, but the New Deal and the Second World War accelerated the American development. At the end of the war, the US was indisputably the leading economic and political power in the world. The basis of the dynamic American development, the establishment of the "pure" white settler state, has been described above in Chapter 2. The high wage level—the large internal market of relatively well-to-do freehold farmers and industrial workers—led to a rapidly growing industrial development.

4   Emmanuel, *Unequal Exchange Revisited*, p. 73.

appropriate more value than they produce. This situation could only arise and continue to exist because there are millions of extremely exploited workers in the surrounding world.[5]

The Welfare State, the considerable ability for consumption, the enormous improvement in productive forces in the rich countries, and the contrasting conditions in the Third World; are all due to the same cause: imperialist exploitation. Primarily, unequal exchange results in a growth in the imperialist countries which is considerably more rapid and extensive than in the Third World. At the same time these economic relations determine the attitude of the working class towards an international system of socialism in the world. The demand for a new economic world order, the demand for socialism, is foreign to the West European and North American working class.

Reformism

Reformists are opposed to revolutionaries in that the former's political ideology and practice do not go further than allowed by the capitalist relations of production and are aimed at being effected on the existing premises of the system. Against that, the revolutionaries organize their policy to overthrow capitalism. Parties which base their policy on the continuous existence of imperialism and ally with a working class with an objective interest in continuing imperialism, cannot be revolutionary. This fact is independent of the forms of the class struggle, i.e. its fierceness etc. The form has nothing to do with the actual basis of the class struggle.

Today, the revolutionaries of the imperialist countries have to base their policy on a class analysis taking its point of departure in global economic conditions. The revolutionaries have to ally with the classes in the world which have an objective interest in overthrowing the imperialist system, no matter where they are geographically.

---

5 On this, Kwame Nkrumah, the late president of Ghana, writes: "Neo-colonialism constitutes the necessary condition for the establishment of welfare states by the imperialist nations. Just as the welfare state is the internal condition, neo-colonialism is the external condition, for the continued hegemony of international finance capital." Nkrumah, Kwame, *Handbook of Revolutionary Warfare*, p. 12.

The Rise of Reformism

It was the economic basis of the class struggle which resulted in the success of reformism within the working classes of the imperialist countries. During the first half of the nineteenth century the capitalists had no economic possibility of satisfying—even partially—the demands of the proletariat for better conditions. At that time the satisfaction of these demands was more than the capitalist system could bear. Therefore, any large demand for improvements had to be ruthlessly suppressed in order not to lead to a subversion of the prevailing conditions of ownership and the state. The bourgeoisie could not allow itself the luxury of introducing parliamentary democracy, the union rights, etc., which would have threatened the very existence of the capitalist system. But this changed with imperialism and the subsequent changes in conditions in the imperialist countries. It became possible for the ruling class to make concessions within the framework of the system. At the same time the high wages, the improved working conditions, and the extended political rights strengthened the faith of the working class in the possibilities of reformism, which again made it less risky for the capitalists to give the working class further political rights. However, the working class had to fight very hard to obtain these improvements in wages and working conditions. As a class, the capitalists will always be against wage increases, as they result in a proportional fall in the rate of profit.

Thus the improved conditions and the considerable political influence which the working class of the imperialist countries obtained were not a result of an ingenious scheme devised by the capitalists or of bribery in order to obtain social calm, but a consequence of the struggle of the working class itself. And it is quite as certain that these demands would never have been satisfied if the imperialist accumulation of capital had not been effected.

Historically, the entire working class did not all at once become a wealthy and bourgeoisified class of the imperialist countries. The development has been gradual. At the end of the last century the improved conditions of the skilled and well-organized part of the working class resulted in the weakening of the revolutionary labor movement concurrently with the advance of reformism. The Paris Commune was defeated and the First International was dissolved in 1871, whereas the industrial and political reformist struggle successfully gained ground. The reformist line turned out to be able to improve the wages and the working conditions of the working class within the framework of the capitalist system. The revolution was no longer on the agenda in Western Europe. Capitalism had regained its vitality and developed dynamically.

Marx and Engels were far from blind to the fact that these changes in the material conditions of the proletariat influenced the policy of the class. They found that the reasons for the insidious reformism within the British working class during the latter part of the nineteenth century were based on the British industrial and colonial monopoly.[6]

> [...] the English proletariat is actually becoming more and more bourgeois, so that this most bourgeois of all nations is apparently aiming ultimately at the possession of a bourgeois aristocracy and a bourgeois proletariat alongside the bourgeoisie. For a nation which exploits the whole world this is of course to a certain extent justifiable. The only thing that would help here would be a few thoroughly bad years, but since the gold discoveries these no longer seem so easy to come by [...].[7]

Concurrently with the improvements in wages and working conditions the working class enforced a political democratization of society. In this way the labor movement was incorporated in the bourgeois parliamentary system by way of political reforms. The improvements in wages, in working conditions, and political reforms against which the bourgeoisie had fought tooth and nail during the 1820s, 30s, and 40s were obtained during the 1870s and 80s, when they no longer presented a menace to the capitalist system.

> As regards the workers it must be stated, to begin with, that no separate political working-class party has existed in England since the downfall of the Chartist Party in the [eighteen] fifties. This is understandable in a country in which the working class has shared more than anywhere else in the advantages of the immense expansion of its large-scale industry. Nor could it have been otherwise in an England that ruled the world market; and certainly not in a country where the ruling classes have set themselves the task of carrying out, parallel with other concessions, one point of the Chartists' programme, the People's Charter, after another. Of the six points of the Charter two have already become law: the secret ballot and the abolition of property qualifications for the suffrage. The third, universal suffrage, has been introduced, at least approximately; the last three points are still entirely unfulfilled: annual parliaments, payments of members, and, most important, equal electoral areas.[8]

Marx and Engels repudiated heavily the reformist line within the labor movement:

---

6 Lenin further develops this conception: "It must be observed that in Great Britain the tendency of imperialism to split the workers, to strengthen opportunism among them and to cause temporary decay in the working-class movement, revealed itself much earlier than the end of the nineteenth and the beginning of the twentieth centuries; for two important distinguishing features of imperialism were already observed in Great Britain in the middle of the nineteenth century—vast colonial possessions and a monopolist position in the world market. Marx and Engels traced this connection between opportunism in the working-class movement and the imperialist features of British capitalism systematically, during the course of several decades." *Imperialism [...]*, p. 283.

7 Friedrich Engels to Karl Marx (Oct. 7, 1858), MESC, p. 110.

8 Engels, 'The English Elections,' MEAB, p. 368.

For a number of years past the English working-class movement has been hopelessly describing a narrow circle of strikes for higher wages and shorter hours, not, however, as an expedient or means of propaganda and organization but as the ultimate aim. The Trades Unions even bar all political action on principle and in their charters, and thereby also ban participation in any general activity of the working class as a class. The workers are divided politically into Conservatives and Liberal Radicals, into supporters of the Disraeli (Beaconsfield) ministry and supporters of the Gladstone ministry. One can speak here of a labor movement only insofar as strikes take place here which, whether they are won or not, do not get the movement one step further [...] No attempt should be made to conceal the fact that at present no real labor movement in the Continental sense exists here [...][9]

★

But the manufacturing monopoly of England is the pivot of the present social system of England. Even while that monopoly lasted the markets could not keep pace with the increasing productivity of English manufacturers; the decennial crises were the consequence. And new markets are getting scarce every day, so much so that even the negroes of the Congo are now forced into the civilisation attendant upon Manchester calicoes, Staffordshire pottery, and Birmingham hardware. How will it be when Continental, and especially American, goods flow in the ever increasing quantities—when the predominating share, still held by British manufactures, will become reduced from year to year? Answer, Free Trade, thou universal panacea? [...]

But what is the consequence? Capitalist production cannot stop. It must go on increasing and expanding, or it must die. Even now, the mere reduction of England's lion's share in the supply of the world's markets means stagnation, distress, excess of capital here, excess of unemployed work people there. What will it be when the increase of yearly production is brought to a complete stop?

Here is the vulnerable place, the heel of Achilles, for capitalist production. Its very basis is the necessity of constant expansion, and this constant expansion now becomes impossible. It ends in a deadlock. Every year England is brought nearer face to face with the question: either the country must go to pieces, or capitalist production must. Which is it to be?

And the working class? If even under the unparalleled commercial and industrial expansion, from 1848 to 1868, they have had to undergo such misery; if even then the great bulk of them experienced at best a temporary improvement of their condition, while only a small, privileged, "protected" minority was permanently benefitted, what will it be when this dazzling period is brought finally to a close; when the present dreary stagnation shall not only become intensified, but this its intensified condition shall become the permanent and normal state of English trade?

The truth is this: during the period of England's industrial monopoly the English working class have to a certain extent shared in the benefits of the monopoly. These benefits were very unequally parceled out amongst them; the privileged minority pocketed most, but even the great mass had at least a temporary share now and then. And that is the reason why since the dying-out of Owenism there has been no Socialism in England. With

---

9 Friedrich Engels to Eduard Bernstein (June 17, 1879), MESC, p. 320.

the breakdown of that monopoly the English working class will lose that privileged position; it will find itself generally—the privileged and leading minority not excepted—on a level with its fellow-workers abroad. And that is the reason why there will be Socialism again in England.[10]

Engels' hopes that the destruction of the British industrial and colonial monopoly by the other advanced capitalist countries would result in the British working class losing its privileged position and again becoming revolutionary, were not fulfilled. As described; capitalism developed in other directions than Marx and Engels had imagined. The British industrial and colonial monopoly was broken before the end of the century. It was broken because it came to include the leading West European powers and the United States. This happened without bringing about a decline in the standard of living of the British proletariat. On the contrary the working class of these countries also succeeded in obtaining higher wages, improved working conditions and more political rights within the framework of the bourgeois parliamentary system. Thus the breach of Britain's monopolistic position only meant that reformism spread to these countries.

At the beginning of our century Lenin had to realize that Engels' hopes that the destruction of the British industrial monopoly would lead to economic conditions which again would place the revolution on the agenda, were not fulfilled. On the contrary Reformism was fortified within the working class. Lenin also realized that this development originated in imperialism. The "treachery" of the leaders of the working class was only expressive of this economic fact. Lenin writes:

> However, as a result of the extensive colonial policy, the European proletarian partly finds himself in a position when it is not his labor, but the labor of the practically enslaved natives in the colonies, that maintains the whole of society. The British bourgeoisie, for example, derives more profit from the many millions of the population of India and other colonies than from the British workers. In certain countries this provides the material and economic basis for infecting the proletariat with colonial chauvinism. Of course, this may be only a temporary phenomenon, but the evil must nonetheless be clearly realized and its causes understood in order to be able to rally the proletariat of all countries for the struggle against such opportunism.[11]

The First World War laid bare the strength of chauvinism within the labor movement, when under the leadership of the Social Democratic parties it followed the national bourgeoisies in the first imperialist war about colonies and spheres of influence. The interests of the bourgeoisie and the upper strata of the working class coincided to a certain degree. The prosperity of the country was

---

10 Engels, Friedrich, 'England in 1845 and in 1885,' MEAB, pp. 393-394.

11 Lenin, V.I. (1907), 'The International Socialist Congress in Stuttgart,' LCW, Vol. 13, p. 77.

their common prosperity.

> By social-chauvinism we mean acceptance of the idea of the defense of the fatherland in the present imperialist war, justification of an alliance between socialists and the bourgeoisie and the governments of their "own" countries in this war, a refusal to propagate and support proletarian revolutionary action against one's "own" bourgeoisie, etc. It is perfectly obvious that social-chauvinism's basic ideological and political content fully coincides with the foundations of opportunism. It is one and the same tendency. In the conditions of the war of 1914-15, opportunism leads to social-chauvinism. The idea of class collaboration is opportunism's main feature [...]

> [...] Opportunism was engendered in the course of decades by the special features in the period of the development of capitalism, when the comparatively peaceful and cultured life of a stratum of privileged working men "bourgeoisified" them, gave them crumbs from the table of their national capitalists, and isolated them from the suffering, misery and revolutionary temper of the impoverished and ruined masses. The imperialist war is the direct continuation and culmination of this state of affairs, because this is a war for the privileges of the Great-Power nations, for the repartition of colonies, and domination over other nations. To defend and strengthen their privileged position as a petty bourgeois "upper stratum" or aristocracy (and bureaucracy) of the working class—such is the natural war-time continuation of petty-bourgeois opportunist hopes and the corresponding tactics, such is the economic foundation of present-day social-imperialism.[12]

THE POLITICAL DEVELOPMENT IN THE INTERWAR PERIOD

Around 1920 Lenin again and again stresses that an understanding of the roots of opportunism and the fight against social-chauvinism are the most important tasks for the West European revolutionaries during this period.

> Is there any connection between imperialism and the monstrous and disgusting victory opportunism (in the form of social-chauvinism) has gained over the labor movement in Europe?
>
> This is the fundamental question of modern socialism.[13]

Lenin does not doubt the answer. In his article 'Revision of the Party Programme,' he writes:

> It would be expedient, perhaps, to emphasize more strongly and to express more vividly in our programme the prominence of the handful of the richest imperialist countries which prosper parasitically by robbing colonies and weaker nations. This is an extremely important feature of imperialism. To a certain extent it facilitates the rise of powerful revolutionary movements in the countries that are subjected to imperialist plunder, and are in danger of being crushed and partitioned by the giant imperialists (such as Russia), and on the other hand, tends to a certain extent to prevent the rise of profound revolutionary movements in the countries that plunder, by imperialist methods, many

---

12 Lenin, V.I., *The Collapse of the Second International*, LCW, Vol. 21, pp. 242-243.

13 Lenin, V.I., *Imperialism and the Split in Socialism*, p. 105.

colonies and foreign lands, and thus make a very large (comparatively) portion of their population participants in the division of the imperialist loot.[14]

Lenin's policy for Western Europe after the First World War was to bypass the highest paid upper strata of the working class and concentrate on the actual proletarians. His strategy did not come to fruition. It was not possible for the revolutionary part of the labor movement to wrest the leadership of the working class from the reformist. In Germany, where the revolutionary line was in a strong position, the Communists tried to revolt in 1918 but were betrayed by the Social Democrats. In 1924 the Social Democracy came into power in Denmark and the Labour Party in Britain, not in order to get rid of capitalism but to resolve its crisis. The majority of the working class wanted reforms, not revolution. In the countries where a Social Democratic policy was pursued, the crisis was eased through government intervention and reforms.[15] In Germany, the loser of the war, stripped of all colonies, and fleeced by the demand of the other imperialist powers for reparations, neither the Communists nor the Social Democrats but the Nazis became victorious.

On the policy of the Comintern during this period, Fritz Sternberg writes:

> As Lenin misjudged the real strength of Reformism so did his epigones even more. He never gave a systematic analysis of the sociological prerequisites which formed the basis of Reformism, and which prevented it from being shaken during the period up to the victory of Fascism. The Comintern has contented itself with slogans. It has never made it clear that the differentiation in the pre-war years within the working class took place on the basis of the increasing wages of the entire class.
>
> The Comintern has not corrected Lenin's mistake as to the question of the labor aristocracy and thus the evaluation of the real strength of Reformism. On the contrary: It has made it even deeper.[16]

The rapid economic growth in the countries of Western Europe during the

---

14 Op. cit., pp. 168-169.

15 The US New Deal and the social reforms of K. K. Steincke in Denmark are examples of this. In the 1930s, as a Danish Social Democratic minister, Steincke put through a large number of reforms for the labor market, the social services, and the health services, and in this way he laid the groundwork for the Danish social security system of today. The New Deal is the name of Franklin D. Roosevelt's reform policy from 1933 to 1938 in the wake of the Great Crash in 1929. It was a policy with a strong social touch, and it was close to the ideas of the European Social Democrats. The basis of the New Deal was an American capitalist society also in the future. But capitalism should be modified and humanized. In accordance with the ideas of the British economist, Keynes, the state should intervene in the economy as a regulating and smoothing factor. Employment on public works was provided to reduce the rate of unemployment. By the Act on Social Security, 1935, old-age and unemployment insurance and public assistance were introduced. In 1938, rules as to maximum working hours and minimum wages were introduced.

16 Sternberg, Fritz, *Der Faschismus an der Macht* [Fascism in Power], p. 91.

period after the Second World War meant considerable increases in prosperity to the working classes of those countries. The Social Democratic parties became one of the strongest political powers. The working class represented by the Social Democratic party often had the government power, and in many cases they administered the capitalist system more efficiently than the antiquated liberal parties did.

THE EFFECTS OF UNEQUAL EXCHANGE ON INTERNATIONAL SOLIDARITY

The effects of imperialist exploitation on the national policy of the exploiting countries did at the same time influence international questions. The policy of the working class of the imperialist countries became still more nationalistic, as the prosperity of the country was the prosperity of the working class.

As already described, this did not mean that the class struggle stopped in the imperialist countries. Whether the wages are high or low, whether the social product is big or small, the wages of the working class and the profit of the bourgeoisie are two amounts which are inversely proportional, and, therefore, the object of continuous struggles.

But when the relative size of the value created by the working classes of the imperialist countries continuously falls compared with the values they receive by way of unequal exchange, and when they appropriate more value than they create because of the low prices of commodities from the exploited countries, then the increase in the national product becomes more important than international solidarity with the members of their own class in the exploited countries. These are the material and economic realities behind the lack of solidarity between the workers of the imperialist countries and the workers of the exploited countries.

Below, a number of concrete examples are given. They illustrate the bloom of chauvinism and the withering of the international solidarity of the working class in some of the countries which participate in the international exploitation. As early as in the latter half of the nineteenth century this chauvinism played a prominent part in the attitude of the British working class to Ireland and the Irish working class. In a letter to Meyer and Vogt (Apr. 9, 1870) Marx writes on this attitude:

> And most important of all! Every industrial and commercial center in England now possesses a working class divided into two hostile camps, English proletarians and Irish proletarians. The ordinary English worker hates the Irish worker as a competitor who lowers his standard of life. In relation to the Irish worker he feels himself a member of the ruling nation and so turns himself into a tool of the aristocrats and capitalists of his

country against Ireland, thus strengthening their domination over himself. He cherishes religious, social, and national prejudices against the Irish worker. His attitude towards him is much the same as that of the "poor whites" to the "niggers" in the former slave states of the U.S.A. The Irishman pays him back with interest in his own money. He sees in the English worker at once the accomplice and the stupid tool of the English rule in Ireland.

[...] This antagonism is the secret of the impotence of the English working class, despite its organization. It is the secret by which the capitalist class maintains its power. [...]

[...] Therefore to hasten the social revolution in England is the most important object of the International Workingmen's Association. The sole means of hastening it is to make Ireland independent. Hence it is the task of the International everywhere to put the conflict between England and Ireland in the foreground, and everywhere to side openly with Ireland. And this is the special task of the Central Council in London to awaken a consciousness in the English workers that for them the national emancipation of Ireland is no question of abstract justice or humanitarian sentiment but the first condition of their own social emancipation.[17]

The Central Council of the First International did not succeed in "provoking" the British working class to be aware of the conditions in the oppressed countries or to be aware of the fact that the emancipation of these countries was a prerequisite of their own emancipation. On the contrary the defense of the colonial empire by the British working class was cemented in the following years.

On the attitude of the British working class to the fight for the emancipation of the oppressed countries Lenin writes:

> I would also like to emphasize the importance of revolutionary work by the Communist parties, not only in their own, but also in the colonial countries, and particularly among the troops employed by the exploiting nations to keep the colonial peoples in subjection.
>
> Comrade Quelch of The British Socialist Party spoke of this in our commission. He said that the rank-and-file British worker would consider it treasonable to help the enslaved nations in their uprisings against British rule. True, the jingoist and chauvinist-minded labor aristocrats of Britain and America present a very great danger to socialism, and

---

17 Karl Marx to Sigfrid Meyer and August Vogt (Apr. 9, 1870), MESC, pp: 236-237. The International Working Men's Association is the same as the First International, formed on 28 September 1864. After the defeat of the Paris Commune in 1871, the First International began to dissolve due to various reasons—partly because of persecution, partly because of internal disagreements (especially between Marx and Bakunin). Formally it was dissolved in 1876. The Second International was founded in 1889. In spite of the many resolutions and assurances that the workers of the various countries would never take up arms against each other, both the German and the French socialist parties voted in favor of war appropriations in their respective parliaments just before the First World War. The national Social Democratic parties made peace with the bourgeoisie and definitively gave up the principles of the Second International. The Third, Communist, International was founded in Moscow in 1919 (generally known as the COMINTERN). "The Second International has died defeated by opportunism." (Lenin at the foundation of the Third International.)

are a bulwark of the Second International. Here we are confronted with the greatest treachery on the part of leaders and workers belonging to this bourgeois International [...] The parties of the Second International have pledged themselves to revolutionary action, but they have given no sign of genuine revolutionary work or of assistance to the exploited and dependent nations in their revolt against the oppressor nations. This, I think, applies also to most of the parties that have withdrawn from the Second International and wish to join the Third International. We must proclaim this publicly for all to hear, and it is irrefutable. We shall see if any attempt is made to deny it.[18]

At the same congress Lenin says about the British Labour Party:

The comrades have emphasized that the labor aristocracy is stronger in Britain than in any other country. That is true. After all, the labor aristocracy has existed in Britain, not for decades but for centuries [...] This stratum is thoroughly imbued with bourgeois prejudices and pursues a definitely bourgeois reformist policy. In Ireland, for instance, there are two hundred thousand British soldiers who are applying ferocious terror methods to suppress the Irish. The British Socialists are not conducting any revolutionary propaganda among these soldiers, though our resolutions clearly state that we can accept into the Communist International only those British parties that conduct genuinely revolutionary propaganda among the British workers and soldiers.[19]

The resolutions of the Third International about the importance of the emancipation of the colonial countries to the world revolution were not followed up. The West European parties were not at all interested in the question.

Ho Chi Minh, who later became the president of the Vietnamese Communist Party, was in Europe at that time. He attended the 5th congress of the Third International (COMINTERN) in 1924, where he severely criticized the West European communist parties, particularly the French for its chauvinist attitude towards the colonial question.

Thus, nine countries with an aggregate population of 320,657,000 and a total area of 11,407,600 square kilometers, are exploiting colonies with a total population of 560,193,000 and covering areas adding up to 55,637,000 square kilometers. The total area of the colonies is five times that of the metropolitan countries whose total population amounts to less than three fifths of that of the colonies [...]

Thus, it is not an exaggeration to say that so long as the French and British Communist Parties do not apply a really, active policy with regard to the colonies, and do not come into contact with the colonial peoples, their vast programmes will remain ineffective, and this, because they go counter to Leninism [...]

According to Lenin, the victory of the revolution in Western Europe depends on its close contact with the national-liberation movement against imperialism in the colonies and dependent countries; the national question, as Lenin taught us, forms a part of the general problem of proletarian revolution and proletarian dictatorship.

Later, Comrade Stalin condemned the counter-revolutionary viewpoint which held

---

18 Lenin, V.I., *The Second Congress*, p. 245.

19 Ibid., p. 261.

> that the European proletariat could achieve success without a direct alliance with the liberation movement in the colonies.
>
> However, if we base our theoretical examination on facts, we are entitled to say that our major proletarian parties, except the Russian Party, still hold to the above-mentioned viewpoint because they are doing nothing in this matter [...]
>
> As for our Communist Parties in Great Britain, Holland, Belgium and other countries whose bourgeoisie have invaded the colonies, what have they done? What have they done since the day they assimilated Lenin's theses in order to educate the proletariat of their countries in the spirit of genuine proletarian internationalism and close contact with the toiling masses in the colonies? What our Parties have done in this domain amounts to almost nothing. As for me, born in a French colony and a member of the French Communist Party, I am sorry to say that our Party has done very little for the colonies.[20]

Ho Chi Minh's criticism was never understood, even less observed by the communist parties of the imperialist countries. They upheld their half-hearted attitude towards the colonial question. But worse than that, the Social Democratic parties, which by then represented the majority of the working class in the West European countries, turned out to be directly pro-imperialist.

At the 6th Congress of the Comintern, July-September 1928, Palmiro Togliatti, who later became the leader of the Italian Communist Party, presented a detailed report on the Social Democratic movement in Western Europe and its attitude towards the colonial question. After the Second World War, Togliatti himself represented a policy which hardly differed from that of the Social Democrats, but at the congress in 1928 he gave a thorough description of the pro-imperialist policy of the Social Democratic parties. Social Democracy, he said, had always had a colonial policy

> which consisted in allying itself with or directly participating in the colonial enterprises of the bourgeoisie [...] the Social Democrats have become colonial politicians. They recognise the possession of colonies as something which their countries could never renounce and that, when their country has no colony it is up to them to demand a colony for it in a more or less open manner. In this field there is not a single Social Democratic Party which is an exception.[21]

In his report Togliatti gives a large number of examples of the pro-imperialist policy of the Social Democrats in proof of his statement.

In France the Socialist Party had always voted in favor of colonial projects. In December 1927 at the congress of the French Socialist Party it was declared

---

20 Ho Chi Minh, 'Report On The National And Colonial Questions At The Fifth Congress Of The Communist International,' pp. 30-32.

21 Togliatti, Palmiro, 'Social Democracy and the Colonial Question,' speech at the 6th congress of the Comintern—quoted from Edwards, H.W., *Labor Aristocracy: Mass Base of Social Democracy*, pp. 36-37.

that "the post-war problems cannot be solved without the colonies." Similarly, the party voted in favor of military appropriations to be used for the suppression of nationalist riots in Syria, when the French troops massacred the population of Damascus.

In Holland the Socialist Party did not even discuss the need for colonies. They were only interested in the methods of government in the colonies. The Dutch Socialist Party warned its government that a revolt was in the offing in Indonesia. When it broke out in 1926 in Western Sumatra and Java under the leadership of the Indonesian Communist Party, it got no support whatsoever from the Dutch socialists. On the contrary, they condemned the revolutionaries in strong terms, "whether they originated from Moscow or Canton." When the revolt was suppressed by mass executions, the Dutch socialists dissociated themselves from these. Only the laborers and the peasants "who were the cause" of the revolt should be executed!

At its conference in 1919 in Germany the Social Democratic Party protested against the fact that Germany had been deprived of her colonies. At the Marseille congress R. Hilferding demanded on the part of the Social Democratic Party colonies for Germany. This demand was repeated in 1928.

In Italy in 1928 the Social Democratic Party passed a resolution protesting against the distribution of colonies after the First World War according to the Treaty of Versailles. They demanded a new agreement about the colonial problem, which considered Italian capitalism.

In the British Labour Party programme of 1918 it appears that they are against the decolonization of the British empire, because the Labour Party considered it its duty to "defend the rights of British citizens who have overseas interests." And finally,

> [...] as for this community of races and peoples of different colors, religions and different stages of civilization which is called the British Empire, the Labour Party is in favor of its maintenance.[22]

Until 1934 the parties of the Third International attacked vigorously this Social Democratic opportunism, chauvinism, and pro-imperialism. But under the impact of fascism they turned to the strategy of the popular front in the middle of the 30s, which meant cooperation with the Social Democrats.

At the end of the Second World War the last remnants of internationalism were disappearing from the West European and American labor movements. Concurrently with the bourgeoisification, the slogan "the proletariat has no na-

---

22 Ibid., p. 39.

tive country" lost its importance to the working class of the Western World completely. It had got somewhat more than its "chains" to lose.

Generally, the British working class has been behind the imperialist policy of the changing British governments. The Labour government under Ramsay MacDonald (1929-31) refused all demands from the Egyptian government for the withdrawal of British soldiers, and politico-economic "advisers," and for the independence of the Suez Canal.

The Labour government under Clement Atlee (1945-51) undertook several dirty tricks to suppress the labor and peasant riots in the British colonies. The Labour government sent its men-of-war to Sudan "to do anything to maintain peace and order."[23] In Kenya, the government of Clement Atlee was responsible for the suppression of labor troubles at the end of the 1940s. In 1947 in Mombasa, The African Workers' Federation and The Railway Staff Union called a general strike. Workers within catering and business as well as servants joined the strike for higher wages and lower rent.

> The Colonial Office under the Labour Government acted with the same ruthlessness as under any Tory Government. Police and troops were called in, the strike was suppressed, and the President of the African Workers' Federation, Chege Kibachia, was banished without trial to a remote village in Northern Kenya.[24]

During a strike later in the same year police shot at the strikers and killed three. During 1949-50 legislation was passed in Kenya which was to stop the labor riots. Wage freezes and forced labor at starvation wages were used. Strikes were made illegal and emergency legislation was introduced. The emergency legislation gave the British governor the right to deport troublemakers. This legislation was passed and introduced by a Labour Government, elected and supported by the majority of the British working class. In the then British colony of Nigeria the coal miners in Enugu were on strike in 1949 demanding higher wages—a completely normal Social Democratic demand. But in the colonies it was not supported by the Social Democratic government, and was met by arms. The result was 21 dead and 50 injured miners. During the war over the Falkland islands in 1982 an almost united British labor movement supported the imperialist war by the Conservative Government against the Argentine.

The French labor movement does not differ from the British as regards lack of solidarity with the proletariat of the Third World and pro-imperialist tendencies. When the Algerian liberation movement FLN fought for a free Algeria in the 1950s and 60s, it found only little sympathy within the French labor move-

---

23 Woddis, Jack, 'Africa and Mr. Wilson's Government,' quoted from Edwards, op. cit., p. 33.

24 Togliatti, 'Social Democracy and the Colonial Question.'

ment. The French Communist Party behaved like a racist party, which must be considered in connection with the fact that it had many members among the European workers in Algeria, who were paid far better than the Algerians—just like the Whites in South Africa today—because they were Europeans. An independent Algeria would mean that they lost their privileges, and, therefore, they fought desperately for a French Algeria: It was also, among these that the terror organization OAS found its assassins.[25] The OAS fought for a French Algeria even after the French Government had given up. It should also be mentioned that the future "socialist" president Mitterand was one of those responsible for the violent attack on the Algerian people in the late 1950s, when he was Minister for Algeria under a Social Democratic government.

The author Simone de Beauvoir writes about the attitude of the French people towards the Algerian liberation struggle:

> It (the French Communist Party) made no effort to combat the racism of the French workers, who considered the 400,000 North Africans settled in France as both intruders doing them out of jobs and as a subproletariat worthy only of contempt [...] What is certain is that by the end of June (1955) all resistance to the war had ceased [...] the entire population of the country—workers and employers, farmers and professional people, civilians and soldiers—were caught up in a great tide of chauvinism and racism [...].
>
> What did appall me was to see the vast majority of the French people turn chauvinist and to realize the depth of their racist attitude.[26]

The American working class has supported American imperialism in general. The American settlers began by putting the original population out of the way, and expanded towards the South on account of Mexico. The African slaves in the South did not meet with any solidarity on the part of the white laborers; on the contrary, the white American working class developed an undisguised racism. The white working class feared that the abolition of slavery would result in a fall in their wages as a consequence of the competition from the emancipated slaves.

As regards the foreign policy of the United States, the American working class has by and large supported it. The dominant position of the United States in the world was a prerequisite of its economic development and therefore of the greatest importance to the labor movement. As part of the fight against "World Communism," the American unions have supported the policy of the United States in Asia, Africa, and Latin America.

---

25 OAS (*Organisation de l'Armée Secrète*.) A terror organization consisting of French officers and colonists who tried to stop the negotiations between the French government and the Algerian liberation movement FLN on the independence of Algeria in the spring of 1962 by means of bomb outrages and assassinations both in Algeria and in France.

26 Ibid., p. 195.

It was students, intellectuals, and Liberals who were behind the demonstrations against the Vietnam war in the 1960s, not the American working class. To the extent that parts of the working class criticized the war at all—and this applied also to the other parts of the population—it was because they did not want to lose "their sons" in the war. The unions even took an active part in the support of the war against the NLF and North Vietnam.

In May 1967 the American seamen's union, the dock laborers, the mechanics, the masons, and several other unions arranged a "Support the Boys" march along the 5th Avenue in New York. They carried bills with the wording "Bomb Moscow," "Bomb Peking," "Throw the H-bomb on Hanoi." Now and then union members left the demonstration to thrash the onlookers who expressed their disapproval.[27]

The American union support of the Vietnam war could also be seen at the union congresses. At 13 union congresses in 10 American states in October and November 1967 attended by a total of 3542 delegates, 1448 voted for a continuation of the policy of the government, 1368 were for an escalation of the war, 471 found that the war efforts should be scaled down, and only 235, less than 7 percent, advocated a complete withdrawal.[28]

In the months of April and May 1970 when the Nixon administration intensified the bombing of North Vietnam and invaded Cambodia and 12 students were killed in anti-war demonstrations in the United States, the unions reacted by escalating their support of the war. J. Beirne, vice-president of the AFL-CIO explained in a speech that opposition to the war was against the interest of the American working class. A termination of the war would lead to unemployment. J. Beirne said among other things:

> Suppose last night, instead of escalating into Cambodia, President Nixon said we are pulling every man out in the quickest manner, with airplanes and ships; if he had said that last night, this morning the Pentagon would have notified thousands of companies and said,—"Your contract is canceled"—by tomorrow millions would be laid off. The effect of our war, while it is going on, is to keep an economic pipeline loaded with a turnover of dollars because people are employed in manufacturing the things of war. If you ended that tomorrow these same people wouldn't start making houses.[29]

George Meany, who was for many years president of the AFL-CIO, announced his unconditional support of Nixon's escalation of the war. The grateful Nixon visited the union headquarters to express his pleasure of the support of the unions. As Meany gave his full support to Nixon, he said: "In this crucial

---

27 Scott, Jack, *Yankee Union Go Home*, p. 261.

28 Ibid., p. 262.

29 Ibid., p. 265.

hour, he should have the full support of the American people. He certainly has ours."[30]

On the 8th of May 1970 the "Hard Hats" (the construction workers) began a hunt for anti-war demonstrators. Anti-war demonstrations were attacked by workers wearing their hard hats and armed with lead pipes and crowbars. Several hundred demonstrators were injured in the following weeks. The police remained totally passive and not one single "Hard Hat" was arrested. The demonstration on the 20th of May proved that it was not a question of a few extremists. An amalgamation of several of the biggest unions in the New York area mobilized more than 100,000 workers for a demonstration in support of Nixon's policy in Indochina. Nixon expressed his gratitude for this "meaningful manifestation of support," and in return he was given a hard hat marked Commander in Chief.

The Danish working class was not immediately in favor of the Vietnam war, but in general it was not against it either: they were more or less indifferent: It was not involved in the same way as the American. However, the then Communist-led seamen's association did not refuse to transport supplies to the regime in Saigon, if they got their war risk allowance according to the tariff.[31] Just like in other places in Europe, the opposition against the Vietnam war came mainly from young people, students, and intellectuals. Any solidarity of importance with liberation movements of other places in the world has not been seen during recent years. Thus, support of the Palestinian liberation movement by the Danish labor movement has been extremely poor. On the contrary, both the Danish Social Democratic Party and the Socialist People's Party have backed the State of Israel massively. The struggles in South Africa have not been favored by the working class either. In spite of numerous requests to the Danish labor movement from the South African liberation movements and the Front Line States for a boycott of trade with South Africa, the Danish Social Democratic Government continued to allow the importation of South African coal and other commodities. These cheap products were more important than the solidarity. In September 1981, when the Angolan ambassador to Scandinavia asked Danish dock laborers to refuse to unload South African vessels because of a South African attack on southern Angola, she received a lot of excuses and a "No." The Latin American anti-imperialist struggle is treated in much the same way by the unions. The solidarity of the Danish working class with the oppressed people of the Third World is certainly not up to much.

---

30 Ibid.

31 *Ny Tid*, April 1969—the Danish seamen's paper.

The Working Class Has Become a "Sacred Cow" to the Left Wing

The Social Democratic parties and the parties which do not differ considerably from these, have had the greatest support from the working class in the imperialist countries. Their nationalist policy has improved the conditions of the working class within the framework of the capitalist system so much that left wing parties of all kinds have had very little or no success at all in their attempts to win the working class over to their policy. The left wing explains away the entry of chauvinism into the working class, even though it ought to regard it as a duty to find out why and to counteract this tendency. Marx and Engels dealt with the first slight signs of the advance of opportunism and chauvinism within the working class. They exposed the causes, condemned these phenomena without hesitation and without "making any excuses" for the working class. In 1916 Lenin wrote that the connection between imperialism and the split in the socialist movement was "the fundamental question within modern socialism." In the 1930s the question of imperialism and the bourgeoisification of the working class was still discussed, but since the Second World War the question has almost been taboo within the left wing of the Western World. Also within the very narrow circle of students and intellectuals who discuss theories of "imperialism," "center-periphery" etc., the question of the consequence of imperialism to the working class of the Western World and consequently to international solidarity has always been avoided. This is not because the question is not of current importance; the cleavage between the working class in the imperialist countries and the working class of the exploited countries has never been wider both as regards standard of living and as regards mentality. The reason why the criticism of the opportunism and chauvinism of the working class has ceased is that those within the left wing who before the Second World War still criticized the bourgeoisification of the working class and its results, have today become the spearheads of the bourgeoisified class. When the Social Democrats demand one Danish Krone more per hour, the extreme left wing demands two. When the Social Democrats demand a reduction of the weekly hours by two hours, they demand five hours with full wage compensation, and so on. To the left wing the working class has become a "sacred cow;" it makes mistakes but this is "not its own fault." The left wing believes that the Danish working class has been misled by Social Democratic traitors, and indoctrinated with bourgeois tendencies through school, television, radio, and newspapers. The task of the revolutionaries is therefore to "disclose this treachery" and these delusions, whereupon the working class will show its "true revolutionary disposition."

It is not quite in accordance with the materialist conception of history to explain the opportunism of generations by the treachery of the Social Democratic leaders. The working class has the leaders it deserves, and it pursues a policy which reflects the will and aim of the class, and as such it must be said that the Social Democratic parties have done well. It is also an extremely superficial and idealistic view that the bourgeoisification should be a result of indoctrination and the propaganda of the media. The question is then why the proletariat of the Third World, who are exposed to a propaganda which is at least as bourgeois, have not fallen into the same ditch. And why the working class of the imperialist world is amenable to this propaganda to such a degree. In Denmark we live in a very democratic society compared to the rest of the world. As a result of its relative economic affluence, the Danish working class has become harmless. It does not present a menace to the capitalist system. The bourgeois parliamentary system agrees well with the working class. In Denmark you can by and large say and write anything you want, the economic and social situation makes this right harmless. The majority of the population of the Third World does not have the same rights, as these very rights present a menace to imperialism and to the ruling class, because of the economic and social conditions in the Third World.

The left wing of the imperialist countries have totally neglected the objective economic causes, which are the basis of the bourgeoisification of the working class of the imperialist countries, and the lack of solidarity with the members of their own class in the exploited countries.[32] The left wing does not want to see that in the last resort the present economic struggle of the working class can only be a success at the expense of the proletariat in the exploited countries. On the contrary, the left wing, on behalf of the Danish working class, avows inter-

---

32 Concerning the situation in Denmark, the left wing—in this case the 'International Forum," a non-party anti-imperialist organization—is blinded by its own "prevarications" to such a degree that in a folder on the relationship between the rich and the poor countries, it writes the following about the economic conditions of the Danish working class during the period from the middle of the 1960s to the oil crisis in 1973: "It is not possible to conclude that the working class has been strengthened economically during this period, as the increase in money wages should be seen in relation to the increases in consumer prices compared with the productivity increases of the same period." (The emphasis is original but quite odd.) "It is not possible to conclude that the working class has been strengthened economically" during this period, when charter trips to Majorca, stereo sets, cars and weekend cottages, bungalows or yachts, became amenities of the working class! The period from 1965 to 73 showed the greatest increase in affluence ever achieved by the Danish working class. On the other hand the same people conclude in the line below the above quotation: "The considerable unemployment of later years (1973-77) has meant an economic weakening of the Danish working class." (Both quotations translated from: International Forum (1977), 'Imperialisme og klassekamp, Perspektiver for en ny verdensorden,' p. 51. Copenhagen.) And this in spite of the fact that during the first years, the "crisis" meant only a stagnation in the increase in real wages. Not until 1977 did a recession set in, and by "recession" is meant a return to the 1973 level!

national solidarity with the proletariat of the Third World in the common fight against imperialism.[33] It is extremely difficult to see any concrete contribution on the part of the West European working class towards the fight against imperialism.

According to the left wing there should be an "organic connection between the struggle in the Third World and the class struggle in Denmark."[34] Again it is very difficult to see for example the connection between the struggle of the Palestinian People for national liberation and the struggle of the Danish working class for higher wages and better working conditions. Apparently the Danish working class also finds it difficult to see the connection, if we are to judge from the lack of sympathy, even hostility, displayed by the majority of the Danish working class towards the struggle of the Palestinian People.

The solidarity expressed by the workers of the Western World with the "members of their own class" in the exploited countries has been very limited. They have by and large been indifferent to the suppression of the proletariat of the Third World. When it has been necessary, they have even offered political support to or participated directly in the suppression of the proletariat of the Third World. Not because they did not know any better, but because it was in accordance with their immediate interests. Economists and politicians from the Third World are much more aware of the real facts. The former president of Tanzania, Julius K. Nyerere, writes as follows:

> "To him that hath shall be given" is a law of capitalist and international economics; wealth produces wealth, and poverty, poverty. Further, the poverty of the poor is a function of the wealth of the rich [...] For the poor nations are now in the position of a worker in nineteenth century Europe [...] The only difference between the two situations is that the beneficiaries in the international situation now are the national economies of the rich nations—which includes the working class of those nations. And the disagreements about division of the spoils, which used to exist between members of the capitalist class in the nineteenth century, are now represented by disagreement about division of the spoils between workers and capitalists in the rich economies.[35]

---

33 For example the following statement from the Youth organization of the so-called Danish Communist Party (DKU): "Today three important forces unite against imperialism: the people who build up socialism and communism, the working class of the developed capitalist countries and the national liberation movements. These three main forces fight on one sector each of the front of the international class struggle. But no matter what immediate problems they face, the struggle against imperialism is a common struggle." (Translated from: DKU (1975), *Kampens Vej*. Copenhagen.)

34 International Forum, op. cit., p. 56.

35 Nyerere, Julius K. (1972), 'A Call to European Socialists,' *Third World*; quoted from Nyerere, Julius K. (1973), *Freedom and Development*, pp. 374-5. Dar es Salaam.

Conclusion for the Imperialist Countries

> No social order ever perishes before all the productive forces for which there is room in it have developed; and new, higher relations of production never appear before the material conditions of their existence have matured in the womb of the old society itself. Therefore mankind always sets itself only such tasks as it can solve; since, looking at the matter more closely, it will always be found that the task itself arises only when the material conditions for its solution already exist or are at least in the process of formation.[36]

As we have described above, imperialism meant a rapid process of change in the economy of the imperialist countries. The productive forces have developed explosively, particularly after the Second World War, concurrently with an increase of the standard of living and political power of the working class. This has changed the perspectives of the class struggle radically in the imperialist countries. While the implementation of demands for higher wages, better working conditions etc. was incompatible with the capitalist relations of production during the first half of the last century, these demands are satisfied today within the framework of the system. The class struggle between workers and bourgeoisie has continued sometimes with the use of very militant means. But concurrently with the improvement of the standard of living of the working class by means of the imperialist exploitation of the poor countries, the class struggle has become a struggle for the share of the loot from the poor countries.

Therefore, a change in the economic situation of the imperialist countries is a prerequisite for restoring a revolutionary socialist aim to the class struggle in these countries. When the economic and political emancipation of the Third World has weakened imperialism to such an extent that the system lands in a deep economic crisis, the possibilities of socialism in the imperialist countries will be present. When unequal exchange disappears, the working class of the imperialist countries will lose its privileged position in the world. The capitalist class will have to turn to the working class in the rich imperialist countries to obtain profit by forcing down wages. The working class of the imperialist countries will again become an exploited class, again be the class which maintains society. The flourishing markets of the rich countries will cease to exist and capitalism will again experience its classic crisis of overproduction. The relations of production will become a fetter on the development of the productive forces. This will result in economic, political, and social crises, which will place socialism on the agenda of these countries again.

The present economic crisis—or rather stagnation—in the imperialist econ-

---

36 Marx, 'Preface,' *A Contribution to the Critique of Political Economy*, MESW, p. 182.

omy has not nearly been serious enough to create such an effect. The economies of the imperialist countries have been capable of "recompensing" about 20 million unemployed and have in this way prevented social unrest and prevented a major decrease in the level of purchasing power. Thus a serious crisis of overproduction has been prevented. The present crisis has not meant any basic change in the economic and social conditions of the working class. The most pessimistic estimates talk about a return to the 1973 standard of living! In spite of the fact that its effect has been weakened by the recirculation of oil incomes, the oil crisis has proved how vulnerable the imperialist economy is to price increases of products from the Third World. Similar price increases of other kinds of raw material from the Third World combined with the spending by these countries of the subsequent profits on a centrally planned development of their own economies would affect the economies of the imperialist countries far more seriously. The vulnerability of the imperialist countries to price increases and threats of decreasing supplies of Third World products also shows that it is not the Third World which depends on the rich countries, as it is often alleged, but vice versa. The rich countries only remain rich because they drain the poor countries of enormous values. The poor countries can easily manage without the rich countries, in fact they would do much better. But the imperialist countries cannot maintain their enormous standard of living if they do not exploit the poor countries. Therefore, the emancipation of the Third World is of vital importance to an outbreak of crises in the imperialist countries—crises which will change the nature of the class struggle and make possible a revolutionary situation.

The Possibilities of Socialism in the Exploited Countries

The development and prosperity, of which imperialism was the basis in the rich countries, have an obligate counterpart in the Third World. The tendency of capitalism towards a concentration of wealth at the one pole and of poverty at the other has become evident internationally. It is only in the imperialist countries that capitalism seems to have solved its contradictions; they still exist globally. The wealth and the rapid development in the imperialist countries and the poverty and underdevelopment in the exploited countries are two interdependent phenomena, two aspects of the same matter, imperialism.

Just as original accumulation—i.e. the immediate violent plundering of America, Africa, and Asia—was one of the prerequisites of the rapid development of capitalism in Britain, plundering and destruction during original accumulation were also the basis of further exploitation of the suppressed countries.

However, during the period from the birth of industrial capitalism and until the last third of the nineteenth century, it seemed (for example to Marx and Engels) as if capitalism would spread all over the world and develop the exploited areas, so that they would reach a level corresponding to that of the old capitalist powers. But with the rise of imperialism and the growth of unequal exchange, this tendency turned towards an increasing inequality. The imperialist countries developed much more rapidly than the colonies and the other exploited countries. As unequal exchange between the old industrialized countries and the exploited countries grew more important, the economic development in the world became still more unequal.

What Are Development and Underdevelopment?

Before we start describing unequal development, it would be appropriate to define the concept of development. By the development of a country is meant the development of its productive forces within all sectors. The development of the productive forces means a development both of human labor, its quantity, knowledge and skill, and of the quality and quantity of the production apparatus (buildings, machinery, tools, etc.) in its widest sense. A development of the productive forces results in an increase in productivity by means of a raising of the quality of labor power through training and education, by means of a better organization of work, and by the use of new and more efficient technology. Thus underdevelopment must be seen in relation to the potentials, existing at a given time in a given society, of the development of the productive forces compared with actual production. If the rate of development of the productive forces is lower, and if, consequently, there is less productive use of the total labor power compared with the limits put by the existing level of technology on a world scale, then it is a question of underdevelopment. The exploited countries can be characterized as underdeveloped in the sense that under the present relations of production it is not possible for them to exploit their human labor power potential.[37]

---

37 Emmanuel finds that, if this definition of development is used—the only logical definition—we have an underdeveloped and poor world in which the rich countries are exceptions and the majority of the countries are poor. He writes:

> If by economic underdevelopment we mean a certain ratio, which may be the ratio, both quantitative and qualitative, between the means of production actually set to work and the potential of the productive forces as shown by the technological level attained at the present time—or, more concisely, between the existing implements of labor and those that could exist—then the world is an underdeveloped planet. In this age of interplanetary rockets and of au-

Development means mechanization, automation, and increase in knowledge and skill within all sectors of production, both within the industrial sector and within agriculture, fishing, and forestry. Too often, development is equated with growth within the industrial sector particularly. However, such countries as Denmark, New Zealand, and Australia have prospered by an industrial development of the agricultural sector, whereas countries/regions with a very big industrial sector, for example Taiwan, Hong Kong, or South Korea, remain comparatively underdeveloped. The superiority of the imperialist world does not consist in industry representing the largest part of the national product. The superiority consists in both their industry, agriculture, and other sectors having

> tomation we have, for a population of nearly 3.5 billion, only 930,000 miles of railway line and an annual production of some 25 million motor vehicles of all kinds, so that several hundred million people continue to travel by the most primitive means or even on foot. Our production of cement and steel does not exceed 450 million tons of each, so that a substantial proportion of the earth's inhabitants live in straw huts or something similar. It has already been pointed out that our world still largely lies fallow. Out of some 27 million square miles of cultivable land, less than one-eighth, a mere 3.38 million is under cultivation, and a large section of this eighth is worked neither by tractors nor even by draught animals. Our world is poor. From the series published in 1955 by Kindleberger we can work out the world net product at about $330 per head per year, which is approximately the average product of Latin America: and Singer is able to declare that the economic well-being of the average person in the world outside the U.S.S.R. was in 1956 less than in 1913 and perhaps less than in 1900. Within this poor and underdeveloped world, however, there are some islets of advanced development, in which approximately nine-tenths of the equipment and, in general, of the human and material productive forces of the entire world are concentrated. As a whole, the world of today offers much the same picture as a European nation at the beginning of industrialization, and history has proceeded as though, instead of the centrifugal forces foreseen by economic science, which were to diffuse progress from the center to the periphery, unforeseen centripetal forces had come into play, drawing all wealth toward certain poles of growth. History has proceeded, too, as if the industrialized countries had succeeded in exporting impoverishment so effectively that the forecasts of Marxism, which have begun to show signs of losing reality within the context of the industrial nations, are being realized to perfection on the scale of world economy. In the face of these inequalities, the same problems that confronted the industrial nations at the end of the eighteenth century and the beginning of the nineteenth now stand before the world as a whole. *Unequal Exchange*, pp. 262-3.

Unequal development must not on any account be confused with Lenin's theory of "different development," by which means the development of the various imperialist powers at various speeds—when one power is in the lead one day, and another power the next day. According to Lenin, this creates unstable conditions and possibilities of war. By "unequal development" is meant a fixed division which is reproduced and deepened between the imperialist powers and the Third World.

been developed. Thus the boundary between over- and underdevelopment is not between industry and agriculture. It is between a highly developed and varied economy and a restrained and one-sided economy.

The Connection Between Unequal Exchange and Unequal Development

Unequal exchange and unequal development have the same basis, namely the international wage variation which has arisen between the rich imperialist and the poor exploited countries. Thus there is no immediate connection between unequal exchange and unequal development. The amounts which are transferred by means of unequal exchange from the poor part of the world to the rich result in a low and a high rate of consumption, respectively.

The basic problem of capitalism is not to produce but to sell. The capitalist crises do not arise as a result of a lack of capital but because of a lack of purchasing power. The circulation of capital is upset by the lack of marketing possibilities. If there is not sufficient purchasing power in society for the sale of manufactured commodities at a price yielding profit, capital will not be attracted. On the cause of the crises of capitalism in the middle of the nineteenth century Marx writes:

> But as matters stand, the replacement of the capital invested in production depends largely upon the consuming power of the non-producing classes; while the consuming power of the workers is limited partly by the laws of wages, partly by the fact that they are used only as long as they can be profitably employed by the capitalist class. The ultimate reason for all real crises always remains the poverty and restricted consumption of the masses as opposed to the drive of capitalist production to develop the productive forces as though only the absolute consuming power of society constituted their limit.[38]

The situation which Marx describes—overproduction in relation to purchasing power—which was the cause of the recurring crises in the middle of the last century, changed in the imperialist countries, as described earlier, through the increases in wages which the working class obtained in the last third of the century. At the same time, this contradiction was intensified in the exploited countries. The low wage level of the poor countries does not represent a market of sufficient purchasing power to attract capital for an industrial development which comes anywhere near the one in Western Europe and the United States.

Capital is attracted when there are openings for profitable investments. This implies a market with purchasing power. The imperialist countries, with their high wage level, represent such a market. It is the enormous purchasing

---

38 Marx, *Capital*, Vol. III, p. 484.

power of the imperialist countries which attracts capital and which is the basis of the more rapid development of the productive forces. Almost three-quarters of the investments of the developed capitalist countries are made in the developed countries.

The low wage level in the exploited countries means a market which is too small to attract any considerable amounts of capital. Thus, only few productions based on the domestic market are established. Even national capitals—for example from OPEC—often seek towards the imperialist countries, where the openings for profitable investments are better. The poor countries which try to develop through capitalist dynamics try in all possible ways to attract capital. For example by establishing free trade areas, by tax concessions, etc. But even under such favorable relations of production, these countries attract only inferior amounts of capital, simply because the domestic market is too limited. The foreign capital which nevertheless is invested in the exploited countries because of the geological conditions, the climatic conditions, or the cheap labor power, is mainly based on exports to the world market, i.e. rich imperialist countries as far as 75 percent is concerned. This applies particularly to investments in the mining and plantation sectors, but lately also to investments in industrial sectors such as the electronics and textile industries. Thus, the productive forces in the Third World often develop very unequally. A modern export industry exists together with widespread subsistence farms and underdeveloped crafts, which are the continuous source of cheap labor power.

Emmanuel describes how investments in the imperialist countries lead to development, and how investments in the exploited countries remain limited and isolated:

> Why is it that European capital in the United States and Australia, and United States capital in Canada, have benefitted these countries by developing their economies, whereas in the Third World they have played a harmful role by forming enclaves? An enclave merely means a foreign investment that refuses to participate in the country's process of expanded reproduction. In less learned terms, it is an investment that restricts itself to the self-financing of the branch in which it is installed and then, once this expansion has been accomplished, repatriates the whole of its profits. The Société Générale de Belgique installed the Union Minière in the Congo and Canadian Petrofina in Canada. The former exploits copper miners, the latter oil wells. When the investment has reached its maximum potential, Canada Petrofina uses its profits to establish a refinery: for this purpose it even increases its capital [...] For several years Canadian Petrofina refrains from paying any money dividend and instead grants stock dividend. This is not displeasing to the Belgian shareholders since, unlike dividends paid in money, a stock dividend is not subject to income tax. Then the company interests itself in the distribution of oil products and buys a network of selling points [...] Next, it sets up a petrochemical industry, followed by a works to produce tank cars; and, after that, what? Perhaps a chain of department stores, or else a shoe factory. If the company does not do this, its shareholders will, by instructing their bankers to use the product of their dividends to purchase a

> wide variety of shares on the Montreal stock exchange [...]
>
> In contrast to all this, the Union Minière du Katanga, once its program for equipping its copper mines is completed, ceases to expand and pays its dividends in money. It becomes an enclave. Why? Are we really to suppose that the heads of the Société Générale in Brussels are solely concerned to overdevelop Canada and "block" development in the Belgian Congo? The reality is different. The simple fact is that in Canada the high standard of living of the people, resulting from the high wage level, constitutes a market for all sorts of products, whereas wages and standard of living in the Congo are such that there is nothing there to interest any fairly large scale capitalist—nothing except the extraction of minerals or the production of certain raw materials for export that have inevitably to be sought where they are to be found.
>
> This situation is the effect, not the cause, of low wages, even though, once established, it becomes, through the capitalist logic of profit-seeking, a cause in its turn by blocking the development of the productive forces [...].[39]

The low wage level and the consequent underdevelopment of the exploited countries is a self-intensifying process. Through unequal exchange and the exportation of the majority of profits to the imperialist countries, the exploited countries are deprived of the conditions for a dynamic capitalist development. The more limited the investments are, the higher the rate of unemployment and the higher the pressure on wages. At the same time this means a further reduction of the market and thus reduced possibilities of attracting capital.

On the other hand, the high wage level means a comparatively high rate of consumption and thus a large market with considerable purchasing power in the imperialist countries. This attracts capital, and a development of the productive forces follows. All this strengthens the industrial and political opportunities of the imperialist working class for further improvements. The rich get richer, and the poor get poorer.

High wages are an incentive to investments in labor-saving mechanization and machinery in the rich countries to a greater extent than in the underdeveloped countries, where it is an immediate advantage to use manual labor because of the cheap labor power.

The enormous incomes of the OPEC countries in connection with the price increases of oil illustrate in a way the importance of the wage level to the attraction of capital and thus to the development of the productive forces. Through OPEC, the oil exporting countries succeeded in enforcing an increase in the price of oil, which improved their exchange conditions.[40] The increase

---

39 Emmanuel, *Unequal Exchange*, pp. 376-7.

40 In spite of the relatively high increases in oil prices during the last 10 years, this is in fact only a minor, insufficient, adjustment of the exchange relations. In 1950 an average Danish worker could buy 14 liters of oil from one hour's wage. In 1982 he could buy 21 liters.

in oil prices was not a result of an increase in the wage level in the oil exporting countries. As the OPEC countries (all belonging to the Third World) held the majority of oil production they could increase prices by a political decision. The increases in oil prices meant an enormous increase in the income of these countries compared to their former national product. However, this income did not result in the rapid development of all OPEC countries that might have been expected. A large part of the increased oil incomes returned to the imperialist countries. Large parts of the outstanding accounts of the OPEC countries actually never left the Western banks, they just changed accounts. OPEC countries like Algeria, Iraq, and Libya, the economies of which to some extent are controlled on the basis of a central plan, were mainly able to spend the increased income on a national development of their economics, even to such an extent that they had to go to the international loan market to get additional capital for their ambitious plans. In a society of planned economy, where investments are not made to gain immediate profits but in accordance with national planning, a low wage level is no obstacle to development—on the contrary.

Here low wages result in the fact that a large part of the national product is accumulated and used for further investments instead of forming part of an unproductive consumption via wages. The case of the OPEC countries Saudi Arabia, Kuwait, and the United Arab Emirates, is different. The majority of the investments of these countries are made with a view to profit. Therefore, the majority of their oil income returns to the imperialist countries, where profitable openings for investments are much more numerous than at home. In 1974 the oil incomes of the Arab countries totalled about $60 billion. Between 43 and 48 of these returned to the Western World as investments in industry and as hot money. The amounts came mainly from Saudi Arabia and Kuwait.

The OPEC countries which have economics guided by capitalist dynamics, have difficulty in transforming the relatively large amounts of capital into a national development. The low level of wages which exists in most of these countries limits the extent of market purchasing power, and thus the profitable openings for investments in industry and agriculture. The oil money thus partly flows back to the imperialist countries as investment capital, or is used by the upper class to import luxury goods.

The development of Venezuela during recent years constitutes an excellent example of these dynamics. During the 1970s Venezuela obtained an increasing income from oil exports, due to the increasing oil prices. In 1980 alone, the revenue from oil amounted to $18 billion. The Government had nationalized the oil industry in the beginning of the 1970s and intended through favorable loans to canalize the revenue into a national development of industry and agriculture. But this failed totally. Only a minor part of the oil income was in fact invested in industrial or agricultural projects, and these few projects mostly showed a deficit. The bulk of the oil revenue went through favorable state loans into the service sector, import business, speculation in land and property, or disappeared abroad, mainly to the US, as financial and currency speculation. The oil revenue supported not only a class of capitalists reluctant to invest in industrial and agricultural development, but also the growth of a large unproductive and corrupt state sector.

In spite of the enormous oil income, the real wages of the majority of the population decreased by about 10 percent from 1974 to 1977, unemployment rose, there was a periodical shortage of important food items, a decline in the level of social welfare, and there were growing urban slums.[41]

The lacking commitment of the private sector to invest inside Venezuela was expressed as a flight of capital and imports of luxury goods. The flight of private capital began in the middle of the 1970s. In 1981 it reached an estimated level of about 100 million dollars per day, and in March 1982 it reached 133 million per day.[42] To finance the resultant deficit of the balance of payments, the state had to secure large foreign loans. Today Venezuela is deeply in debt.

> The Venezuelan bourgeoisie also invested heavily in luxury dwellings in the United States, channeling an estimated $2.3 billion in 1977, for example, into the purchase of weekend houses and condominiums in southern Florida. Meanwhile, even conservative estimates agreed that at least 25 per cent of the population lived in substandard housing. The large urban centers also experienced a decline in public services: water and electricity shortages, inadequate educational facilities, serious and persistent unemployment, and a notable contraction in available state-funded health facilities.
>
> The low purchasing power of the mass of the Venezuelan population contributed to the inability of the economy to absorb the petrodollar wealth. Instead, the government acted to channel the surplus financial resources abroad in the form of interest-bearing loans and investments.[43]

By the end of 1978 about 40 percent of Venezuela's oil income was being invested in financial operations abroad, and only 60 percent in Venezuela. This resulted in a stagnation of the Venezuelan economy by the end of the 1970s. The rate of growth of the gross domestic product was 8.4 percent in 1976, declined to 6.8 percent in 1977, and in 1980 it became negative: 1.2 percent—the lowest rate of growth in the oil-rich country for decades.

---

41 See: Petras J. P. and Morley, M. H. (1983): "Petrodollars and the State: The failure of state capitalist development in Venezuela, *Third World Quarterly*, Vol. 5, no. 1, p. 7. London.

42 Ibid., pp. 14, 16.

43 Ibid., p. 15.

> In a word, state ownership serves as a mechanism for redistributing economic surplus among segments of the national and foreign bourgeoisie, increasing their profit opportunities but not necessarily expanding the productive forces in either industry or agriculture [...] It is clear that neither oil wealth nor state ownership have laid the basis for a more equitable and productive society. In addition, the vaunted economic independence which the oil wealth was supposed to have bestowed has turned into a chimera; Venezuela has now become as dependent on finance capital as it was earlier on investment capital.[44]

Emmanuel describes the situation of the capitalist OPEC countries in the following way:

> After having been, for a long time, too poor to sell their oil at a normal price, it happens that when they are finally able to adjust the prices they are too poor to collect the real money these prices represent.
>
> This deadlock is one of the signs of capitalism's basic contradiction between social production and private appropriation.[45]

Capitalism, as it appears in the Third World, is not capable of extending the productive forces to a social extent—and not capable of releasing the enormous resources of human labor power of the Third World. The continuous drain on capital prevents directly and unequal exchange prevents indirectly the investments which are necessary for the development of the productive forces. However, this does not mean that there is no development at all in the Third World. But the countries of the Third World are prevented from developing at the same speed as the imperialist countries—they fall more and more behind. Therefore, the social and political conflicts become more and more serious. Several countries of the Third World approach a situation in which development is no longer possible within the framework of capitalism. This is the basis of the revolutionary changes which take place in the Third World.

For a New World Order—What is Progressive?

The problems of development in the Third World cannot be solved within the framework of the present economic world order. The solution demands partly national planning, which encourages national development benefitting the masses in the exploited countries, and partly a new economic world order which eliminates the unequal exchange between the rich and the poor parts of the world. The present international unequal accumulation of capital results in the exploited countries being in continual economic, political, and social

---

44   Ibid., pp. 26-7.

45   Emmanuel, *Unequal Exchange Revisited*, pp. 72-3.

crises, which intensify both the national class struggle and the antagonism to the imperialist countries. This situation has been reflected by a number of revolutionary situations in the Third World. The struggle of the exploited and oppressed masses has been aimed partly at the imperialist powers in the form of wars of national liberation, and partly at the ruling classes at home.

Of course it is not accidental that the revolution is on the agenda in the Third World. Because of the very small rate of consumption on the part of the population in these countries, the production is restrained to such an extent that the relations of production have become a fetter which must be broken in order that the productive forces can continue to develop. This is the cause of the social unrest and the revolutionary changes in the Third World. If these changes are to lead to improvements, they must be directed towards socialism, which means that society owns the production apparatus so that a social planning of production and consumption can be made under the leadership of the proletariat. Thus, under socialism the contradiction between social production and private appropriation disappears, a contradiction which is characteristic of the capitalist mode of production. Under socialism the contradiction between production and consumption takes another shape because a market with purchasing power, i.e. an unproductive consumption, is not a prerequisite of investments and thus of development. The connection between consumption and development which exists under capitalist relations of production does not exist under socialism. On the contrary, consumption and investments are treated as the inversely proportional quantities they are. In a society of planned economy a low wage level is an accelerating factor for development. A comparatively large part of the social production can be accumulated, which means that it can be invested productively in the development of an industrial basis or agricultural production. In this way the basis of a long-term increase in the standard of living of the masses is created. The Russian and Chinese revolutions are historical examples of this.

The Russian revolution meant the establishment of new relations of production, and the Soviet Union was the first society of a planned economy under the leadership of the proletariat. This resulted in a rapid development of the Soviet Union from a comparatively underdeveloped country to a modern industrial state. The rapid development of the Soviet Union in the 1930s was partly achieved by keeping down wages and thus unproductive consumption. Through this strategy, the majority of the production could be set aside for new investments.

After the revolution, the People's Republic of China developed at a speed never seen before in the Third World. From the first Five Year Plan in 1953 until the end of the 1970s, China had a ratio of accumulation to consumption which meant a rate of accumulation of 35-40 percent. This resulted in an average annual growth in the industrial production of 13.5 percent and in agriculture of 5.5 percent, which is higher than the growth of any capitalist country.[46]

FOR A SOCIALIST WORLD ORDER

National development is one thing, international economic relations is another. The exploited countries can establish planned economies internally and thus create a certain basis for an increased speed of national development to the benefit of the population. However, the wretchedness of the Third World is closely related to the connection with the capitalist world market. The price at which Angola sells its coffee on the world market did not change because MPLA defeated the Portuguese colonial power and established a people's republic introducing a planned economy to a certain extent. At first Angola could only spend its income in another way.

There is a growing consciousness in the exploited countries of this situation. Slowly and hesitantly the cooperation between the poor countries is beginning to be established. The "Group of 77" countries within UNCTAD[47] and the demand for a "New Economic World Order" which was made at the extraordinary general meeting of the United Nations in 1974 are some of the signs of a growing consciousness.[48] No matter what economic policy the poor countries

---

46 The Beijing daily *Guangming Ribao*, 9 May 1980. During recent years a change of this policy has taken place. The leading economist in China, Xue Mubiao, wrote in the October 1981 issue of *Jing Guanli* (Economic Leadership): "The drawback of the Chinese economic policy during 30 years (1949-1979) was the ratio of accumulation to consumption. During the period from 1952 to 1978 Chinese industrial production increased by 11.2 percent annually, which is more than in any capitalist country. However, the standard of living saw only few improvements between 1957 and 1978, because the rate of accumulation was so high and the economic effect of production so low." (The somewhat lower percentage is due to the fact that Xue uses 1952 as basic year, whereas *Guangming* uses 1950) Thus from 1979 to 1980 the rate of accumulation began to fall to around 30 percent and the industrial growth rate was reduced to 6-8 percent, whereas unproductive consumption increased. (The information comes from an article on "The New Economic Policy of China" by Dino Raymond Hansen in the Danish newspaper *Information*, 1981.)

47 The Group of 77 was founded on the basis of the need of the Third World for speaking with one voice at UNCTAD conferences and at similar international meetings about the economic situation in the world. Since the first meeting in 1967 in Algeria, the group has been increased from 77 to 120 Third World countries.

48 On behalf of the non-aligned states, Algeria called this conference, where the subject was "Raw Materials and Development Problems." In spite of strong opposition from the Western coun-

have pursued, they have had to see how their individual efforts to develop their economies have been checked by the conditions prevailing on the world market. The conditions of the world market cause the poor countries to sell their products at a low price and buy their imports at a high price. At a meeting of the Group of 77 in 1979, Julius Nyerere said:

> Nations which have just freed themselves from colonialism and old countries in Latin America, have all inherited the same opinion from the prevailing Euro-American culture: "Work hard and you will become rich." But gradually, we have all learned that hard work and wealth were not cause and effect. External forces always seemed to break the alleged connection! The so-called neutrality of the world market turned out to be the neutral relationship between the exploiter and the exploited, between a bird and its prey [...] Even though we have not tried to do anything but to sell our traditional exports and buy our traditional imports, we can buy continuously less for continuously more of our hard work.[49]

On the demand for a New Economic World Order Nyerere says:

> [...] the complaint of poor nations against the present system is not only that we are poor, both in absolute terms and in comparison with the rich nations; it is that within the existing structure of economic interaction, we must remain poor and get relatively poorer. The poor nations of the world remain poor because they are poor and because they operate as if they were equals in a world dominated by the rich. The demand for a new international economic order is a way of saying that the poor nations must be enabled to develop themselves according to their own interests and to benefit from the efforts which they make.[50]

The main demand of the poor countries at the UNCTAD negotiations during the so-called "North-South" dialogue and in similar situations has always been: A fair and just connection between the prices of the commodities exported by the exploited countries and the prices of the imports. Furthermore the action programme of a New Economic World Order attaches importance to the sovereign right of disposal by the exploited countries of their own natural resources. Fidel Castro sums up the ten most important demands of the underdeveloped countries in the following way:

1. Unequal exchange is impoverishing our peoples; and it should cease!
2. Inflation, which is being exported to us, is impoverishing our peoples; and it should cease!
3. Protectionism is impoverishing our peoples; and it should cease!
4. The disequilibrium that exists concerning the exploitation of sea resources is abu-

---

tries two resolutions were passed, which are known as "A New Economic World Order."

49 Julius K. Nyerere at a pre-UNCTAD V conference, translated from the Danish magazine *Kontakt*, no. 3, 1980-81.

50 "The Plea of the Poor: new economic order needed for the world community," in *New Direction* 4, October 1977; here quoted from *Third World Quarterly*, Vol. 3, no. 3, p. 511.

sive; and it should be abolished!
5. The financial resources received by the developing countries are insufficient; and should be increased!
6. Arms expenditures are irrational. They should cease, and the funds thus released should be used to finance development!
7. The international monetary system that prevails today is bankrupt; and it should be replaced!
8. The debts of the least developed countries and those in disadvantageous positions are impossible to bear and have no solution. They should be canceled!
9. Indebtedness oppresses the rest of the developing countries economically; and it should be relieved!
10. The wide economic gap between developed countries and the countries that seek development is growing rather than diminishing; and it should be closed![51]

After almost ten years of negotiations about the majority of these demands, the poor countries have only achieved very inferior results. Only the OPEC countries have had sufficient power to obtain a change in the exchange of one single commodity: oil. It becomes more and more clear to the exploited countries that even though most of the imperialist countries speak of a need for a New Economic World Order, they do not at all contemplate satisfying the demands. The exploited countries slowly recognize that it is not possible to obtain fundamental changes in the economic world system by means of negotiations. Because there is no consensus of interests but a conflict of interests between the rich and the poor countries.

Therefore, a new economic world order will not be reached as a result of negotiations and supranational control, but as a result of a confrontation between the imperialist countries and the exploited countries. A change in the present system presupposes that the exploited countries can put force behind their demands. One of the forcible means, which the poor countries could use is production cartels. OPEC has shown both the strength and the weakness of such cartels. On the one hand it has been possible to introduce considerable price increases, in spite of the fact that OPEC far from has the monopoly of oil production. On the other hand OPEC has turned out to be weak in the long run, because reactionary regimes dominate the organization. The demand of the nationalist regimes for higher prices have been weakened by the dual position of the reactionaries. Countries such as Saudi Arabia and Kuwait have by now considerable investments in the West and their upper classes are allied with imperialism to such an extent that they do not want to harm the imperialist countries. A car-

---

51 Castro, Fidel (Sept. 27, 1981), "Speech at the Conference of the Inter-Parliamentary Union in Havana, 15-23 September 1981," *Granma*.

tel which consists only of states under the leadership of the proletariat would be much more effective.

As more and more of the Third World countries obtain the internal conditions of development by doing away with the capitalist relations of production and replacing them by planned economy, the possibilities of effective international co-operation between the exploited countries are also increased. This can be established not only as cartels but first and foremost as increased trade and technical and political cooperation directed against imperialism.

Conclusion Concerning the Perspectives of Socialism in the Exploited Countries

In Latin America, Africa, and Asia, imperialism and capitalism stand in the way of progress and development. Therefore, it is here that the struggle against this system takes place. This struggle against the imperialist world order is the most important progressive force in today's world, and it opens the possibilities of socialism both in the exploited countries and, in the long run, in the imperialist countries.

6

What Can Communists in the Imperialist Countries do?

As INHABITANTS of one of the richest countries in the world, our possibilities of promoting socialism are limited because of very special conditions. In the richest imperialist countries there are no classes today which are objectively interested in overthrowing the imperialist system, because all classes in these countries profit by this system. Any social movement in the rich imperialist countries must be seen in the light of this fact. A mass movement has only a socialist perspective if it is directed against imperialism. Such a mass movement does not exist in the imperialist countries.

For decades left-wing parties in Western Europe and North America have set themselves the task of leading the struggle of the working class for higher wages, improved conditions, etc. This practice has been followed irrespective of the special position of the working class in the imperialist countries. Therefore they are reformists, no matter what international ideals they have had, whether they were pro-Soviet, Chinese, or Albanian, and regardless of their names. It cannot be the task of the Communists to lead the struggle of the labor aristocracy and thus to maintain or increase its privileges.

Support the Anti-Imperialist Movements in the Exploited Countries!

As anti-imperialist mass movements are only found where imperialism means exploitation and impoverishment, the task of the Communists is to support the movements there. The most effective practice of Communists in an imperialist country today is to support the anti-imperialist liberation movements in the

Third World who fight against capitalism and international exploitation and for socialism. By supporting movements who pursue an anti-imperialist policy and who have the necessary political strength because of a mass basis, or who have the possibilities of developing such a strength, we can do our share towards impairing imperialism.

We support the national revolutionary movements in the underdeveloped countries because these social movements represent the biggest possible social improvement in their countries; because, through a revolution, they have the possibilities of liberating enormous productive forces, especially in the form of human labor power; because, through the efforts of establishing a socialist society in their own country, they take a step towards the establishment of socialism in the whole world, also if these countries are not in a situation in which they can establish a socialist society immediately. There is no direct or easy way from an underdeveloped and exploited economy to socialism. In spite of this, the national movements in these countries represent the greatest threat to the imperialist system today. They do their share towards creating crises in imperialism. These crises are of crucial importance, if a revolutionary situation ever is to arise in the rich part of the world.

Unlike the capital and the labor aristocracy, the Communists are interested in crises in capitalism. Therefore, when the crises arise, it is not the task of the Communists to defend the privileged position of the labor aristocracy by making plans to protect the capitalist system against crises. Communists in the imperialist countries should not try to reduce the extent of such crises and their consequences such as unemployment, decreases in wages, etc. Even today, when the economic crisis has meant only a comparatively small decrease in the standard of living of the population in the rich countries, the "fear of crisis" is widespread. The left-wing parties, from the Social Democratic party to the extreme left wing, compete with the right-wing parties to suggest the most efficient methods of solving the problems of capitalism. To them it is first and foremost a question of defending the standard of living achieved. The revolutionary perspective of the crisis has been completely forgotten. From a revolutionary point of view, crises are necessary. When the crisis is really felt, the Communists must oppose chauvinism, racism and hatred towards immigrant workers, and support anti-imperialist movements and progressive states in the Third World.

In the long view, the crises can only be removed by an elimination of capitalism through a global revolutionary socialist development. It is however evident that only economic development itself can convince the labor aristocracy of this. The labor aristocracy, which helps to administer imperialism, cannot be transformed into a revolutionary class exclusively by means of agitation and propaganda. It is primarily the economic development that determines the policy of a class.

Support the Liberation Movements Materially!

The way in which Communists of imperialist countries can support the liberation movements is of course specific from country to country. However, one thing is sure: if the support is to be of any importance, it must primarily be of a material nature. At the end of the 1960s, members of our organization participated in and tried to influence the big demonstrations directed against the warfare of the United States in Vietnam. But even though much was written about it and there were many discussions, and even though thousands of people were engaged in the work even in a small country like Denmark, the material support to the Vietnamese liberation movement was surprisingly small.

During this period the left wing devoted quite some time to liberation movements all over the world, but there was a striking disproportion between the often very militant and uncompromising slogans and the minimal value it had to the liberation movements and their struggle. The majority of the left wing did not concern themselves with the liberation movements with the primary aim of supporting them, but rather because they hoped to mobilize more people. People whom they could engage in their work for the labor aristocracy in Denmark with the illusory purpose of leading its wage struggle in a socialist direction. In the 1970s this became even more obvious. It was not possible to transfer the few anti-imperialist forces from the Vietnam work to the support of the liberation struggle in Southern Africa, Palestine, etc. Other questions have caught the main interest of the left wing. Anti-EEC and anti-nuclear power campaigns, pollution problems, environmental questions, unemployment problems etc. Anti-imperialism is no longer an important aspect of the political activity of the left wing. There is a very limited number of people that can be mobilized for anti-imperialist work in Denmark today.

However, it is positive that here and there in the imperialist countries there are supporting groups which attach the greatest importance to material support. By this work, the possibilities of the liberation movements for defeating imperialism are improved. Talks with representatives of the liberation movements and visits to the movements have confirmed that it is of use to offer material support, as they often lack the most elementary things to be able to carry on their struggle and to be able to mitigate the hardships of the masses.

What Do We Work For?

It is our aim to gather anti-imperialists in order to support the struggle against the suppression and exploitation of the Third World. As things are now it must be a matter of individuals, as there is no objective basis for mass movements with anti-imperialist views in Denmark today.

The solidarity for which we work is not based on pity or bourgeois humanitarianism, but on the awareness that the emancipation of the proletariat, in the exploited countries, is a condition of the destruction of the imperialist system and the introduction of socialism in Denmark.

We regard the two aspects of the political struggle, theory and practice, as inseparable. It is necessary continuously to investigate the economic and political conditions in the world in our endeavors to increase and improve our support, and to find new ways in which we can give this support. We have to study which contradictions are the most important, so that our efforts are concentrated on the areas which will be of most benefit to the struggle for socialism. We shall communicate our views to the anti-imperialist movements and states in the Third World and to anti-imperialist groups and organizations in all countries. In particular, we shall discuss our opinion of imperialism and the economic and political conditions in Western Europe. For a long time the left wing has passed on its illusions about the conditions in Europe and the solidarity of the working class with the liberation movements. We shall continue to tell the liberation movements not to count on an active support of their struggle on the part of the labor aristocracy. On the contrary, they must expect opposition, and this is not due to ignorance or lack of information about the struggle, but to the position of the working class of the imperialist countries as a labor aristocracy—a global upper class.

THE STARVING AND EXPLOITED MASSES SHALL BE VICTORIOUS!

Epilogue

The Task of the New Stage

Torkil Lauesen

The End of Our Praxis

Up through the 1980s the illegal work was intensified. At the same time our small organization, together with sympathizers ran the café and restaurant "Liberation." The development of theory continued with studies of the capitalist crises, and the developments in the Soviet Union and the Third World. This was reflected in publications from "Manifest Press."

At the end of the 1980s, with the decline of Third World liberation struggles, and the general crises in the struggle for socialism, it became difficult to mobilize new activists for the café and find new prospects to become members of M-CWG. Between the increased workload and getting older, we might have been feeling a bit tired and incautious.

Our illegal practice ended suddenly on April 13, 1989, when six comrades, including me, were arrested. There was not one single mistake that led to the arrest, but cumulative incidents over the years, and our occasional negligence allowed the police to track us down. However, there was no hard evidence, and we were to be released within 48 hours. But shortly after our arrest, a comrade—in the process of "cleaning up" evidence—was gravely injured in an automobile accident. His car was full of incriminating evidence, including a phone bill with the address of our safe house. This allowed the authorities to put us on trial. We were found guilty of one robbery and other criminal acts, and sentenced to ten years in prison, effectively meaning the end of our group.[1]

---

1 For an account of the group's practice and history, see For the history of CWC and CWG, see: Kuhn, (ed.) (2014), *Turning Money into Rebellion*. Montreal: PM/Kersplebedeb.

Reflection and Evaluation

At this point, it might be appropriate to reflect on the question raised by CWC: *Is it possible to build a revolutionary organization in a capitalist welfare state like Denmark?* Furthermore, we should re-evaluate the strategy and game-plan of CWC: supporting the Third World revolution, to cut the pipeline of value-transfer to the imperialist center, in order to create a revolutionary situation at home.

Concerning the first question: Is it possible to build a revolutionary organization in a country where the socio-economic conditions do not make radical change an imperative? The transition towards socialism is not an act of will alone, nor is it a mechanical process of history. It is driven by the dialectic between the objective conditions for transformation and the subjective forces.

There are many reasons why people want socialism. Some want socialism because they can hardly earn a living despite hard work. Others want socialism because capitalism is in the process of destroying the earth's ecosystem, or because it leads to war. Without anger and a burning desire to change the world (subjective forces), it is not possible to mobilize and organize the objective forces that will create a radical change. However, it is also a common experience that revolutions do not occur just because people want it. In North America and Europe, the movements of 1968 put socialism on the agenda. However, this wave fizzled out. The possibility of radical change depends on not only the will of the subjective forces. It also depends on the development of the contradictions within the mode of production: the possibility for the development of the productive forces, on one side, and on the other side, that of the relations of production. The prospects of revolution are determined by whether the relations of production promote or inhibit the development of the productive forces. The status of that contradiction is what we call the material or objective conditions for revolution. As Marx states:

> At a certain stage of development, the material productive forces of society come into conflict with the existing relations of production [...] From forms of development of the productive forces these relations turn into their fetters. Then begins an era of social revolution [...] [However] no social order is ever destroyed before all the productive forces for which it is sufficient have been developed, and new superior relations of production never replace older ones before the material conditions for their existence have matured within the framework of the old society.[2]

A positive—socialist—outcome is not given, and it is not only determined

---

2   Marx (1859), *'Preface,' A Contribution to the Critique of Political Economy*, MESW.

by the contradiction between the productive forces and the relations of production. The outcome also depends on how prepared the proletariat is ideologically, politically, and organizationally. Thus, the development of capitalism is determined by the dialectical relationship between the economic laws that govern accumulation and the class struggle induced by the social consequences of these laws.

By polarizing the world-system in an imperialist center and exploited periphery, capitalism managed to find a mode of production in which the development of the productive forces could continue. The productive forces in Europe and North America developed rapidly based on the combination of imperialist gains and a growing domestic market. This dynamic duo would prolong the existence of global capitalism for more than a century. The objective conditions for revolution declined in the center, while the polarizing dynamics of capitalism trapped the periphery in a deadlock, which made it impossible for it to develop its productive forces and hence creating a revolutionary situation. This is the reason for the wave of revolution in the Third World in the long sixties, and the difficulties for building revolutionary organizations in the imperialist center.[3]

So, I think Appel's conclusion after the split in CWC, would be no, it is not possible to build a revolutionary organization in an imperialist country, nor are the conditions ripe for revolution. I agree with Appel, to the extent that it was certainly not possible to build a revolutionary party based on a mass movement at the time. However, it was possible to make some preparation for this process, made by small, dedicated organizations. We managed to continue from 1978 to 1989, and history has shown that such counter-currents have always existed in the imperialist center. In Denmark there were clandestine support networks for the Spanish communists during the civil war, and for the Algerian liberation struggle in the beginning of the 60s. In the U.S., the Black Panther Party and the Weathermen are examples of communist organizations with a clear anti-imperialist profile.

To sustain such organizations, dedication and discipline is needed. In other organizations, I have seen comrades coming and going as it fit their career and other interests. In my part of the world, you can choose to be an anti-imperialist and drop out again as you please; it is not necessary for your existence, nor embedded in the social conditions—as in Gaza. However, we do not need dogmatism, but innovation and initiative. We need democracy and procedures to solve conflict that are able to secure the stability of the organization.

---

3 Lauesen, Torkil (2019), "The Prospects for Revolution and the End of Capitalism." *Labor and Society* no. 22, pp. 407-440. Wiley.

Evaluation of the Strategy

When I read our book today, one thing strikes me. It presents an analysis of economic imperialism and the political situation around 1970. However, the book was written ten years later in the beginning of the 1980s when things were already changing. From approximately 1965 to 1975 the contradiction 'imperialism—anti-imperialism' was the principal contradiction in the world-system. The anti-imperialist struggle from Vietnam to the Middle East, from Africa to Chile caused problems for U.S. neocolonialism. We hoped that the victory for the liberation struggle in the Third World would cut the suction pipe of imperialism and thereby create a world economic crisis that would put revolution on the agenda, even in the imperialist states. Needless to say, things did not work out that way. The anti-imperialist offensive of the 1960s did not continue in an unabated and continuous course. The opposite aspect of the principal contradiction, "imperialism," evolved and changed character. From the middle of the 1970s, the liberation struggles and the socialist-oriented states of the Third World were put on the defensive. The anti-imperialist aspect of the contradiction was weakened rapidly during the 1980s, a development our analysis had not anticipated and could not explain. One explanation to "excuse" our poor dialectical analysis might be found in the following quote by French philosopher and friend of Che Guevara, Régis Debray:

> We are never completely contemporaneous with our present. History advances in disguise; it appears on stage wearing the mask of the preceding scene, and we tend to lose the meaning of the play. Each time the curtain rises, continuity has to be re-established. The blame, of course is not history's, but lies in our vision, encumbered with memory and images learned in the past. We see the past superimposed on the present, even when the present is a revolution.[4]

We had been so preoccupied with the analysis of the "anti-imperialist" aspect and of the functioning and consequences of imperialism in the Third World that we had overlooked the evolution of the 'imperialism' aspect itself. Emmanuel had warned us that socialism was not on the agenda in Africa. The development of the productive forces in the newly liberated countries was not sufficient to challenge the capitalist force of the world market.

The anti-colonial movements were well aware that the struggle to develop the forces of production was a necessary continuation of national liberation towards socialism. But national self-determination and the ambition to create socialism were not enough to bring about socialism in reality. The conditions

---

4 Debray, Régis (1967), *Revolution in the Revolution? Armed Struggle and Political Struggle In Latin America*, p. 19. New York: Monthly Review Press.

were even more difficult for the smaller Third-World countries than it was for huge countries like Russia and China, where more diverse economies, land reforms, and planning made it possible to create more viable transitional economies and mount a defense against hostile imperialist encirclement.

The most important barrier for transition towards socialism was the polarizing dynamic caused by the "unequal exchange" in global capitalism. Raw materials and agricultural products produced by low-wage labor in the Third World were exchanged by industrial products produced by relatively high-wage labor in the imperialist center. The newborn revolutionary states did not have the power to change this dynamic. They could not simply increase wages and thereby prices for the raw materials and agricultural products they supplied to the world market. They stood in competition with one another and were forced into a race to the bottom. Without the necessary development and diversity of the productive forces, delinking themselves from the world market and trying to produce solely for the domestic market, in the interest of the workers and peasants, risked throwing their economies into ruin. They had inherited the economic structures established by their former colonial oppressors—these were not designed to serve their interests. They were stuck with monocultures and industries limited to processing a few raw materials. No matter their aspirations, the economies of the newly independent countries were determined by the dominant capitalist realities.

Political independence led, in most cases, to capitalist applications of "development economics." Unlike their Western colonial predecessors, they could not just transfer the costs of industrialization and welfare to other nations, and therefore most were caught in the "development trap," leading to huge debt and sliding back to an exploited position in global capitalism. The periphery states managed to achieve national independence, but they did not liberate themselves from imperialist exploitation and they did not manage to develop a socialist mode of production.

It is easy to say that this was inevitable, and that the anticolonial movements should have known better. However, they had little choice. Seizing state power was necessary to at least change the balance of power in international relations. Various attempts to strengthen the political position of the former colonies and newly independent nations shows that at the time, it seemed possible to collectively make a difference.

Up until the mid-1970s, global capitalism was actually under pressure. The struggle against colonialism and imperialism grew stronger as U.S. neocolonialism penetrated the Third World, replacing the old colonial powers. This contradiction of imperialism versus anti-imperialism interacted with the confrontation between the U.S. and the "actually existing socialism" of the Soviet Union. Although the split between China and the Soviet Union weakened the socialist bloc, and socialist movements in general, the two positions, in some peculiar ways, also supplemented each other. While China's Cultural Revolution and Vietnam's armed struggle provided a new revolutionary spirit, the Soviet Union was the necessary nuclear military power which could counterbalance U.S. imperialism on a global scale, so that the revolutionary spirit had the necessary space to flourish without being crushed. The Soviet Union's ability to reciprocate a nuclear attack deterred the U.S. from using nuclear weapons in its imperialist wars.

Vietnam took advantage of "the best of both worlds." The Soviet Union provided them with anti-aircraft missiles and heavy artillery alongside existential guarantees to counterbalance the U.S. and avoid a nuclear attack on Hanoi. At the same time, Vietnam waged a "protracted people's war" on the ground without compromise, until its final victory, in tune with Maoist principles. However, the new global wave which came into being was not a world socialist revolution, but neoliberalism. Capitalism still had options for expansion—a new spatial fix in the international division of labor. The forces of the Third World were too fragmented and weak to cut the pipelines of imperialism. The socialist camp was split, and the '68-rebellion in the West was, in the end, more rhetoric than deeds.

The G77—77 developing countries within the United Nations system—demanded a "New International Economic World Order" to give them control over their natural resources and to allow the development of a more equal world-system. However, the UN-system was blunted; the power rested in the imperialist center, led by the U.S. Formulated in the language of historical materialism was the overarching factor that ended the revolutionary wave of the long sixties, the inability of "actually existing socialism," both the Soviet and Chinese versions, and in the new states in the Third World, to develop their productive forces to a sufficient degree to break the dominance of the global capitalist market forces. Because of this, the neoliberal counter-offensive was able to do what the U.S. army could not in Vietnam—put the Third World on its knees.[5]

Multinational corporations embraced neoliberalism as it promised to relieve the pressure of nation-state regulations on investment and trade; they wanted to move from being multinational to transnational. Neoliberal global-

---

5 Lauesen, Torkil (2024), 'The Crises of Imperialism and the Prospect of Socialism,' forthcoming in *Imperialism: domination, unequal development and dependence*. Mexico City: Revista de Estudios Globales. Análisis Histórico y Cambio Social (REG), de la Universidad de Murcia.

ization of industrial production would not have been possible without a certain development of the productive forces, especially in transport, information processing, and communications. The introduction of the standard-size container, which could easily be moved from ships to trains and trucks, was one such innovation. The unloading of cargo ships, which once took days, could now be completed within hours. Costs for long-distance shipping were reduced by 97 percent. Since 1980, container transport by sea has grown by 1,550 percent: 95 percent of the foodstuffs, clothes, cars, and electronics we consume are shipped in containers. More than twenty million of them circumnavigate the globe. The biggest cargo ships can carry twenty thousand, which translates into forty thousand cars, 117 million pairs of shoes, or 745 million bananas.[6]

The development of computers, mobile phones, email, the Internet, and other forms of communication technology have revolutionized the global stream of information and communication. It became possible to manage and control production over long distances and in detail. One example is the "just-in-time" managing model, which minimizes production time as well as storage costs by delivering the material used in production at exactly the right time to the right place. In short, the new communications and logistics innovations became central to the production process. They made it possible to divide the production process into numerous steps that don't need to be closely geographically linked. The components of a car or a refrigerator could be produced and assembled in many different countries. The globalization of production made it possible for capital to free itself from the nation-state's embrace. Production is coordinated in networks and chains—whether they connect different floors in a building, or offices, workshops, or factories across the globe. Due to the development of the productive forces in production and transport, the geographic connection between the site of production and consumption became of less importance. The container became the hidden link between the producer countries in the South and the consumer countries in the North.

What matters is the price of the factors of production—independent of geographical location—most important being the price of labor power. Capital could employ labor wherever it makes production most profitable. Laborers, on the other hand, are bound to the places where they earn a living by the borders of the national state.

Neoliberalism was not just a technical development, it was also about pol-

---

[6] Kneller, Richard, Bernhofen, Daniel and El-Sahli, Zouheir (2016), 'Estimating the effects of the container revolution on world trade,' *Journal of International Economics*, Vol. 98, pp. 36-50.

itics. The neoliberal breakthrough occurred when liberal think tanks and lobbyists from multinational corporations connected with conservative political forces. In England, Margaret Thatcher ran against the Labour Party in the 1979 election with the slogan: "There is no alternative." She immediately set about cutting away services provided by the welfare state, privatizing public companies and seeking in every way to curtail the influence of the trade union movement. When Ronald Reagan won the U.S. presidential election in 1980, it signaled the global breakthrough of neoliberalism.

Neoliberalism combined a market-oriented critique of state regulation of capitalism with an emphasis on individualism rather than community. The social democratic state was criticized for being patronizing and bureaucratic and for depriving people of freedom, responsibility and initiative. Thatcher wanted to replace what she called the "Nanny State" and its cradle-to-grave "coddling" with the "competition state." Governments across the world-system adopted neoliberal policies, "modernizing" the workflows of the public sector according to the principles of New Public Management and Public Choice. They sold off public assets as social housing, railway and bus companies, telecommunications companies, electricity, heating—everything from the water supply to the sewers.

The main priority of the "competition state" is to secure the best possible conditions for capital, in competition with other states in the world-system. Free from the grip of the social state, from its control of the flow of capital and trade, and from the power of the trade unions, capital could initiate a new transformation of the global division of labor.

The New Global Division of Labor

During the past forty years, there has been a fundamental change in the global division of labor. From capitalism's very beginning up to the 1970s, the countries of the periphery mainly served as sources of raw materials and tropical agricultural products. In the 1950s, industrial goods made up only 15 percent of the exports of all Third World countries combined. By 2009, the number had risen to 70 percent.[7]

Outsourcing of industrial production began in the 1970s with trade capital (represented by corporations such as Tesco and Walmart) moved the production of shoes, clothes, toys, and kitchenware to low-wage countries. The next wave in the beginning of the 80s saw the U.S. electronics giants such as Cisco,

---

7 UNCTAD (2009). *Handbook of Statistics, 1980—2009*. Geneva: United Nations.

Sun Microsystems, Garmin, and AT&T moving their production to South Korea and Taiwan in response to increasing competition from Japan. The latest, and strongest, wave was prompted when China entered the global market in the 1990s.[8]

In total, the global labor force engaged in capitalist production rose from 1.9 to 3.1 billion people between 1980 and 2011. That is an increase of 61 percent. Three-quarters of this workforce live in the Global South. Together, China and India account for 40 percent of the world's labor force.[9] India joined the WTO in 1995, China in 2001, and the former Soviet republics and the countries of Eastern Europe were integrated into the global capitalist market around the same time. This meant an expansion of capitalism of historic magnitude, and a shift in geographic balance between North and South. In 1980, the numbers of industrial workers in the Global South and Global North were about equal. In 2010, there were 541 million industrial workers in the Global South, while only 145 million remained in the Global North.[10] The center of gravity for global industrial production no longer lies in the Global North, but in the Global South.

According to Ruy Mauro Marini, capitalist exploitation in the dependent country was mainly based on absolute surplus value (long working time with high intensity—blood, sweat, and tears). With the change in the international division of labor, created by the neoliberal industrialization of the Global South, the relative surplus value (new technology and organization of work) was *added* to the forms of exploitation, not swapped, as it happened to a certain degree in the center throughout the twentieth century. In the Global South, absolute surplus value continued to play a significant role. The wage-level remained low, and the consumption power, which is needed to realize profit, was mainly located in the Global North, hence no need for an expansion of the domestic market.

In the 1970s, dependency theory showed how the development of the periphery—or, more precisely, the lack of it—was dependent on the core countries. By the first decade of the twenty-first century, the core countries have become dependent on production in the periphery, and the periphery dependent on consumption in the center. To speak of "producer economies" and "consumer economies"—connected via global chains of production—more ac-

---

8 Smith, John (2016), *Imperialism in the Twenty-First Century*. New York: Monthly Review Press.

9 International Labour Organization (2011), *World of Work Report 2011: Making Markets Work for Jobs*. Geneva: International Labour Organization.

10 Suwandi, Intan and Foster, John Bellamy (2016), 'Multinational Corporations and the Globalization of Monopoly Capital,' *Monthly Review*, Vol. 68, no. 3, July-August 2016.

curately describes current global economic relationships than the terminology formerly used by dependency theorists.[11]

We did not perceive the shift in the relationship between "imperialism" (transnational monopoly capital) and the "social national state" in the imperialist countries. Having previously accepted a division of power and a social compromise with the working class in the imperialist countries, capital, now in the form of neoliberalism, launched an offensive against the social national state. This special form of state had helped capitalism to solve the economic crises of the 1930s and it had facilitated the development of capitalism in the aftermath of the Second World War. The consumption power of the welfare state guaranteed the realization of the profits made by imperialism as well as the loyalty of the working class in the confrontation with the socialist bloc. However, the social nation state and its control and regulation of the movement of capital, goods, and currency was no longer an asset, but turning into a problem for burgeoning transnational capital by the 1980s. The bulwark of the nation state against the forces of the world market was becoming an intolerable barrier for the development of a more globalized capitalism.

We were so preoccupied with our analysis of the anti-imperialist aspect and of imperialism's impact on the Third World that we forgot to analyze what was going on in the center. We were aware of the growing significance of transnational corporations in the Global South but not of the increasing contradiction with the "social state" in the Global North. After accepting a class compromise and entering a power-sharing agreement with labor, capital was on the offensive once again in the form of neoliberalism. The shackles of the welfare state with its regulations and control of capital were to be shed. The "capital vs. the national state" contradiction was on the rise, as "U.S-imperialism vs. anti-imperialism" declined as the world's principal contradiction.

The neoliberal offensive became obvious in the center with Reagan and Thatcher's tax cuts, privatizations, dismantling of public services, and attacks on the trade union movement. Soon, the neoliberal logic spread across the globe. Industrial production was relocated to the Global South, and the era of global chains of production and finance capital's exponential growth began. The dialectical relationship between neoliberal politics/ideology and neoliberal economics became a very potent constellation. Neoliberal politics (as a mode of production) unleashed a huge expansion of the productive forces both in qualitative terms (computers, communications, management, and logistics) and in quantitative terms (establishment of global production chains). This

---

11 Kerswell, Timothy (2006), *The Global Division of Labour and Division in Global Labour* (Ph.D. thesis). Brisbane: Queensland University of Technology.

economic and technological upswing in turn strengthened neoliberal politics and ideology. The capitalist counter-attack was forceful. Neoliberalism became so dominant that capitalism seemed to have conquered the world and was here to stay. On the left, Antonio Negri and Michael Hardt declared that globalization would lead to the death of the nation-state and the rise of a global "empire." But contradictions develop—the strength of their aspects change, they fight, and are always in flux, even if we tend to forget that. It often only becomes clear when a certain historical period is over. "The owl of Minerva spreads its wings only with the falling of the dusk," as Hegel put it.[12]

Neoliberal Lessons for Dependency Theory

When we in M-CWG in the late 1970s were studying *Unequal Exchange*, we were wondering why capital did not move much more industrial production to the Global South to take advantage of low wages. We discussed this with Emmanuel in 1982, going through the draft for our book. He cited several practical, technical, cultural, and political reasons. Transport and communications barriers posed much bigger obstacles than today, as mentioned above. The trade unions still had the strength to resist outsourcing, and the social democratic-led states had the ambition to regulate multinational companies.[13]

The polarizing dynamic in global capitalism from the second half of the nineteenth century and up through the twentieth century led the "dependency" theorists of the 1970s to conclude that the industrialization of the Third World was impossible within the imperialist system. They assumed that a substantial domestic market for consumer products had to be developed before industrialization could occur. The Third World countries had to delink to unblock the development of the productive forces, as Russia in 1917 and China in 1949 had tried. However, this was only an option for very large diverse economies. Most Third World countries would continue to supply raw materials, tropical agricultural products, and simple, labor-intensive industrial commodities; their economies would remain dependent, and they would still constitute the periphery of a world system dominated by capitalist states.

However, these barriers for industrialization of the Global South were knocked down, and this analysis fell apart with the breakthrough of neoliberal

---

12 Minerva is the Greek god of wisdom. Hegel, G.W.F. (1820), 'Preface,' *Philosophy of Right*. London: G. Bell & Sons.

13 Lauesen, Torkil (2023), 'Emmanuel and us.' Arghiri Emmanuel Association, https://unequalexchange.org/2023/07/06/emmanuel-and-us/.

globalization. Capitalism was still a dynamic system. It had an ace to play. Its need to expand and its hunger for profit led it to outsource industrial production on a massive scale from the North to the Global South. The management of globalized production-chains became possible by new forms of communication and new forms of transport, which solved the problem of the geographic distance between the site of production and consumption. The domestic market for consumer goods became less relevant for the industrialization of the South, as it could be substituted by export to the Global North. It seemed unthinkable for most dependency theorists in the 70s that only a few decades later, 80 percent of the world's industrial proletariat would live and work in the Global South, and that the Global North would be partly deindustrialized. However, Emmanuel somehow anticipated this development in 1976:

> Another specific feature of the multinational company (MNC) which is vaguely considered to generate prejudice but which, if it really exists, is eminently advantageous, is its independence of the domestic market of the receiving country. Since the main problem of capitalism is not to produce but to sell, less traditional capital was attracted by the low wage rates of certain countries than was discouraged by the narrowness of the local market associated with such wages. This lack of capital in turn prevented growth and hence wage increases. The result was deadlock. In theory the solution was production for exports alone. But except for standardized primary products, such an operation appeared to transcend the fief of the traditional capitalist. In any case, it has never occurred.
>
> The MNC, with its own sales network abroad and, even more, its own consumption in the case of a conglomerate, would not be put off by the lack of 'pre-existing' local outlets. It would take advantage of both the low wages of the periphery and the high wages of the center. I have no idea of the relative importance of the phenomenon. Here, as elsewhere, statistical information is lacking. Albert Michalet considers that it is very extensive in quantity and very important from the point of view of quality. All I can say is that, if this is so, this gives us for the first time the possibility of breaking the most pernicious, vicious circle which was holding up the development of the Third World. It is rather a matter for rejoicing.[14]

Emmanuel was aware of the role that the transnational companies had in the Third World both in terms of value transfer, but also in terms of developing the productive forces and technology transfer. He shared Marx's dialectical approach concerning the development of capitalism. Marx on the one hand affirms the positive, progressive features of capitalism: new technology and development of science, industrialization, urbanization, mass literacy, and so on. On the other hand, he denounces the exploitation, the human alienation, the commodification of social relations, false ideology, and colonialist genocide, all of which are inherent in the modernization process.

This dialectical conception of capitalism permeated Marx's writings. In

---

14 Emmanuel, Arghiri (1976a), 'The Multinational corporations and inequality of development,' *International Social Science Journal*, XXVIII, 4, p. 754-772. Paris: UNESCO.

the *Communist Manifesto*, Marx describes the rise of capitalism as a progressive stage of historical development. In the first pages he describes 'modern industry,' 'modern bourgeois society,' 'modern workers,' 'modern state power,' 'modern productive forces,' and 'modern relations of production.'[15] In the preface to *Capital*, Marx writes that the 'purpose' of the book is to "disclose the economic law of motion of modern society."[16] Marx defended modernity because it prepared the way to a more fully developed modernity—socialism.[17]

When we analyze the role of transnational companies in development, we must make sure to distinguish between when we discuss development inside the framework of the capitalist mode of production, or when we discuss the possibility of the appropriation of the productive forces by the people—the transfer to a new mode of production. In the end of the 20th century, the capitalist mode of production was for sure still vital and dominated the world system. A transformation of the mode of production was not on the agenda. Capitalism in the Global North was bad, but underdeveloped capitalism in the South was worse.[18]

THE DECLINE OF NEOLIBERALISM

From the mid-1970s, until the turn of the millennium, neoliberalism was on the offensive. At first, it weakened the state "at home" through the deregulation of transnational movements of capital and trade, privatization, and cuts in welfare. Then transnational capital outsourced jobs to low-wage countries for higher profits. However, the social consequences of these acts began to change the balance between aspects. The outsourcing of jobs, erosion of the welfare state, and migration problems generated nationalism in the North, demanding a stronger national state as a bulwark against the negative impact of global market forces. The "structural adjustments" of neoliberalism in the Global South had the same effect. By the turn of the millennium, the negative social consequences of neoliberalism began to weaken the political dominance of its institutions. The financial crisis of 2007-2008 further strengthened the demand for state control of capital. The balance in the neoliberal contradiction tipped to-

---

15 Marx, Karl and Engels, Friedrich (1848), *The Communist Manifesto*, MESW, Vol. I.

16 Marx (1867), *Capital*, Vol. I.

17 Therborn, Göran (1996), 'Dialectics of Modernity: On Critical Theory and the Legacy of Twentieth Century Marxism,' *New Left Review*, I/215 Jan/Feb. 1996.

18 Lauesen (2014), 'The Crises of Imperialism and the Prospect of Socialism,' forthcoming in: *Imperialism*. Mexico City: Revista de Estudios Globales. Análisis Histórico y Cambio Social (REG), de la Universidad de Murcia.

wards nationalism and the nation-state.

The financial crisis was a wake-up call to the Chinese leadership. They realized that neoliberalism was no longer a dynamic force to develop the productive forces, but increasingly a problem in the form of economic stagnation, social inequality, and environmental problems. With Xi Jinping in power in 2012, China began to shift the cycle of capital accumulation from being focused on the world-market to more emphasis on domestic circulation, by tripling the wage level and massive state programs for internal investment that have pulled millions out of poverty in the countryside.

After its encounter with neoliberalism, China emerged as a major economic power. China was able for the first time in two hundred years to break the polarizing dynamic of capitalism between the center and the periphery. It is a historical break of significant size. A nation of 1.4 billion people made the change from one of the poorest countries on earth in 1949 to the leading industrial power in the world-system, with 35% of the world's gross production, compared with the U.S.'s 12%.[19] The consequence was an increasing discordance between global capitalism and China's national project of development.

FROM NEOLIBERAL GLOBALIZATION TO GEOPOLITICAL CONFRONTATION

With the crises of global neoliberalism from 2007, the decline of the U.S. hegemony, the rise of China, and the development towards a multipolar world-system, the world is undergoing a profound change, not seen in the past hundred years.

The global trade pattern is under transformation. After two hundred years, North—South trade is declining, and South—South trade is on the rise. This is manifested by huge development in transport and infrastructure projects in the Global South, facilitating this new trade pattern. The global value transfer of unequal exchange from South to North has begun to decline for the first time in the past 150 years, from a zenith in 2011 of 2.9 trillion dollars to 2.3 dollars in 2017.[20] The rising wage-levels in China are contributing

---

19 Baldwin, Richard (Jan. 17, 2024), 'China is the world's sole manufacturing superpower: A line sketch of the rise.' VoxEU, https://cepr.org/voxeu/columns/china-worlds-sole-manufacturing-superpower-line-sketch-rise.

20 Hickel, Jason, Sullivan, Dylan and Zoomkawala, Huzaifa (2021), 'Plunder in the Post-Colonial Era: Quantifying Drain from the Global South through Unequal Exchange, 1960-2018,' *New Political Economy*, Vol. 26, no. 6, pp. 1030-1047.

to this decline:

> Between 1978 and 2018, on average, one hour of work in the United States was exchanged for almost forty hours of Chinese work. However, from the middle of the 1990s [...] we observed a very marked decrease in unequal exchange, without it completely disappearing. In 2018, 6.4 hours of Chinese labor were still exchanged for 1 hour of U.S. labor.[21]

Besides the transfer of value from South to North by unequal exchange, debt has contributed to solving the problem of lack of consumption power in the global capitalist accumulation circuit, by pushing the problem of imbalance between production and consumption into the future.[22] The amount of debt has grown steadily in the history of capitalism and accelerated in the past decade, not least during the Covid-19 epidemic. Global debt (of governments, corporations, and households) stood at 120% of global GDP in 1980. By 2021 global debt reached 355% of global GDP,[23] which means that during the neoliberal era, debt grew three times faster than global production. This debt bubble can burst in a major financial crisis and throw the system into deep crises.[24]

A special form of creating consumption power is printing money without backing in expanded production, as the U.S. has done in the past fifty years. The U.S. can do this because the dollar has the status of "world-money" in trade and international finance, a position reached by U.S. political dominance in the Bretton Woods institutions: the IMF and the World Bank. Trillions of dollars are circulating as payment in trade and financial transactions, and are stored as deposits in banks. The U.S. gets commodities and services for these dollars, as they enter the world market, but they never return as claims on commodities produced in the U.S. A precondition for this advantage is the continued U.S. dominance in world finance; however, this has changed. The transformation in trade structure is accompanied by changes in finance and banking in the world-system. Alternatives to the Bretton Woods institutions are being developed in the context of BRICS+. This gives the Global South possibilities to invest and trade in their own currency instead of dollars and lend money without "structural adjustments" and other political conditions.

---

21 Long, Zhiming; Feng, Xhixuan; Li, Bangxi and Herrera, Rémy (2020), 'U.S.-China Trade War. Has the Real "Thief" Finally Been Unmasked?' pp. 8-9, *Monthly Review*, Vol. 72, no. 5, October 2020, pp. 6-14.

22 Emmanuel, Arghiri (1984), *Profit and Crises*, p. 356. London: Heinemann.

23 IMF (2021), 'Global Debt Reaches a Record $226 Trillion.' IMF, https://www.imf.org/en/Blogs/Articles/2021/12/15/blog-global-debt-reaches-a-record-226-trillion.

24 Smith, John (2022), 'A supernova looms: world debt reaches critical mass.' openDemocracy, https://www.opendemocracy.net/en/oureconomy/global-debt-interest-rate-hikes-capitalist-supernova/.

In the 1970s we hoped that the Third World liberation movements would cut off the pipelines of value transfer. But capitalism was still vital. Neoliberal globalization offered an escape route. However, now it seems that the capitalist mode of production has reached the limit of exploitation of the proletariat in the periphery, and it is on a collision course with the global ecosystem. Capitalism is no longer progressive in terms of development of the productive forces—it is becoming irrational, destructive and prevents progress for humanity. We are approaching the situation where they are becoming fetters of development.

The center no longer has the advantage of a monopoly of high-tech industrial production, and they are losing the grip of global finance. To uphold its hegemony, the U.S. is now splitting and eroding the neoliberal world market, which has served them so well for fifty years, providing huge profits and cheap commodities for consumers in the Global North. They are doing it by trade wars, sanctions, and blockades. The formerly mighty World Trade Organization, which settles international trade disputes, has been weakened by Trump and Biden, as its verdicts now go counter to US interests. The U.S turned to political pressure and military means in a geopolitical struggle for dominance. This strategy is not an expression of strength, but of weakness.

The division of labor created by neoliberal globalization, with Asia as the "factory of the world" and the West as consumer societies, meant that the geopolitical importance of controlling trading routes became paramount. Hence the importance of the gateway to Asia in the North—Ukraine—and in the South—Palestine, the Suez, the Persian Gulf, and Red Sea. In a geopolitical struggle, NATO led by the U.S. is trying to secure dominance of the Euro-Asian corridor, and get a regime change in Russia and China, to pro-Western Yeltsin-type governments.

Through the proxy-war on Ukrainian soil between Russia and NATO, the US has disciplined Europe back under its command. The U.S. is dragging Europe into the confrontation with Russia, China, Iran, Cuba, Venezuela, and the Global South in general. NATO membership is not an *a la carte* dish; Europe must swallow the whole American menu, including U.S. policy in the Middle and Far East.

The Contradiction of the End Game

Marx underestimated the longevity of capitalism, as did Lenin and Mao. Many of us in the "1968 generation" have predicted the end of capitalism several times, and our hopes for world revolution were frustrated. This has led to the mistaken belief that capitalism can assimilate all critiques and innovate out of all problems.

Universalization of the present denies the historical specificity and transitory character of capitalist social relations. Capitalism has successfully reproduced its existence for 200 years, but there are limits to this reproduction. It is not a system in balance. The polarized development between center and periphery generated by the imperialist value transfer enabled it to reproduce itself. However, this dynamic is challenged by the rise of China.

Like the late Immanuel Wallerstein (1930-2019), I believe that the decline of U.S. hegemony forebodes the end of capitalism.[25] This will not take place within a decade, but it seems clear that the twenty-first century is the autumn of the capitalist system. The industrialization of the Global South in recent decades signals a significant change in the dynamics of global capitalism itself. The system is losing the balancing force of the center-periphery dichotomy.

Certainly, an industrialized Global South will not develop into a prosperous capitalism as in Northwestern Europe and North America. Neither China, India, Indonesia, nor Brazil has a periphery to exploit, substantial enough to feed the development of welfare capitalism, and ecologically, the world cannot sustain such a capitalist world-system. However, the development of the productive forces in the Global South will threaten the privileged positions of the U.S. and the E.U. and accelerate the crises of global capitalism.

From the Global North, the U.S., in its desperate struggle to uphold its hegemony, is disrupting the imperialist pipeline system of globalized production and trade. From the Southern flank, China has succeeded in diminishing the imperial rent of unequal exchange, while simultaneously breaking the technological monopoly of Western corporations and financial institutions, providing an alternative for the Global South in their economic development.

In "the end game," global capitalism will be haunted by economic crises generated by the inherent contradiction between the need to expand production and the lack of corresponding consumption power. Profits will decline and accumulation will come to a halt.

The development of the productive forces in the Global South signals not only a shift in the dynamics of capitalism, but also enhances the material conditions for the development of socialism.

---

25 Wallerstein, Immanuel (2013), 'Structural Crisis, or why capitalists may no longer find capitalism rewarding.' in: Wallerstein, Collins, Mann, Derluguian, and Calhoun (2013), *Does Capitalism has a Future?*, pp. 23-24. Oxford: Oxford University Press.

The Current Principal Contradiction

What is the driving force in this transition? The first step in answering this question is to identify the principal contradiction, as this will tell us where to start and is a guide for further analysis. If the development of global capitalism and the world system of states is one process, then at any given point in time, this process has a principal contradiction emerging from the multiple contradictions in the capitalist mode of production, driving its development forward. The principal contradiction affects regional, national, and local contradictions decisively. However, the interaction between the principal contradiction and national and local contradictions is not one-sided. Due to the feedback effects, local contradictions affect the principal contradiction, as they push and change the relations between the aspects of the principal contradiction.[26]

Since the late 1970s, the principal contradiction has been between transnational capital's neoliberal globalization project and the nation-state's attempt to regulate capitalism. Until the turn of the millennium, transnational capital was the dominant aspect of this contradiction. However, the consequences of neoliberalism, in both the Global North and South, generated nationalist demands for a stronger state, as bulwarks against globalization. In the past decades, globalized capitalism and its institutions came under increasing pressure from both right and left-wing nationalist forces.

The international division of labor, created by neoliberal outsourcing, has changed the power structure in the world-system. Northern transnational capital turned China into "the factory of the world," but it did not manage to keep China as a periphery of the center. China broke the historical polarizing tendency in the capitalist mode of production. China used the neoliberal intrusion to develop its national project—"Socialism with Chinese Characteristics."

The US, the EU, Japan, New Zealand, and Australia, have united to uphold U.S. hegemony. They constitute one aspect of the current principal contradiction. The other aspect is headed by China allied with a conglomerate of states which, for different reasons, are opposed to the continuation of U.S. hegemony and want a multipolar world system. They are united in the ambition to change the North-South structure, which has dominated the world-system for the last two centuries and expand South-South relations.

The U.S. can no longer uphold its hegemony by economic and financial means, but must rely on its military power. The decline of neoliberalism is not

---

26 Lauesen, Torkil (2020), *The Principal Contradiction*. Montreal: Kersplebedeb.

in the interest of transnational capital, which is dependent on their global production chains to generate surplus value, and access to the entire world market to realize the profit. If the 2007-8 crisis was the crisis of financial neoliberalism, then the current crisis is the crisis of globalized production. However, transnational capital cannot distance itself from its political leadership, which provides security for its operation. There is no way out of the dilemma for transnational capital, as it is the crisis of neoliberalism itself which has created this situation. The immediate need of political imperialism overrides the interests of transnational capital.

U.S. policy is becoming self-destructive; it shatters the world market, on which it has built its power since the end of the Second World War. Its political system erodes from within, as the elite is split, a split that continues down to the people of the U.S. The only vision is "making America great again," which is not shared by the rest of the world.

The disintegration of globalization is a reconfiguration of the power structure in the world-system. In retrospect, China was admitted into the global trade regime in 1972 because of the U.S. rivalry with its chief opponent, the Soviet Union. Beating the Soviets first, then China, was the plan. US superiority in technology and finance at the time gave it the confidence to open its global trade regime to any country willing to play the game, regardless of ideology. In this phase, the globalization regime was a gigantic profit machine based on global production chains and extraction of cheap production factors from the Global South. Today, as the U.S. is no longer economically competitive, it uses instead its military power in alliance with Europe and Japan for geopolitical struggle to rule the world-system.

"Socialism or Barbarism"

Two months before his death in 2019, Immanuel Wallerstein wrote his ultimate commentary: "This is the end; this is the beginning," leaving his final reflection:

> The world might go down further by-paths. Or it may not. I have indicated in the past that I thought the crucial struggle was a class struggle, using class in a very broadly defined sense. What those who will be alive in the future can do is to struggle with themselves so this change may be a real one. I still think that and therefore I think there is a 50-50 chance that we'll make it to transformatory change, but only 50-50.[27]

This is a bit like Rosa Luxemburg's statement in her 1916 anti-war pam-

---

27 Wallerstein, Immanuel (July 1st, 2019), 'This is the end; this is the beginning.' Immanuel Wallerstein, https://iwallerstein.com/this-is-the-end-this-is-the-beginning/.

phlet, 'The Crisis of German Social Democracy,' "Bourgeois society stands at the crossroads, either transition to Socialism or regression into Barbarism,"[28] or Marx and Engels in the *Communist Manifesto*, speaking of class struggles resulting in "either a revolutionary constitution of society at large or the common ruin of the contending classes." [29]

The endgame of capitalism takes place within a framework of its structural crisis economically, politically, and ecologically. The structural crisis entails that the system is out of balance and that conjunctions do not come in regular waves, but by sudden uncontrollable swings. We have reached the stage in the history of planet earth where capitalism is the main driver of systemic changes, disrupting ecological balances and expediting gradual changes over millennia to now occur in decades. A revolutionary break with capitalism is not just a question of removing capitalism's fetters on human development; it is necessary to stop the destruction of the earth.

Climate change is a reality; it is the rate of destruction that is unclear. Where will the next disaster strike, and how big will it be? The growing ecological and climatic problems as well as the scramble for the Earth's natural resources can trigger revolutionary situations, as it changes living conditions, causing natural disasters and refugee movement. We are under time pressure to make the transition, due to capitalism's continued impact on climate change. If we move into the second half of this century, some kind of "lifeboat socialism" may be the only solution to climate change and destruction of the earth's ecosystem.

Then there is the danger of nuclear war, in a world system with intensified geopolitical struggle, induced by the declining hegemon. The U.S. is the world's mightiest military power. Europe is arming at an unprecedented scale. NATO stands for 60% of the world's total military expenses, Russia 4 %, and China 13%.[30] It is the U.S. which has more 900 military bases all over the world, with the common slogan: "No beach out of reach."

Many states in the world-system have, and more states are acquiring, nuclear weapons and the means to launch them, increasing the mathematical risks of mass destruction. A war between the world's leading powers could very well become the world's principal contradiction if they escalate into the use of nu-

---

28 Luxemburg, Rosa (1916), *The Junius Pamphlet: The Crisis in German Social Democracy*, Ch. 1. Marxists Internet Archive, https://www.marxists.org/archive/luxemburg/1915/junius/ch01.htm.

29 Marx and Engels (1848), *Manifesto of the Communist Party*, MESW.

30 SIPRI (2023), 'Trends in the World's Military Expenditure.' SIPRI, https://www.sipri.org/sites/default/files/2023-04/2304_fs_milex_2022.pdf.

clear weapons. While nuclear weapons are essentially defensive weapons, the decision to use nuclear weapons is in the hands of individual, sometimes irrational human beings. The end of capitalism can be chaos or a transition to socialism; it depends on the outcome of our struggle.

Anti-Imperialism Today

Anti-imperialism today cannot be the same as it was in "the long 1960s." History does not repeat itself; it moves ahead. The high revolutionary spirit, and the success of the anti-colonial struggle, from the late 1940s until mid-70s, were due to a combination of contradictions in the world-system: the contradiction between the Socialist Bloc versus the U.S., and the contradiction between the emerging Third World on one side, and U.S. neocolonialism on the other side. This set of interlinked global contradictions opened up a wave of anti-imperialist liberation struggles, with a socialist perspective, across Asia, Africa, and Latin America.

All this changed with the counter-offensive of neoliberal globalization from the mid-1970s. It became difficult to continue national liberation into a socialist transformation. However, neoliberalism was not "the end of history." The result of outsourcing of industrial production was, on the one hand, the transfer of value from South to North. However, on the other hand, the development of productive forces in the Global South began to break up, the century old polarization between a rich North and poor South. In the 70s, the Third World demanded a "New World Order," which came to nothing. Today the Global South is creating a new world order.

One example is BRICS. The cooperation between Brazil, Russia, India, China, and South Africa, which was enlarged in September 2022, now comprising 46 percent of the world's population, and 36 percent of the world economy, counterbalancing the G7 (U.S., Canada, the UK, France, Italy, Germany, and Japan.) with only 10 percent of the world population and 30 percent of the world economy. In the future BRICS+ will further outweigh the G7. BRICS+ is not an anti-capitalist organization. But it is a step in the right direction. The emerging multipolar world system consists of a complex of contradictory currents—between hegemonism and counter-hegemonism, conservative and progressive, capitalist and socialist forces. This is how the world looks. We have to keep in mind Marx's words, that no social order disappears before all the productive forces, for which there is space, have been developed. We are reaching this point. Then—as Marx continues—comes the period of social revolution.[31] The challenge is to navigate in this sea of interconnected contradictions.

---

31 Marx (1859), *'Preface,' A Contribution to the Critique of Political Economy*, MESW.

Like in the sixties, the contradiction between the North, trying to uphold its hegemony, and the Global South, can create space for movements and nations advancing towards socialism. The development of the productive forces in the Global South has placed them in a much better position to achieve this goal than in the sixties. The U.S. is still the dominant aspect in the principal contradiction, but the South is on the offensive, encircling the center. While the transformative power of the Third World in the sixties was based on the "revolutionary spirit"—the attempted ideological dominance over the economic development—the current transformative power of the Global South is based on its economic strength.

Things may develop faster than we expect. The next decades will be dramatic and dangerous. The transition will not be a tea party. We will see sudden changes in political alliances and in this scenario, we need to stay the course and stick to a clear socialist perspective. At the same time, we are working under time pressure due to climate change.

From Utopian Socialism to Realizing Socialism

A rigid and idealistic perception of socialism in national and international struggles obscures the complexity and changeability of current class behaviors and interests. Again, with Marx's words in mind: the new relations of production never appear before the material conditions of their existence have matured in the womb of the old society. There is not and has never been any "pure" socialism in the world—it is not possible. It cannot exist in the real world of dominating capitalism. Only transitional modes of production and states have existed. Socialism is a project under construction, and the first step is to cut loose from the shackles of capitalism controlled by the U.S.

We are not to be utopians; our development of socialism must be based on dialectical and historical materialism. The attempts to build socialism in the past two centuries, must be seen as part of a long transition process, rather than a row of failures, attempts which have contributed to the progress of the transition by modifying capitalism as well as a learning process for building socialism.[32] The development of socialism contains negations, imperfections, and impurities, as it is developed from the reality of the capitalist mode of production.

Anti-imperialist strategy must contain *real existing concrete* counter-hegemonic forces capable of challenging the dominant power structure. It is not enough to wish for some pure self-organized workers movement to take

---

32 Lauesen, Torkil (2024), *The Long Transition to Socialism and the End of Capitalism*. Washington: Iskra Books.

state power from below, if you cannot point to its real existence. Western Marxists are often trapped in a utopian world where the idea of socialism is superior to the transitional regimes and modes of production, which have emerged in the past hundred years, struggling against a dominant capitalist world system. The Brazilian communist Jones Manoel writes:

> Nothing is socialist transition, and everything is state capitalism [...] The contradictions, the problems, the failures, the mistakes, sometimes even the crimes, mainly happen during this moment of building the new order. So, when the time comes to evaluate the building of a new social order - which is where, apparently, the practice always appears to stray from the purity of theory - the specific appears corrupted in the face of the universal.[33]

The support for a multi-polar world system does not imply avoiding criticism of reactionary tendencies within the BRICS+ states. We must support the Chinese peasants and workers in their class struggle to move towards socialism, which means getting rid of remaining capitalist elements, national or transnational. Forty years of "opening up" to neoliberalism has had an impact on Chinese society; this must be changed.

However, an understanding of the dilemmas and the balance between the need for national development, within the capitalist mode of production, versus advancing socialism nationally and globally, is important on how to relate to the transitional states, in order to defend them against imperialism, but also to advance the transition to socialism. We must support the transitional states' nationalist aspect, against the hostile capitalist states, not only to defend their attempt to develop socialism, but also because they are an essential anti-imperialist component, balancing imperialism and providing breathing space for socialist movements in the remaining capitalist world system. However, we must also push for a socialist transformation by class struggle, wherever we can, to ensure that the socialist aspect dominates the national aspect in the contradictions of the transitional state.

Just as the Soviet Union balanced U.S.-imperialism, making national liberation possible, China balances the U.S., making economic delinking from Western capitalist dominance possible. To avoid the collapse of capitalism into a chaotic abyss, a strong China will be of decisive importance for a global transformation to socialism.

---

33 Manoel, Jones (June 10, 2020), 'Western Marxism Loves Purity and Martyrdom, But Not Real Revolution.' Black Agenda Report, https://www.blackagendareport.com/western-marxism-loves-purity-and martyrdom-not-real-revolution.

The Prospects of Socialism

In the past century, only a revolutionary process, led by communist parties, could unblock the development of the productive forces in the periphery of the world-system, and get the wheels of the economy running again by initiating the development of a "transitional" mode of production. It had to be a "transitional mode" because the world-system was dominated by capitalism. The lack of development of productive forces in the periphery and the hostile world-system hindered an immediate transition to a more advanced socialist modernity. This is the history of the Soviet and Chinese revolutions, and other efforts to move towards socialism in the 20th century. In developing this transitional mode of production, they had to adopt the same dialectic as expressed by Marx, between the progressive role of capitalism and the agony it produces.

Lenin did not believe that socialism was equivalent to the collectivization of poverty. To overcome mass poverty, the Soviet Union was compelled to develop the productive forces. In the New Economic Policy [NEP], the Bolsheviks used the technology and management associated with capitalism to boost production. However, the "commanding heights" of the economy—finance, infrastructure, large industry, and mining—remained in the hands of the state.[34] To avoid getting crushed by German imperialism, the Soviet Union had go through an accelerated industrialization during the 1930s, with huge human costs.

In 1949, China was in a similar position as Russia in 1917. The development of productive forces and technology was among the lowest in the world. China was forcefully isolated and could not import technology from the West. However, the Soviet Union came to its rescue in 1950 and provided China access to its technology. But, due to political disagreements, Soviet technology was cut off in the late 1950s, and China was again isolated from the surrounding world economy.

In the 1970s, under pressure from neoliberal globalization, China had no choice but to build its peculiar form of state capitalism and market socialism to maintain its national project. It could not develop its productive forces without investments and trading with capitalist countries. China had to "open up" to acquire the appropriate technology to develop its productive forces to continue the development of "Socialism with Chinese Characteristics."

---

34 Lenin, V. I. (1922), 'The Role and Functions of the Trade Unions Under the New Economic Policy,' LCW, Vol. 33, p. 188.

Deng Xiaoping's reform strategy does not stem from a necliberal perspective. He advocated for the acceleration of foreign investment capital believing that planning and markets could be applied to serve the development of a socialist system. Nor did Deng introduce economic shock therapy as Yeltsin did in the post-Soviet era. With a reference to Lenin's NEP policy in the Soviet Union, Deng said that "Socialism does not mean shared poverty." In an interview with CBS in 1986, he explained his approach:

> According to Marxism, communist society is based on material abundance. Only when there is material abundance can the principle of a communist society—that is, 'from each according to his ability, to each according to his needs'—be applied [...] There can be no communism with pauperism, or socialism with pauperism. [..] Wealth in a socialist society belongs to the people. To get rich in a socialist society means prosperity for the entire people. The principles of socialism are first, development of production, and second, common prosperity. We permit some people and some regions to become prosperous first, for the purpose of achieving common prosperity faster.[35]

Hence, China, or any other transitionary state should not attempt to avoid contact with globalized capitalism, as they cannot carry on the transformation process towards socialism in isolation from a capitalist mode of production, which is still vital, developing the productive forces and hence a source of advanced technology. In addition, the transitional state's interaction with global capitalism is part of the transition process, as it modifies and presents itself as an alternative to capitalism.

However, "Socialism with Chinese Characteristics" or in any other national form, is only one step. Socialism does not only imply the eradication of poverty within the national framework, but also global equality. It is not possible to raise the living standard of billions of people in the Global South to the level of the U.S. or Germany within the capitalist mode of production. To accommodate their needs, it is not only a change in the relation of productions and patterns of consumption which is needed to develop socialism on a global scale—it is also a continued development of the productive forces and the implementations of the most advanced technology. On this Emmanuel writes:

> Steel, aluminum and copper of which the masses of the center consume today such extravagant quantities, do not serve only to produce automobiles and gadgets. They produce doctors or books as well (it takes a tremendous amount of steel, cement or energy to produce a doctor or to school a village). While no one up to now has laid out the model of this "anti-consumption" society, there exists at least one point on which everyone agrees. That is the absolute priority of the maximization of available leisure, time being the prerequisite for the quality of life. How then can we rid ourselves of "productivism" since for any given physical consumption, whatever its volume, leisure time is an increasing function of the return on time passed at work? [...] Naturally,

---

35 Xiaoping, Deng (Sep. 2, 1986), 'Interview with Mike Wallace of CBS 60 Minutes.' CBS. Here from: *All Asia Times* (Dec. 13, 2006).

if it is shown that the 'consumer society' is in any case a material impossibility on a world scale, the question of choice no longer presents itself for four-fifths of humanity. However, the idea that the remaining one fifth which has the privilege of this type of society would profit from the change is not a statement so obvious that one could excuse oneself from demonstrating.[36]

Global socialism cannot be developed by underdeveloped technology—it requires the most advanced forms of technology.

Advanced Socialism

To move onwards to an advanced socialist mode of production, we need in addition to the "national characteristic of socialism" to develop the universal and global dimension of socialism. An advanced socialist mode of production has to be realized on the global level, as it has to solve the historically inherited problem of inequality between center and periphery in the world-system, as well as the global ecological and climate problems. On the international level, investment and trade should promote global equality and sustainability. A globally planned economy has to be introduced, by a global political institution.

The current transitional mode of production has, respectively, the nationalist development perspective and the universal socialist perspective. An advanced socialist mode of production must be global, but the global transformation has to go through the national state, as the current world-system is politically organized in national states. However, the national framework constitutes a historical constraint that must be taken into account as a necessity, not something we should make into a virtue. China can—and has to—continue the first part of the way to socialism on the national road, as "Socialism with Chinese Characteristics," but the Communist Party has to keep in mind that a developed socialist mode of production can only be realized on the global level.

To realize an advanced socialist mode of production requires not only that China moves in that direction, but also the majority of states in the world-system join the effort. A multipolar world-system will make space for movements and nations to move along this path. In the coming decades, we might see the development of different socialisms with national characteristics, based on different histories and cultures. However, it is essential to move on from the nationalist version towards global socialism, as the national component contains ma-

---

36 Emmanuel, Arghiri (1976b), *Europe-Asia Colloquium. For the use by the Commission on International Relations. Some guidelines for the "problematique" of world economy*, pp. 3-4. IEDES. Dated Oct. 6, 1976. Manuscript found in Emmanuel's archive. Green portfolio marked "Imperialism."

terial for future national disputes. For a transitional state—like China—it is important to keep the right balance between the national interest and socialist transformation, in relation to the surrounding world-system. The nationalist aspect should not dominate the socialist perspective. Nationalist disputes between transitional states will not only benefit capitalism, but also increase the risk of nuclear warfare, and disturb the process to solve the urgent environmental and climate problems. It will block the transition towards advanced global socialism.

The fact that humanity has transitioned from scattered local places, then from states and empires, towards a more and more globalized world-system, equipped with advanced productive forces, means that we have developed a way of living that has damaged the planet, and we have acquired weapons with the ability to destroy human life on earth. But it has also contributed the knowledge and ability to organize and manage the world-system as a whole, needed for an advanced socialist mode of production.[37] The transformation of the relations of production towards socialism does not mean going back to productive forces organized within the national framework. The world's unification has ceased to be an option. It has become a condition of its existence.

What Can Communists in the Imperialist Countries Do?

In this final part, I will update chapter VI in our book: What can communists in the imperialist countries do? Being imprisoned in 1989, the world outside the walls underwent significant changes, as described above. However, at the same time, the basic structure remained the same. The world-system was still divided into a center-periphery structure, although there were pockets of the "Third World" in the center, and "an imperial mode of living" in certain countries and class-layers in the Global South, for example in the Arab Gulf. The effects of globalization of production required that the "parasite state theory," and its related strategy had to be updated.

The strategy should be able to tell us "what is to be done" in concrete practical terms. On the organizational level, we must prepare ourselves and get the necessary skills for the future struggles. We act where we are, what else can we do? However, as the "local" is an integrated part of the world-system, this praxis

---

37 Shigong, Jiang (2021), *A History of Empire Without Empire*. Preface to the Chinese edition of Darwin, John (2008), *After Tamerlane: The Global History of Empire Since 1405*. Red Sails, https://redsails.org/jiang-on-empire/.

will most likely be a consequence of the global principal contradiction. Hence the importance of identifying and analyzing how it interferes with our local contradictions. Which practice can move the principal contradiction in the right direction, to achieve our goals?

There Will Come a Day…

The emergence of the labor aristocracy and the bourgeoisification of the working class is a historical development, and as such, it can and does change. We need to see the imperialist exploitation, in relation to the capitalist exploitation by wage labor in the center, in a dynamic and ever-changing perspective.

Unequal exchange developed up through the 19th century as colonialism divided the world into rich and poor countries, with growing differences in wage levels. Unequal exchange accelerated throughout the 20th century, providing super-profits for capital and cheap goods, based on low-wage labor in the periphery, for the consumers in the imperialist core.

The acquired value, through the consumption of goods produced in the Global South has throughout the 20th century been greater than the surplus value created by labor in the imperialist countries. The balance between appropriation by consumption on one side, and the exploitation of labor in the Global North on the other, is quite concrete and can be calculated, both in terms of transfer on the national level and for individuals.[38]

This perspective of a balance between appropriation of value through consumption, and exploitation by wage labor, must also be applied to the political consequences of imperialism in the Global North. In the description of unequal exchange's political consequences, in the form of the "parasite state," and the "imperial mode of living," it is important to keep in mind that these phenomena are historical. Just as unequal exchange can explain the emergence of these political trends, changes in the balance between appropriation through consumption and exploitation by wage labor, in a national context, will have political consequences.

There is of course no one-to-one relationship between the above-mentioned economic balance and the revolutionary potential of a given working class. Want and misery do not necessarily lead to a left turn, sometimes the opposite. The erosion of the "imperial mode of living" in the past decade

---

38 Lauesen, Torkil (2023), *Unequal Exchange on the Individual Level*. Arghiri Emmanuel Association, https://unequalexchange.org/2023/07/06/unequal-exchange-on-the-individual-level/.

has led to the development of populist right-wing movements and even fascism in the Northern working class, allying themselves with the ruling class in the attempt to uphold imperialist dominance. In the coming decades, with a deepening economic crisis, it will be an important task to convince the working class that their long-term interest is to join the anti-imperialist struggle, to put an end to global capitalism. The struggle against fascism may, as in the 1930s, be of paramount importance.

The explanation of bourgeoisification as a historical, economic, and political development in capitalism opens up the possibility of change in the position and attitude of the working class.

Without this historical perspective, the "parasite state" theory becomes static and loses its revolutionary content. Via this double perspective on the relation between exploitation in the national framework and international exploitation, the theory can explain both the historical process of bourgeoisification and the working class's support for colonialism and imperialism up through the 20th century, but at the same time maintain a future possibility of this class as gravediggers of capitalism.

If one denies the significance and consequences of imperialism's transfusion of value to the working class in the Global North, one falls into the fog of seeing the purely economic struggle as a revolutionary struggle on the road to socialism. If one denies that the highly paid workers in the imperialist countries produce value, surplus value, and so profit, then you reject the possibility that the working class, in my part of the world, can play a role in the struggle against capitalism. Moreover, one loses sight of political activity, and gives up on Lenin's assignment for us:

> To be able to seek, find and correctly determine the specific path or the particular turn of events that will *lead* the masses to the real, decisive and final revolutionary struggle— such is the main objective of communism in Western Europe and in America today.[39]

The hallmark of a Marxist is that you have a political analysis, strategy, and praxis wherever you are.

For twenty years, the "parasite state" theory gave us sufficient knowledge and basis to support the anti-imperialist struggle of the Third World, with the perspective that their victory would create a revolutionary situation in our part of the world by cutting off the possibilities of imperialism's exploitation. The plan did not come through. The world changed while we were busy with our activities. However, I do not have regret. The national liberation struggle moved the world in the right direction and prepared for the next stage in the struggle.

---

39 Lenin, V. I. (1920), "*Left-Wing" Communism: an Infantile Disorder*, LCW, Vol. 31, p. 112.

After half a century of economic globalization, imperialism is once again dividing the world into economic and political blocs, such as the West against the Rest. In some ways, we stand in the same situation as in "the long sixties." The Third World then—the Global South now—are demanding a new World Order. The difference is that in the 70s, it was a demand that the imperialist center could, and did, ignore. Today, the Global South has acquired the productive forces to build a new world order. In the Global South, there is again a striving for political and not least economic independence from imperial dictates.

Anti-imperialism today can take the form of the de-linking of nations in the South from the global production chains and the US-dominated finance, banking, and the use of dollars as world currency. The U.S. declining hegemony and China's emergence as a major global economic and political power makes space for new social movements and opportunities for nations to develop socialism. This change is already creating a political and economic crisis in our part of the world on top of the ecological crisis of capitalism.

How will this affect the political struggle? Will the working class move to the right and support imperialism to defend its "imperial mode of living"? Alternatively, will it go to the left and stand by the nations and movements in the Global South, based on a common position as exploited labor?

As the endgame of capitalism develops in the coming decades, the anti-imperialist struggle will intensify in the center itself. It might begin as efforts to limit imperialist intervention in the Global South, but as the economic and political crises gets deeper, the struggle for another world order will enter the center. Capitalism needs to be uprooted in the center to put an end to imperialism.

Amílcar Cabral led the struggle against the Portuguese colonizers in Guinea Bissau and Cape Verde from 1963 until he was assassinated by Portuguese agents in 1973. He had an important message for the European left about its tasks in the revolutionary struggle:

> Another thing you can do is to support the really revolutionary national liberation movements by all possible means. You must analyze and study these movements and combat in Europe, by all possible means, everything which can be used to further the repression against our peoples. [...] If we are fighting together, then I think the main aspect of our solidarity is extremely simple: it is to fight—I don't think there is any need to discuss this very much. We are struggling in Guinea with guns in our hands, you must struggle in your countries as well—I don't say with guns in your hands, I'm not going to tell you how to struggle, that's your business; but you must find the best means and the best forms of fighting against our common enemy: this is the best form of solidarity. There are, of course, other secondary forms of solidarity: publishing material, sending medicine, etc.; I can guarantee you that if tomorrow we make a breakthrough, and you are engaged in an armed struggle against imperialism in Europe we will send you some

medicine too.[40]

The war in Gaza since October 2023 has created a new generation of anti-imperialists in the Global North, not seen since the protests against the Vietnam War. The mobilization of solidarity with the Palestinian struggle is also a schooling in organization, and learning about how the system works: the powerful instruments of the state, the media, and imperialism in general. Anti-imperialists will be a minority, but an important minority. In the solidarity movement with Palestine, we see the local people standing shoulder to shoulder with Palestinians in the diaspora. Refugees and migrant workers can be an anti-imperialist Trojan Horse within the Global North. Because of their position in production and services, they are not powerless, and their affiliation with family and hope for the economic development of their homelands in the Global South may be stronger than their loyalty to a state that barely tolerates their stay.

Let me end this text by summing up what communists in the Global North can do in a programme:

BASIC TENETS

1. Capitalism has been imperialistic since its beginning as the dominant mode of production in the world-system. As such, it cannot reproduce nor maintain itself without imperialism.

2. Imperialism is a global system of value transfer characterized by a hierarchical system of states that compete with each other for their share in captured value.

3. Value transfer is facilitated by economic mechanisms, while war, geopolitics, culture, and ideology reproduce it and maintain it.

4. The value flows from the periphery to the core and, beyond capitalist profits, provides a material basis for higher living standards of the working and middle strata of the states pertaining to the core. Hence, imperialism proposes material incentives to the Global North workers to maintain the status quo and improve its position within the existing political and economic order, constituting the so-called "labor aristocracy."

5. Any action, ideology, and movement that challenges the existing capitalist world-system and aims to transform it to abolish imperialism in favor of a new, just society free of oppression and exploitation, we denote as anti-systemic.

---

40 Cabral, Amilcar (1964), 'Brief Analysis of the Social Structure in Guinea.' Marxists Internet Archive, https://www.marxists.org/subject/africa/cabral/1964/bassg.htm.

IDEOLOGY

6. We oppose the ideological tendencies identified as Western Marxism that negate the role, importance or even existence of imperialism in the world-system; that deny the agency of the people of Third World in systemic change; that oppose the national and anti-colonial struggle of the oppressed people, and that reject the legacy and lessons (positive and negative, equally) of actually existing socialist states.

7. We oppose all other ideologies that perpetuate national, racial, ethnic, gendered, religious division and oppression, as it is a basis for super-exploitation and as such, for the reproduction of the imperialist system.

8. We are firm in defense of ideas, movements, communities and states that wage the anti-systemic struggle for a new world-system without imperialism.

9. We are open to all ideas that follow the above parameters.

STRATEGY

10. If capitalism is globalized in the economic sense, and if we consider the development of the world-system as one process, then this process, according to dialectic materialism, has a principal contradiction emerging from contradictions in the capitalist mode of production and is reflected in world politics.

11. These successive principal contradictions affected all regional, national, and local contradictions decisively. However, the interaction between the principal contradiction and national and local contradictions is not one-sided. Due to the feedback effects, and the struggle between the aspects, the principal contradiction changes in the course of history. The local situation is defined by the interaction between the global principal contradiction and the contradiction on the regional, national, and local levels.

12. Hence the importance of identifying the principal contradiction as the starting point of developing a strategy.

13. The result of neoliberal globalization was on the one hand an increase of the transfer of value from South to North. However, on the other hand, the development of productive forces in the Global South, began to break up the century old polarization between the Global North and South. China became the leading industrial power in the world. Hence

the current principal contradiction is between declining US hegemony versus the rise of China and its attempt to build a multipolar world system.

14. In the current phase, the decline of US hegemony is a condition for advancing a socialist transition. Just as the Soviet Union, balancing imperialism, made decolonization possible, a multipolar world system will strengthen the anti-imperialist struggle globally. To avoid the collapse of capitalism into a chaotic abyss, a strong China will be of decisive importance, for a global transformation to socialism.

15. The U.S. is still the dominant aspect in the principal contradiction, but the South is on the offensive. While the transformative power of the Third World, in the sixties, was based on the "revolutionary spirit"—the attempted ideological dominance over the economic development, the current transformative power of the Global South is based on its economic strength. This places them in a better position in the future struggle.

16. Since the aim is not only to understand the world, but to change it, the strategy should be able to tell us "what is to be done" in concrete practical terms to push the principal contradiction in the right direction.

Praxis

17. Imperialism is a global system and requires a global anti-systemic response. Imperialism cannot be fought exclusively within nation-state borders in isolation from other struggles.

18. Anti-systemic movement must be globally coordinated, and its priorities must be set accordingly, and not opportunistically for local short-term objectives.

19. The anti-imperialist struggle is centered in the Global South, where exploitation and oppression are most urgent, and environmental destruction greatest. We must support popular struggles in the Global South not only in words, but in deeds, and by material means.

20. We in the Global North should not be passive bystanders, waiting for the proletariat in the Global South to create a revolutionary situation in our part of the world. We must make sure that the North is no safe "hinterland" for imperialism, which means struggle against right-wing nationalism, racism, and most importantly against imperialist political and military intervention in the Global South.

21. If our struggle is more than words, it will have consequences. We should plan and be prepared for this, on the personal and the organizational level.

How will the global struggle develop in the next decade? How can I, and my organization, fit into the analysis of the objective and subjective forces of transition? What kind of support can we deliver? The specific ways and which means to use in the struggle depend on the type of organization, and the specific political situation and place.

22. The criminalization of anti-imperialism will be increased. We will be considered national traitors—but that is better than being class traitors. On a personal level, it is not easy to be at odds, not only with the state, but also with mainstream society. There are strong forces, which aim to integrate us in the system. It will be difficult to maintain a clear-cut opposition to the system and accept that economic and political crises are part of the "endgame" of capitalism, and we should welcome it. It will not be a walk in the park.

23. The objective conditions—material—conditions for a transformation towards socialism are excellent. The capitalist system is in a deep structural crisis, economically, politically and ecologically. The alternative is not some blurred vision in the haze. As you are reading it is under concrete development—economically, and politically. We are in a revolutionary epoch. The socialist subjective forces are developing.

Bibliography

Abbreviations

LCW Lenin, V.I., Collected Works, Vols. 1-45. Moscow: Progress Publishers.

MEAB Marx, Karl and Engels, Frederick (1971), Articles on Britain. Moscow: Progress Publishers.

MECW Marx, Karl and Engels, Frederick, Collected Works, Vols. 1-50. Moscow: Progress Publishers.

MEOC Marx, Karl and Engels, Frederick (1968), On Colonialism. Moscow: Progress Publishers.

MESC Marx, Karl and Engels, Frederick (1965), Selected Correspondence. Moscow: Progress Publishers.

MESW Marx, Karl and Engels, Frederick (1970), Selected Works. Moscow: Progress Publishers.

Literature

Amin, Samir (1976), *Unequal Development*. New York: Monthly Review Press.

Bunting, Brian (1969), *The Rise of the South African Reich*. London: Penguin.

Busch, Klaus (1972), 'Problemen des Klassenkampfes,' *Deutsches Institut für Wirtschaftsforschung*, Wochenbericht, 22/72. Berlin.

Castro, Fidel (Sept. 27 1981), 'Speech at the Conference of the Inter-Parliamentary Union in Havana, 15-23 September 1981,' *Granma*. Havana.

Dandekar, V.M. (Jan. 12, 1980), 'Bourgeois Politics of the Working Class,' *Economic and Political Weekly*, Vol. XV. Bombay.

Davis, Robert (1973), 'The White Working Class in South Africa,' *New Left Review*, no. 82, Dec. 1973. London.

Dillard, Dudley (1967), *Economic Development of the North Atlantic Community*. New Jersey: Prentice-Hall.

DKU (1975), *Kampens Vej*. Copenhagen.

Dunning, John H. (1970), *Studies in International Investment*. London.

Edwards, H.W. (1978), *Labor Aristocracy: Mass Base of Social Democracy*. Stockholm: Aurora.

Emmanuel, Arghiri (see also 'Works By Arghiri Emmanuel,' below)

— (1976), 'The Socialist Project in a Disintegrated Capitalist World,' *Socialist Thought and Practice*, no. 9, September 1976.

— (1972), *Unequal Exchange: A Study of the Imperialist Trade*. New York: Monthly Review Press.

— (1975), 'The Unequal Exchange (A Summary),' unpublished paper presented at the Conference on 'New Approaches to Trade' at IDS, University of Sussex.

— (1975), *Unequal Exchange Revisited*, IDS Discussion Paper no. 77. Brighton: Institute of Development Studies at the University of Sussex.

— (1972), 'White Settler Colonialism and the Myth of Investment Imperialism,' *New Left Review*, no. 73. London.

Engels, Friedrich, 'England in 1845 and in 1885,' MEAB.

—, 'The English Elections,' MEAB.

—, 'Karl Marx: A Contribution to the Critique of Political Economy' MECW, Vol. 16.

—, 'The Movements of 1847,' MECW, Vol. 6.

—, 'Socialism: Utopian and Scientific,' MESW.

Engels, Friedrich, Lafargue, Paul, Lafargue Laura (1959), *Frederick Engels-Paul and Laura Lafargue: Correspondence*, Vol. I. Moscow: Foreign Languages Publishing House.

Frank, A.G. (1981), *Crisis in the Third World*. London: Heinemann.

Fröbel, F., Heinrichs, J. and Kreye, O. (1980), *The New International Division of Labour*. Cambridge

GATT (1976), *International Trade 1975/76*. Geneva

— (1978), *International Trade 1977/78*. Geneva.

Gundersen, Gerald, *A New Economic History of America*.

Hobsbawm, E.J., 'The British Standard of Living, 1790-1850,' in A.J. Taylor (ed.) (1975), *Standard of Living in Britain in the Industrial Revolution*. London: Methuen.

Ho Chi Minh (1973), 'Report on the National and Colonial Question at the Fifth Congress of the Communist International,' *Selected Writings*. Hanoi.

International Forum (1977), *Imperialisme og klassekamp*. Copenhagen.

Jones, R. B. (1979), *Economic and Social History of Britain*, 1770-1977. London: Longman.

Lenin, V.I., *The Collapse of the Second International*, LCW, Vol. 21.

—, *Imperialism and the Split in Socialism*, LCW, Vol. 23.

—, *Imperialism, the Highest Stage of Capitalism*, LCW, Vol. 22.

—, 'The International Socialist Congress in Stuttgart,' LCW, Vol. 13.

—, 'Karl Marx,' LCW, Vol. 21.

—, 'Revision of the Party Programme,' LCW, Vol. 26.

—, 'The Second Congress of the Communist International.' *LCW, Vol*. 31.

Malthus Thomas Robert (1872), *An Essay on the Principle of Population*. London.

Mao Tse-tung (1967), 'On Practice,' *Selected Readings from the Works of Mao Tse-tung*. Peking.

Marx, Karl, 'British Commerce,' MECW, Vol. 15.

—, *Capital*, Vols. I-III. Moscow: Progress Publishers.

—, 'Preface', *A Contribution to the Critique of Political Economy*, MESW.

—, 'The Future Results of the British Rule in India,' MEOC.

— (1973), *Grundrisse*. London: Pelican.

— (1843), Letter to Arnold Ruge, MECW, Vol. 3.

—, *Theories of Surplus Value*, Parts I-III. Moscow: Progress Publishers.

Marx, Karl, Engels, Friedrich, *The German Ideology*, MECW, Vol. 5.

—, *Manifesto of the Communist Party*, MESW.

Nkrumah, Kwame (1968), *Handbook of Revolutionary Warfare*. New York: International Publishers.

Nyerere, Julius K. (1973), 'A Call to European Socialists,' *Freedom and Development*. Dar es Salaam.

— (1981), 'The Plea of the Poor: New Economic Order Needed for the World Community,' *Third World Quarterly*, Vol. 3, no. 3. London.

Petras, J.P., Morley M.H. (1983), 'Petrodollars and the State: The failure of state capitalist development in Venezuela,' *Third World Quarterly*, Vol. 5, no. 1. London

Say, J.B. (1821), *A Treatise on Political Economy*. London.

Scott, J. (1978), *Yankee Unions, Go Home!* Vancouver: New Star Books.

Smith, Adam (1814), *The Wealth of Nations*. Edinburgh.

Sternberg, Fritz (1935), *Der Faschismus an der Macht*. Amsterdam: Contact.

Sweezy, P.M. (1956), *Theory of Capitalist Development*. New York: Monthly Review Press.

United Nations (1984), *Monthly Bulletin of Statistics*, no. 5, May 1984.

— (1979), *Statistical Yearbook* 1978. New York.

— (1982), *Statistical Yearbook* 1981. New York.

— (1975), *Transnational Corporations in World Development*. New York.

Works by Arghiri Emmanuel

Emmanuel, Arghiri (1937), 'L'or, interdit de séjour,' *Proia*, July 1937. In Greek. Athens.

— (1954), 'Les Groupements d'achat,' *Le Stanleyvillois*, Sept. 24, 1954. Congo.

— (1954), 'La Productivité,' *Le Stanleyvillois*, Oct. 2, 1954. Congo.

Emmanuel, Arghiri, Bettelheim, Charles (1962), 'Échange inégal et politique de développement,'. Paris: Centre d'étude de planification socialiste.

Emmanuel, Arghiri (1963), 'L'Échange inégal,' *Problèmes de Planification*, no. 2. Paris.

— (1964), 'El intercambio desigual,' *Economica*, Febr. 1964. Havana.

— (1964), "Commerce extérieur et sous-développement' de Guy de Lacharrière,' *Présence Africaine*, no. 4. Paris.

— (1965), 'Le Dollar c'est indésirable,' *Le Monde*, 9/10, May 1965. Paris.

— (1965), 'The Franc and the Currency War,' *International Socialist Journal*, Sept.-Dec. 1965. Rome.

— (1965), 'Der Weltmarktpreis and der internationals sozialistische Markt,' *Beitrage zur Wissenschaft*, Oct. 1965. Berlin: Fak. Außenhandel.

— (1966), 'La Division Internationale du travail et la marche socialiste,' *Problèmes de Planification*, no. 7. Paris.

— (1966), 'Le Taux de profit et les incompatibilités Marx-Keynes,' *Annales*, no. 6, Nov.-Dec 1966. Paris.

— (1969), 'Le Prolétariat des Nations priviligiées participe à l'exploitation du tiers monde,' *Le Monde*, Nov. 11, 1969. Paris.

— (1970), 'Démystifier les antagonismes entre les nations,' *Politique Aujourd'hui*, Jan. 1970. Paris.

— (1970), 'The Delusions of Internationalism,' *Monthly Review*, June 1970. New York.

— (1970), 'Échange inégal et développement inégal,' *Politique aujourd'hui*, Nov. 1970. Paris.

— (1970), 'La Question de l'échange inégal,' *L'Homme et la Société*, no. 18. Paris.

— (1971), 'Les Causes de la variation des termes de l'échange,' *Doc. de l'I.R.E.P.*, Jan. 1971. Grenoble.

— (1971), 'L'échange inégal: Réponse a J. Lahire,' *La Quatrième Internationale*, March 1971. Paris.

— (1971), 'Scambio ineguale e sviluppo ineguale,' *Problemi del Socialismo*, July-Aug. 1971. Rome.

— (1971), 'Pour l'or estampille,' *Le Monde*, Sept. 7, 1971. Paris.

— (1971), 'Le Colonialisme des 'poor-whites' et le mythe de l'impérialisme de l'investissement,' *L'Homme et la Société*, no. 22. Paris.

— (1972), *L'Echange inégal*, 2nd revised and enlarged ed.; 1st ed. 1969— (Maspero, Paris 1972). Translation: *Unequal Exchange* (Monthly Review Press, New York 1972; NLB, London 1972).

— (1972), *Interrogations récentes sur la théorie du commerce international*. Paris: Cujas.

— (1972), 'C'est parce qu'il est pauvre que le tiers monde vend bon marché,' *Croissance des jeunes Nations*, Mar. 1972. Paris.

— (1972), 'Les Termes de l'échange obéissant à une disparité préétablie par l'impérialisme mercantile,' *Le Monde Diplomatique*, Apr. 1972. Paris.

— (1972), 'White Settler Colonialism and the Myth of Investment Imperialism,' *New Left Review*, no. 73, May-June 1972. London.

— (1972), 'Plus-value et équilibre,' *Doc. de l'I.R.E.P.* Sept. 1972. Grenoble.

Emmanuel, Arghiri, Boggio, Luciano, Salvati, Michele, Somaini, Eugenio (1973), *Salari, sottosviluppo, imperialismo*. Turin: Einaudi.

Emmanuel, Arghiri (1973), 'Les Variations tendancièlles du taux de profit,' *Cahiers du C.E.R.E.L.*, June 1973. Lille.

— (1974), 'Les Prix de production et la notion de l'exploitation dans de le marxisme.'

— (1974), 'Myths of Development Versus Myths of Underdevelopment,' *New Left Review*, May-June 1974. London.

— (1975), *Le Profit et les crises*. Paris: Maspero. Translation: 1984, *Profit and Crises*. London: Heinemann.

— (1975), *Unequal Exchange Revisited*, IDS Discussion Paper no. 77. Brighton: Institute of Development Studies at the University of Sussex.

— (1975), 'The Dynamics of Unequal Exchange.' Contribution to the Conference on 'New Approaches to Trade'. Brighton: Institute of Development Studies at the University of Sussex.

— (1975), 'The Unequal Exchange (A Summary).' Paper presented to the Conference on 'New Approaches to Trade'. Brighton: Institute of Development Studies at the University of Sussex.

— (Nov. 2, 1975), 'The Wage in the Marxist Outlook.' Paper presented to the Wage Conference. Sussex.

— (Nov. 2, 1975), 'The Wage in the Marxist Outlook.' Transcription of the oral presentation. Sussex.

— (1975), 'Le Développement économique et les objectifs des mouvements populaires,' *Anti*, Sept. 1975. In Greek. Athens.

— (1976), 'La 'Stabilisation' alibi de l'exploitation internationale,' *Tiers Monde*, no. 66, Apr.-June 1976. Paris.

— (1976), "Production, Circulation and Value'—A critical comment.' Unpublished answer to Ira Gerstein's article in *Economy and Society*, Vol. 5, no. 3.

— (1976), 'Le Projet socialiste dans un monde capitaliste désintègre,' *Questions actuelle du Socialisme*, Sept. 1976. Belgrade. Translation: 'The Socialist Project in a Disintegrated Capitalist World,' *Socialist Thought and Practice* (Sept. 1976).

— (1976), 'Les Sociétés multinationales et le développement inégal,' *Revue Intern. des Sc. Soc.*, no. 4. Paris: UNESCO. Translation: 1976, 'The Multinational Corporations and Inequality of Development,' *Intern. Soc. Sc. J.*, no. 4. Paris: UNESCO.

— (1977), 'L'Etat de la 'transition',' *L'Homme et la Société*, nos. 45-46. Paris. Translation: 'The State in the Transitional Period,' *New Left Review*, no. 113-114, Jan.-Apr. 1979. London.

— (1977), 'Gains And Losses from the International Division of Labour: Reply to Paul Samuelsson,' *Review*, Vol. I, no. 2 New York: Fern. Br. Cent.

— (1977), 'La Contradiction intérieure de la mode de production socialiste,' *Socialism in the World*, no. 7.

— (1977), 'Vergopoulos: Le Capitalisme difformé et la nouvelle question agraire', *L'Homme et la Société*, no. 43. Paris

— (1978), 'Le Profit et les crises—Réponse à quelques questions,' *Annales de l'économie publique sociale et coopérative*, Vol. 66, no. 1, Jan.-March (Liège 1978).

— (1978), 'Le 'Prix rémunérateur'.' A research project submitted to the OECD in Paris.

— (1978), 'A Note on Trade Pattern Reversals,' *Journal of International Economics*, no. 8.

— (1979), 'The Dynamics of Unequal Exchange/Uneven Development.' Paper presented to a conference at the London School of Economics. London.

— (1979), 'The Variations of the Wage and the Breakdown of the Capitalist System. Reply to Spraos.' London: London School of Economics.

— (1979), 'The Surprises of 'Stagflation.' Outline of a research-project submitted to Ford Foundation and turned down by that organization.

— (1980), 'Le 'Prix rémunérateur' épilogue à 'L'Échange inégal',' *Tiers Monde*, Vol. 21, no. 81, Jan.-March 1980. Paris.

— (1980), 'Technologie appropriée—Mirage ou réalité?' Contribution to the Working Group Multinationales et développement (European Association of Development Research and Training Institutes).

— (1980), 'Réponse à la critique de Serge Latouche.' Contribution to the Working Group Multinationales et développement (European Association of Development Research and Training Institutes).

— (1982), *Technologie appropriée ou technologie sous-développée?* Translation: *Appropriate or Underdeveloped Technology?* Chichester: John Wiley.

— (1982), 'Les Avatars du révisionnisme.' Paper presented to the Table Ronde at Cavtat, Yugoslavia, Sept. 13, 1982.

— (1984), 'Indebtedness as Vehicle for Transfer of Resources,' *Tiers Monde*, March. Paris.

— (1986), 'The Economic Crisis and the Way to Get Out of it'. Published in Danish as a pamphlet: 1986, *Krisepolitikkens fallit*. Copenhagen: Manifest, Copenhagen.

www.ingramcontent.com/pod-product-compliance
Lightning Source LLC
LaVergne TN
LVHW091549070526
838199LV00030B/613/J